PRAISE FOR ANNAHID DA[
BREAKING THE OCEAN

"A profound and candid reflection on the realities of race today, *Breaking the Ocean* pulls no punches in calling out the power structures upholding racism. By sharing her life's story, Annahid Dashtgard effectively examines the complex intersection of culture, class, and colour. As a mixed-race person, I found her story deeply resonant, and felt an immediate kinship with her and her loved ones."

—Waubgeshig Rice, author of *Moon of the Crusted Snow*

"A powerful memoir about the making of a leader and the rise of her passion for justice and equity. This is a stunning personal reflection on one woman's growth to claim her own power and the dedication she makes to social change."

—Carrianne Leung, author of *That Time I Loved You*

"*Breaking the Ocean* is a deeply intimate and provocative memoir about the explorations of a young immigrant mixed-race woman trying to find her way to belonging through social change. A profound and important read at this time of the intersections of our struggles. We need more voices like hers."

—Judy Rebick, author of *Heroes in My Head*

"A bold and intimate memoir about growing up mixed-race, overcoming adversities, and fighting for social change, *Breaking the Ocean* deftly illuminates the pain and loss of immigration and what it means to feel like you don't belong. At its core, this is a book about trauma and resilience and the power of storytelling to heal and connect us all."

— Ayelet Tsabari, author of *The Art of Leaving*

"*Breaking the Ocean* is imbued with a passion that arises from a life of sorrow, bravery, and great joy. Franz Kafka once said, 'A book must be the axe for the frozen sea within us.' With this memoir, Dashtgard takes the axe to the frozen sea of indifference and inequality, and leads us on a journey towards healing."
— Sensei Koshin Paley Ellison, author of
Wholehearted: Slow Down, Help Out, Wake Up

"In direct contrast to the dominant narrative of the fortunate immigrant, Annahid Dashtgard reveals the trauma she experienced after leaving Iran, and the abhorrent rejection and racist abuse she suffered as a child once her family arrived in Canada. With incredible courage, Dashtgard gives us a memoir that alters the way stories are told. *Breaking the Ocean* will change the way we look at each other."
— Suzanne Desrochers, author of *Bride of New France*

"Poetic, raw, and incisive, *Breaking the Ocean* will be a developmental bedrock for anyone wanting to complicate and explore their place in the tapestry of Western society. Dashtgard takes us under her skin, bravely offering readers the rare chance to feel the world through her body."
— Julie Devaney, author *My Leaky Body:*
Tales from the Gurney

"*Breaking the Ocean* took my breath away. In strong, raw prose, Dashtgard recounts what it is to lose not only home and country, but cultural identity, safety, and the security of belonging. This brave and beautiful book is an absolute must-read—a powerful lesson for a world struggling to come to grips with cultural and racial difference."
— Dr. Julie Diamond, author of *Power: A User's Guide*

"A beautifully written and enduring memoir that immerses readers in the struggles of growing up while searching for a place to belong, *Breaking the Ocean* is a welcome addition to the literature of race, power, privilege, and oppression."

—Dr. Eddie Moore, Jr., founder and program director of the White Privilege Conference

"*Breaking the Ocean* applies a relentless magnifying glass to the everyday bias of decent people and the unjust systems that we sustain with our silence. At once an intimate memoir, an impassioned social critique, and a call to dismantle the hierarchies in ourselves and our communities, it is a fierce and compassionate invitation to rethink 'belonging.'"

—Barb Thomas, co-author of *Dancing on Live Embers: Challenging Racism in Organizations*

"Beautifully written from a deep personal wellspring of strength and courage, *Breaking the Ocean* is the vulnerable story of one woman's journey to her authentic self. It will have a profound personal and social impact."

—Berns Galloway, Somatic Experiencing Trauma Institute

"*Breaking the Ocean* is a testament to the transformative power of embracing our vulnerability and writing from a deep place of conscious subjectivity. This book has changed me; I recommend it as essential reading for anyone interested in dislocation, diversity, and inclusion."

—Imam Timothy J. Gianotti, author of *In the Light of a Blessed Tree: Illuminations of Islamic Belief, Practice, and History*

BREAKING THE OCEAN

A Memoir of Race, Rebellion, and Reconciliation

ANNAHID DASHTGARD

ANANSI

Published in Canada in 2019 and the USA in 2019 by
House of Anansi Press Inc.
www.houseofanansi.com

House of Anansi Press is committed to protecting our natural
environment. As part of our efforts, this book is made of material
from well-managed FSC®-certified forests, recycled materials,
and other controlled sources.

23 22 21 20 19   1 2 3 4 5

Library and Archives Canada Cataloguing in Publication

Title: Breaking the ocean : race, rebellion, and reconciliation /
Annahid Dashtgard.
Names: Dashtgard, Annahid, author.
Identifiers: Canadiana (print) 20189067047 | Canadiana (ebook)
20189067055 | ISBN 9781487006471
(softcover) | ISBN 9781487006488 (EPUB) | ISBN 9781487006495
(Kindle)
Subjects: LCSH: Dashtgard, Annahid. | CSH: Iranian
Canadians—Biography. | Iranian Canadians—Social conditions.
| LCSH: Political refugees—Iran—Biography. | LCSH: Political
refugees—Canada—Biography. | LCSH: Political activists—
Canada—Biography. | LCGFT: Autobiographies.
Classification: LCC FC106.I5 Z7 2019 | DDC 971/.00491550092—dc23

Library of Congress Control Number: 2019930410

Book design: Alysia Shewchuk

 Canada Council
for the Arts
Conseil des Arts
du Canada
 ONTARIO ARTS COUNCIL
CONSEIL DES ARTS DE L'ONTARIO
an Ontario government agency
un organisme du gouvernement de l'Ontario

We acknowledge for their financial support of our publishing
program the Canada Council for the Arts, the Ontario Arts Council,
and the Government of Canada.

Printed and bound in Canada

 MIX
Paper from
responsible sources
FSC® C004071

For my family.

And for anyone who has ever
struggled to belong.

Contents

Author's Note

NAMES OF FAMILY MEMBERS and close friends have been kept; all the rest have been changed to obscure the identity of the person or organization mentioned. In some cases, the person mentioned is an amalgam, created to serve narrative purposes. As most lives are touched by countless others, I had to sort through to find the key characters necessary for this particular story. Had I written on a different theme, others may have appeared, or the same, but to varying degrees. Lastly, it is not my intent to cast any blame, embellish, or manipulate, but to tell this story as plainly as it is in my power to do. I leave you to the journey.

Prologue

IT IS THE BEGINNING of September, the first day of school, and the sun is flirting with making an appearance. Butterflies fill my stomach, but in a good way. Today marks my four-year-old daughter's first day of attending the "big school" at the end of our street. She's wearing the robin's-egg-blue dress I bought for her birthday earlier this year with the silver filigree design down the front—an echo of her Middle Eastern roots. My husband Shakil and I leave the house to drop her off together. With her marching gait, laser-beam gaze, and set mouth, she seems fine. Better off than her mama.

I feel alone. The paralyzing isolation I felt during the early years of motherhood has given way to tenuous new connections with many other parents—through daycare, local Facebook groups, and community gatherings—but I'm still off balance. Despite reaching middle age, despite having achieved professional success, despite all the wonderful things and people in my life, this moment undoes me.

The sight of monkey bars and green playing field makes me feel tight and floaty at the same time. I know it's because a part of me was left behind in a place just like this, where I learned that in order to survive I had to make myself disappear. I can't catch my breath. I feel dislocated.

My daughter runs into the play area without a backward glance, and I call her back to give her one last hug. "Enjoy your first day at your new school, Baba. I love you so much," I whisper. I can't tell if it's her or some earlier version of myself that I watch twist and spin away, the past collapsing into the present. All I know is that my daughter's story begins with my story. And my story begins with my people.

PART I

RACE

you broke the ocean in
half to be here.
only to meet nothing that wants you.

— NAYYIRAH WAHEED, "IMMIGRANT"

ONE

Persian Girl

I'VE ALWAYS LOVED FAIRY tales, yet I never saw myself in one, never pictured myself as a princess. Sleeping Beauty, Rapunzel, and Cinderella seemed so far away, so fantastical, until I started to write my own story. As I embarked on this journey, I realized how many frogs I'd had to kiss in my lifetime, how many spells I'd had to break, how many monsters lying in wait had been slain—and how many monsters were still lurking in the shadows. I found red dancing shoes, and a pea under many mattresses. I stumbled upon a recipe for fairy dust. And I discovered that even if I'm not a princess I can still make my own happy ending—or at least a version of one, because this journey doesn't end. Like all fairy tales, though, it does start with...

Once upon a time, at the turn of the twentieth century, a boy named Abdullah escaped from his nomadic community to the big city of Shiraz in Iran in search of a better

future. He was just twelve, a member of one of the northern Indigenous tribes, the Ghashghaei. As in many other
countries, this itinerant population represented the poorest,
least-educated segment of Iranian society. When Abdullah
was asked his last name for a potential job, he made one
up on the spot (tribal culture had no use for surnames).
"Dashtgard," he said, coining a phrase meaning "wanderer
of the desert." He lost any further contact with his family
and tribe.

Abdullah was my father's father. He fell in love with the
first car he ever saw, a Rolls-Royce, and got a job chauf-
feuring rich people around Shiraz. He would jump at
any job that came his way, and so it was that some years
later he was driving a bus, taking a family to a picnic in
nearby Persepolis, when he momentarily lost control of the
vehicle. But it wasn't his fault. He'd looked in the overhead
mirror and caught a glimpse of my Mamanbozourg (grandmother), Talat, sitting in the second row. Later, during the
picnic, he approached Talat's mother to ask if he could
visit the next day. That was the beginning of their—and
my—story. My grandmother was from a working-class
family—her father was a bread maker—and they were
devout Muslims. Abdullah and Talat were married soon
after they met, he at eighteen and she at thirteen. Early
in their marriage they moved to the capital so he could
drive a bigger, better car for another rich family. Tehran
became their home.

In another country, on another continent, there was a
second man, an Englishman and a Methodist lay preacher,
who was born around the same time as his nomadic peer.

This was Allan Exton, my mother's father. When Britain entered the Second World War, my maternal grandfather's religious convictions concerning non-violence led him to register as a conscientious objector, and his refusal to bear arms in military service made him a social pariah. Conscientious objectors were required to serve in other ways, often doing farmwork for little to no remuneration, and this enforced servitude continued at least ten years past the end of the war.

Allan had met my grandmother, Elsie, just before the war. She came from a working-class family where it was often a struggle to put nourishing food on the table, never mind pay for grammar school necessities. My grandmother was the lone scholarship student who travelled daily from her small town of Irthlingborough to the nearby larger town of Kettering. She entered teaching college at age twenty-nine, and married my grandfather a year later. After the war, she gave up her profession to settle with my grandfather on a plot of land they bought in a small village called Skellingthorpe, making ends meet with a small market garden.

Though their worlds were far apart, what my grandparents had in common was a character and drive that led them to sacrifice for a higher vision, giving up status, family support, even home, in service of a better and brighter future. Their renegade genes were passed to the next generation, and eventually to me.

My mother, Janet, grew up in the village of Skellingthorpe, where she attended the Methodist church. She was the second of two daughters. My father, Jamshid, grew up in the big city of Tehran. He was a Muslim and Persian, the third of six children. They were brought together in the dirty industrial city of Birmingham, England.

Dad had scored in the top seven in a nationwide math competition sponsored by Bank Markazi, the Central Bank of Iran. The prize for the winning candidates was to go to England to study chartered accountancy. He arrived in Birmingham in the mid 1960s, when anyone brown-skinned (or darker) was routinely turned away by landlords, mocked openly in the streets, and rarely deemed eligible for white-collar jobs. Most of the men in this group of seven contest winners found English wives, my father among them. I often wonder if part of the appeal of a fairer-skinned wife was the bump in social status that came with marrying "up the racial ladder."

My parents' meeting in January 1967 transpired in an old house on Moseley Road in central Birmingham. My mother was teaching kindergarten at an inner-city school while renting an apartment on the third floor of a house, when my father happened to move in next door. One day the man with the exotically darker skin, belying the Scandinavian-sounding "Dashtgard" on the nameplate outside his door, met my mother on the landing between their apartments. After an initial greeting he offered in heavily accented English, "I'm going to the laundrette. Do you have any clothes I can help you with?" He finished by proudly bran-dishing his own laundry bag as proof of his sincerity. The family joke goes that this was the first and only time my father ever dirtied his hands with a domestic task (I think he may have been hoping she'd make a counter-offer).

My mother was slightly flabbergasted as she searched for the words to let him down politely. Not for the last time, my father's dazzling smile managed to override any hesitation on her part. She said no to his offer but invited him to join her and her roommate for dinner. Thus began their courtship.

If it was a coup for my father to secure a British wife, for my mother to marry out of the Christian tradition she'd grown up in was considerably more controversial. Both her parents travelled frequently across the English countryside as preachers to spread the gospel of Christ, a local form of community building. To their credit, my maternal grandparents accepted my foreign-born father, though the differences between Jamshid Dashtgard and Janet Exton — differences in background, values, and experiences — extended far beyond skin colour.

My father, a cultural, non-practising Muslim, is a materialist, a risk-taker, and something of a hedonist. His modus operandi is always to push for more, to be the life of the party. He enjoys nothing more than a heated argument — especially if he gets to take both sides. By contrast, my mother is grounded, organized, and frugal — a quintessential salt-of-the-earth type. Intimacy for my mother is measured through calm connection; overt conflict is not a comfortable arena. Though she might come across at first as quiet, she also shares the British love of pantomime, theatre, singing, and games. She will never pass up an opportunity to create a family skit — birthdays, church services, a twenty-minute oeuvre performed at my marriage ceremony. In their partnership each of them changed: my father learned to play Scrabble (with my grandmother), while my mother learned to drink (socially). He now eats pork crackling; she makes *tadeeg* (an Iranian delicacy of crispy rice). He drinks his tea with milk; she arrives on "Persian time" (read: late).

What they share is an open-mindedness, a pull towards adventure, and a (sometimes miraculous) ability to get things done. I am still surprised by what each of my parents is able to accomplish, both of them now over seventy. My mother will call to tell me she's writing and directing a Christmas play for her church. And my father still works long hours as an accountant, doubling his hours each tax season.

In 1972, after four years together in England while my father completed his chartered accountancy training, my parents relocated to the Middle East. My father owed service to the Central Bank of Iran in payment for his British training. They travelled in their aqua VW Beetle from my grandparents' bungalow in their tiny northern village, crossed on a ferry to Belgium, drove through western Europe to Yugoslavia, and from there made their way through Turkey into northern Iran. The story goes that soon after they had said tearful goodbyes and set out on the English back-country lanes, my mother sighted a pheasant in the middle of the road. "Stop!" she cried. My father, of course, swerved right into the unfortunate fowl. They hightailed it back to my Grandma Elsie and Grandpa Allan's house, bird in hand, and knocked on the windowpane, holding up their unexpected gift. Although my mother and father departed again shortly afterwards, this time they left laughter in their wake and dinner in the oven.

Somewhere on this drive from my mother's homeland

to my father's, from England to Iran, I was conceived. Even in utero, neurons were shaped in the dialogue between my mother's English body and the sounds, smells, and foods of the Persian culture that would welcome me into my first home. I was hatched in a space suspended between two cultures, not fully one or the other, arriving in the Tehran General Hospital on May 25, 1973. My brother Shahin and sister Fariba were born in the same hospital, in 1976 and 1979, respectively. We are Persian by birth, if not fully by blood.

⌐

I HAVE ONLY PATCHWORK memories of my first seven years in Iran. My father had five other siblings, who at various times all had spouses or partners, so our regular family gatherings were high-volume affairs. On these occasions my body would be squeezed like a loaf of fresh bread to cries of "*dokhtar khoshgel*" ("pretty girl") and "*kheili gashang!*" ("very beautiful"), while no exposed flesh was left unpinched. Persians are not known for social restraint.

Before I could speak English or Farsi, I was immersed in the universal language of unconditional love and held in the centre of a family tribe. As the oldest cousin and the ringleader, I was free to jump into whatever puddles of trouble appeared, secure in the knowledge that I would be dried off on the other side. On weekdays, I attended the English-speaking Rustum Abadian International School, where my mother worked. We had Farsi classes each morning as part of the curriculum, although I was competent in the language early on.

I remember buying crusty flat bread—*sangak*—from hole-in-the-wall, one-man bakeries, watching as the steamy bread was pulled out of a stonewall oven, dotted across the top with small pebbles to prevent it from rising too high. There would be scuffling in the back seat all the way home as my siblings and I fought over the scraps. A piece secured with a stone was a bonus—extra ammunition!

My mother would often take the three of us on nature walks in the hills behind our newly built mansion in northern Tehran, and we'd search for tadpoles to carry home in glass jars. There was no one else around during these times, only the four of us in the green-scented air. I remember a feeling of freedom and expansiveness that contrasted with the chaos of the city below.

Eid is the cultural equivalent of Christmas in a society organized around the Islamic religion, but the Persian New Year—*Nowruz*—was the most elaborate event in our calendar. A pre-Islamic holiday rooted in pagan traditions and taking place on the first day of spring, *Nowruz* was like all the best days at summer camp (how I imagined it, anyway) spread over a two-week period. I remember gleefully jumping over fires in the gathering darkness as part of the annual *Chaharshanbe Suri*, or festival of fire, that took place on the Wednesday before *Nowruz*, a mass ritual signifying purification. Thirteen days later we'd communally picnic near a river for *Sizdah Be-dar* ("Nature's Day"), which marks the end of the *Nowruz* holidays. The ritual of dumping our plate of *sabzeh* (sprouts) into the flowing water was the only calm moment in a day otherwise dominated by games and food, that ended finally with sleepy children's bodies draped over adult shoulders. My belly was always full of *sholeh zard* (saffron rice pudding), beef kebabs, and the delicious *sangak* that I stuffed into my mouth at regular intervals. My skin was left tingling from tickles, pinches, and hugs. I never stopped moving, basking in the silent music that's made when family and friends gather.

Once, when I was six years old, we visited Shiraz, the city where my grandparents met and fell in love. It was 1979, and I can recall in vivid detail the bazaar full of sparkling clothes, rainbow-coloured spices, and woven carpets of all shapes and sizes, where the city's beggars sat with their hands outstretched for money. This is the Iran I remember: one of great extremes, often side by side. Colour and poverty. Tiny stone bakeries and lavish mansions. Crowded streets and open hills.

There are two photos of me taken during this trip. I'm wearing traditional Ghashghaei nomadic dress. In one, my head is tipped to the side as I coyly stare up at the camera; in the other, I am nestled in my father's arms, mouth wide open, laughing. I have this outfit folded in a drawer now, the only physical object I have left from that time. I have no coherent narrative of my formative years in Iran, only these inchoate images appearing like bright koi fish darting through the murky waters of memory. As an adult, I am left waiting, watching for flashes of gold, glimpses of the girl I once was in a land far away.

⌐

MY FATHER WAS THE emotionally colourful parent, most often dressed up in charm or volatile in anger, while my mother was a stereotypical Brit, emotionally distant yet always persevering. In our household, the gender roles were clearly divided: my mother took care of domestic responsibilities, and my father played the "how to become a millionaire by forty" game, determined to improve our family's social status, remembering his own childhood spent in poverty.

During my early childhood years my mother kept busy holding her new family together while grieving the loss of all that was familiar to her. My mom is complicated. Although she isn't assertive, she has a fierce determination to deal with what life sends her way. She learned to drive in a city where everyone made up their own rules ("Ignore the red light!") and got into only one accident during her eight years there — not bad odds. She started a job as head of the English department at the Kooros International School when I was four months old, a position that called on her considerable teaching and management skills. Such was her influence in our extended Muslim family that every Christmas everyone would gather to exchange presents and witness Santa's (a.k.a. my father's) annual visit.

In addition to dealing with severe homesickness and the difficulties associated with adjusting to a completely new life in an unfamiliar country, my mother suffered a crippling blow just two years after I was born. In 1975, before Shahin and Fariba were born, she gave birth to a second child, a son they named Barbak. Within days the baby contracted meningitis, and he passed away after a week in hospital. My father was in New York for work at the time, and he missed his first-born son's entire lifespan. My mother suffered heartache alone at a time and place where women were expected to "just get over it." To this day, when I ask my mother what we were like as young children she claims that she cannot recall, as if her memories are hostage to something other than age. Denied emotions—unnamed trauma—can often block access to the past.

It's easy to espouse the optimism of cross-cultural relationships, but the actual work of bridging difference is extremely difficult, even with strong self-awareness and communication skills—which were not readily available to my parents' generation. From its very beginning, their marriage was marred by my mother's guilt for marrying outside the Christian faith and my father's shame for having the wrong skin colour. Commitment to family was the glue that held them together, as well as love.

Of course, much of this was left unspoken, so I became gifted at reading signals. I learned very early on that I was responsible for changing the emotional channel in our house. I wanted to save my mother from the emptiness of my father's frequent absences and the fury of his authority when present. And at the same time, I strove to earn my father's approval. I was always trying to fix my world—the curse of the first-born child. But it came at a cost: trust in my own "enough-ness." In a kindergarten report card, my teacher commented, "Annahid is very capable, but she often seeks approval for things that she already knows how to do." My earliest sense of self was shaped by the desire to make others happy. Later, this became a coping mechanism.

⌒

WHEN MY FATHER WAS in New York in 1975, missing the birth and death of his second child, it was because he was on a truly remarkable assignment for the Central Bank of Iran. With the support of Merrill Lynch, the largest American brokerage house, he was given two months to study the workings of the mammoth New York Stock Exchange. My dad, a numerical genius, was tasked with learning the inner workings of American capital markets so he could establish the first public trading market in Iran. When he returned and formed the Tehran Stock Exchange (TSE) there was no place to house it, until my father scoped out a room in one of the branches of Bank Melli on Saidi Street. In its humble beginnings, the TSE consisted of my father sitting at the head of a giant table with about ten brokers, mostly from the other banks. He would begin each session by calling on someone to offer some shares, then wait for the others in the room to bid. Once the transaction was complete, he would enter the details in a large ledger book using a pencil (so they could later be erased, if necessary). In 2012, the TSE represented more than three hundred companies with a combined worth of $104 billion, and for many consecutive years at the beginning of the new millennium it was one of the world's best-performing stock exchanges.

As I was writing this, enthralled by this unique piece of family history — how many people can say they set up a country's stock market?—I asked my father if he still had his *Sal Nahmeh*, or first annual ledger book. He grew serious, then replied, "Yes, it's one of the things I made sure to bring with me. All in Persian, of course."

My father quickly moved up the ranks at the Central Bank of Iran. When he left, in 1977, it was to take the prestigious position of Iran's auditor general, with responsibility for a staff of over 350 employees. He was at the top of the financial food chain, a position that came with a private car and chauffeur. Yet in his spare time he still had the energy and drive to start a successful construction business, building houses with his father and brother. Years later, when our family had relocated to Canada, he offhandedly remarked that if he could go back in time he would choose to be an engineer rather than an accountant. He was more an innovator than a manager, but, being one of the eldest brothers in a large and impoverished family, he had prioritized security over pursuing his own passions.

By 1978 my mother had left the Kooros International School and risen to the role of assistant-principal at the Rustum Abadian International School in downtown Tehran. She was thriving as well, using her tremendous organizational skills to shape the elementary school curriculum, manage a staff of about ten people, and ensure success for the two hundred students in her care. The three of us kids accompanied her to school each morning. My younger brother and sister would be handed to a caregiver, while I attended classes from pre-kindergarten to grade two. My mother's British credentials served her in good stead in a country rapidly moving towards Western-focused industrialization. Behind the scenes, however, not everyone was happy with the shifts towards urbanization.

⌒

IN THE 1970S, IRAN'S reigning monarch, Shah Mohammad Reza Pahlavi, was modernizing the country, building roads, libraries, and universities, primarily using wealth from oil exports. Iran became 90 percent self-sufficient in food production, and in 1978, the average Iranian earned $2,540 annually, compared to $160 just a quarter century earlier. A significant pro-Western, anti-Communist ally, he was a major force for Middle East stability, supporting peace with Israel and supplying oil to them. He even legalized abortion in Iran—a decision that was very contentious with the country's Shia Muslim majority. But there were many who believed he was shaping the country too strongly in the image of the distrusted West, specifically the United States. The Shah came to be viewed increasingly as a Western puppet, ensconced in privilege and out of touch with Iranians struggling with daily life in a rapidly shifting economy that benefitted city dwellers to the detriment of everyone else. The rift between the educated, urban elite and the majority of Iran's population—poorer citizens in rural parts of the country—grew hopelessly wider. And as the relationship between the ruler and the governed began to fester, the Shah proved that he could be dictatorial, using his secret police and state propaganda to squash dissent.

Ayatollah Khomeini, a political rival to the Shah, leveraged this divide. Though he had been outcast years earlier, in 1964, he organized the rural Muslim majority from exile. In August 1978, a group of four men set fire to a movie theatre in Abadan, in the southwest of Iran, killing the 422 people inside. The incident was blamed on the Shah, quickly stoking revolutionary sentiments, despite the arsonists themselves claiming they did it to further the revolutionary cause. The Shah, once again influenced by the ideals of Western democracy, chose not to crack down on this opposition and allowed the protests to grow in strength and size, hoping to negotiate a peaceful conclusion. During the revolutionary days of action in December 1978, between six and nine million protesters marched throughout the country, more than 10 percent of the population, possibly a higher percentage than in any other revolution. They demanded the abdication of the Shah and the transition of power to Ayatollah Khomeini.

The United States, which until then had supported the Shah's reign, switched to backing Khomeini, hypothesizing that a different regime would better favour their interests. Some have speculated that the United States acted on the knowledge the Shah's days were numbered, as he had been diagnosed with terminal cancer; others theorize that there was concern that the Shah's regime had simply become too powerful. And the world's media fell for Khomeini's mystical Eastern rhetoric. Initially conciliatory, Khomeini seemed more like a spiritual guide than a despot.

The Iranian Revolution surprised many around the world, as it was not heralded by the usual signposts. It seemed impossible, right up until it became inevitable. And if few people saw the revolution coming, fewer still anticipated that when Khomeini seized power in February 1979 he would mould the country almost overnight into a hardline Shiite Islamist state, governing through absolute military rule. My father remembers that when Khomeini got off the plane upon his arrival in Tehran, a French reporter asked him what it felt like to be back in the country after so many years in exile. His response: *"Hich,"* or *"Nothing."*

Anyone affiliated with the Shah was immediately blacklisted, including my father, a high-ranking official in the Iranian government. It soon emerged that many of those sympathetic to the Shah—anyone deemed a threat, including journalists—were being imprisoned or executed. "There was no doubt he was an evil man," my father reflected years later.

By then, my father had finished building his dream house on the outskirts of Tehran: a three-storey, white-marble mansion edged by a garden boasting rose bushes alongside orange trees, and with a full swimming pool at the southern edge of the property. He had finally arrived at the doorstep of success, only to have the rug violently pulled out from under him.

My father, like many urban professionals, had believed whispers of the revolution to be nothing more than insubstantial rumours, and so he had not taken any precautions. Iranian millionaires had started to move their investments out early on, betting against their own country. According to my father, many of these people continue to reap a profit off the existing regime. But none of my father's savings had been sent away into secure foreign banks, nothing had been sold off in preparation for a hasty and imminent departure.

At the time, I didn't know any of the specifics, but I remember a lot of talk, most of it in hushed tones: at home, when we were thought to be asleep; at school, as the teachers huddled in doorways; and between neighbours, as they passed one another in the street. Even though I didn't know what people were saying, the image of heads bent together twisted my stomach in a way I hadn't felt before.

Although we didn't know what sweeping changes were awaiting every aspect of secular Iranian society, the first announcements offered strong clues. Western influences — books, music, and alcohol — were banned. Women and girls as young as my seven-year-old self would soon be required to wear the head-to-toe chador in public. The punishment for non-compliance was imprisonment. I couldn't visualize myself cloaked in such a way. In my childhood imagination there couldn't be a worse sentence. The restriction of movement, having to wear something not imposed on my brother and male cousins, seemed outrageously unfair.

Additionally, daily classes devoted to the study of the Quran would become mandatory in schools. And classes would be divided by gender, boys segregated from girls. Only female teachers could teach female students. My mother would be unable to continue working outside the home. She would not be able to identify publicly as a Christian, and it was questionable whether it would be safe even in private. Yet, despite an impulse to rebel that was growing inside me, I vehemently did not want to leave our home in Iran. I didn't understand that we had no choice.

FOR YEARS AFTERWARDS, I was told how lucky it was that we were able to get out of Iran when we did, but I did not feel this. What I mostly felt was the absence of everything familiar, everything we'd been forced to leave behind. After my parents informed me of our impending exile, I remember walking in our backyard garden surrounded by orange blossoms and persimmon trees, repeating to myself, "I hate Khomeini! I hate Khomeini!" relishing the bitter taste of his name on my tongue. Though I knew nothing of him beyond an image of a man with a long beard and turban, he became the focus of my anger and someone I could blame for evicting us from our home.

My mother left Iran in June 1980, eighteen months after Khomeini took power, heading back to England with the three of us in tow. The international school had just closed, and things were moving in an increasingly fundamentalist direction, with worsening consequences for failing to obey. My father had left his position as auditor general and returned to his previous job with the Central Bank, treading water for a few months while making plans to leave the country himself. In November 1980, while my father was still trying to get out, fifty-two Americans remained hostage in the American embassy in Tehran by a pro-Islamist, anti-Western student group (it had been a year since their detainment). Khomeini had stoked anti-Western sentiment to ride into power, and once in control he fanned the flames even more strongly. The hostage crisis seemed to justify increased security measures and crackdowns, jeopardizing my father's safety even further. He remembers driving by the American embassy regularly seeing the kidnappers on the roof of the building.

In January 1981, my father told everyone he was leaving for a three-week "holiday" in England. Because so much was still up in the air, he still believed that returning to Iran was a possibility. He didn't tell his family in Iran he was leaving until the night before his departure, to save them from any complicity in his escape, and perhaps also to minimize the likelihood that his plans would become known—a whisper in the wrong ear could place him under suspicion. Little did he know that it would be another quarter century before he would come face to face with most of them again. Sadly, he never had a chance to say a proper goodbye to his own father, who passed away a few years after we left. The price of exile is loss.

Up to the very last minute, my father didn't know if he'd be allowed to pass through airport security, or whether instead he would face arrest as an enemy of the state. Had that come to pass, it's unlikely he would ever have made it out of prison, never mind the country. Most of my father's hard-won wealth was lost after emigrating. Though he did manage to sell the mansion he'd built, the international exchange rate reduced the value substantially. When the Shah was still in power, the rate was seven Persian tomans to the American dollar; when we left, it was thirty-one, and dropping further every day. As I write this, it's now over a thousand tomans. The revolution did not come cheap. Yet, ultimately, the price my father paid was less than what many others lost. He was lucky enough to escape with his life, though not his fortune.

TWO

Dislocations

WE FOUND OURSELVES TRANSPLANTED for the first year to a tiny village deep in northeast England, the place where my mother grew up. It wasn't an especially good time to be Iranian, assuming people even had an inkling of what or where the country was. The Iran hostage crisis was still in play, lasting for 444 days under the watchful eyes of the global media (a story capitalized on in the Academy Award–winning movie *Argo*). The eight-year Iran-Iraq War started in 1980, a year after the revolution, with America and most other Western nations siding with Iraq. Iranians were, for the purposes of cultural stereotyping, seen as religious zealots and all-round bad guys. And while my mother was back in her childhood home, mostly immune to such perceptions, the rest of us stood out uncomfortably.

Arriving in Britain, I felt as though someone had turned down the volume on the radio, or painted over all the vibrant jewel tones with pastels. I had travelled from the land of samovars to cozy-covered teapots, from a place where people sucked searing black tea through sugar cubes held between their front teeth to a place where tea was sipped with milk, saucer in hand. I had left behind a culture where everything was always spilling over the edges, a chaotic city of over five million in which people made a sport of being louder, more opinionated, funnier.

As a child in Iran, there was always so much of everything coming my way: pistachios shoved in my pockets by my Bababozourg (grandfather), stinging cheeks from too many aunts pinching them in greeting, a ringing in my ears hours after raucous family gatherings. I had grown up bossy, forthright, and loud in a matriarchal culture where these traits were encouraged as a sign of healthy growth. Most of all, no matter where I went in Tehran, I knew implicitly that I was always welcome.

In contrast, the tiny village of Skellingthorpe, home to a population of roughly a thousand people in 1980, was extremely quiet. The skies were grey, the streets still. When locals spoke, it was hard to tell what they were thinking or if they were happy to see me. It was as if they wore a mask over any kind of spontaneous expression. The first day we arrived, I sat watching my grandmother pouring tea, measuring out the proper amount of milk, a tiny teaspoon of sugar, sipping carefully. There was a different order here, one governed by constraint rather than excess, a legacy in part of the long, difficult years of rationing brought on by the Second World War.

Nevertheless, it was an adventure to be staying with

my Grandma Elsie and Grandpa Allan. They lived in a tiny three-bedroom bungalow on a small farm about a half-hour walk from the village proper. Each morning I'd put on my swimsuit printed with purple daisies and scamper into their bedroom to perform an impromptu ballet routine. At their home, I was nursed through chicken pox, learned to identify a butter knife, and enjoyed the freedom of exploring the old woods behind their home, imagining myself surrounded by fairies, gnomes, elves, and the occasional toadstool troll.

Entering first grade at the local school was a shock. My classmates, with few exceptions, had never left the village. Iran might as well have been on the moon, it seemed that alien. Into this small puddle of Emilys, Clares, Toms, and Georges came the Dashtgards: Annahid, Shahin, and Fariba. My mother added an extra *n* to my name, supposedly to help others with pronunciation, so I went from Ah-nah-*heed* (spelled Anahid) to *A*-na-heed. I still find it hard to understand why so many people have difficulty pronouncing *ah* (as in "ball") instead of *a* (as in "cat"). Nevertheless, at age seven I dutifully began anglicizing my name to fit in, stretching out each deep *ah* sound to a flat *a*, and even then I often had to repeat it multiple times.

To be honest, I don't remember much of this time. And from the little I do recall, I don't remember feeling welcomed. It wasn't that the other kids called me names, it was the invisible ways they shunned me: not inviting me to join in at recess, sitting farther away than they needed to in class, casting suspicious looks in my direction. My Grandmother Elsie later told me that I would come home most days from school crying that my lunch money had been stolen. What I remember most clearly is standing alone in the school playground, wearing the uniform of grey pinafore and white shirt. From a passerby's perspective, I would have been unremarkable—another little girl, albeit darker featured, watching the world pass her by. Yet I felt as if I had travelled outside myself. Exiled from my familiar tribe, from a place where I knew the wild steps to the culture's chaotic rhythm, in Skellingthorpe I found my feet bolted to the ground. I moved from studying Arabic-style writing, with its loops and dots flowing from right to left, to straight up-and-down letters marching in the opposite direction. I felt betrayed. I was not prepared for—and there was nothing to cushion—the fall into this radical new world order.

I don't remember talking to anyone about my growing feelings of loneliness and fear. A notebook from 1981, a few months after our arrival when I was seven years old, contains two stories that reveal what I wasn't able to articulate to my family, to anyone. The first, called "My Island," is dated October 2:

One day I was going on a voyage. I was going on the sunflower ship. We were far out to sea. Suddenly a big storm came. The waves tossed about. Suddenly the ship fell over. All the others died. I found myself swimming. Suddenly I found myself washed up on the shore. I got up and looked around, there were big trees with fruit on. I explored the island. There was only a few animals and some other trees. I felt hungry. I ate some fruit. It tasted nice, then I went up a tree. I went to the highest branch. In the morning, I went fishing, then I saw a can. I said somebody's been here. I am sure I didn't see it yesterday. This went on for two or three days. I saw a ship in the distance. I lit a fire with two pieces of flint. The ship came to the island. They were my people. I went to them and they welcomed me then they took me home. I lived happily ever after.

The second, following a short while later, is called "A Surprise":

I was so shocked I did not know what to do. I felt so frightened that my heart started to beat loudly in my head. So, I decided to jump out the window. The strange creature was a ghost. I landed on a car. The car suddenly went off all by itself. I thought, that's strange. I looked through the window but I had to lean down because on the top of the car I saw it was the ghost. I climbed down to where the front window was, then we got caught in a traffic jam. I heard the ghost. He sounded furious and angry. The traffic jam was still blocked. I jumped off the car. I saw a bus coming. It was going to my house. I ran to the bus stop and I quickly jumped on the bus. I saw the driver was the ghost. I yelled and screamed. I pulled out my pocket knife and got hold of the ghost and cut him in two. It was only a sheet. Then I woke up.

On top of the sense of threat I implicitly absorbed as a young child after our family's flight from Iran was the growing sense that perhaps I was doing something wrong, that the problem lay with me. Shame is a secretive emotion. Was it my fault that we had moved? Did I deserve what was happening to me? My mother was busy holding everything together, and my father wasn't there. At one point during those first months in Britain my siblings and I were playing in my grandparents' living room. I was glued to the final pages of a dog-eared copy of *Robin Hood* that I'd found on the shelf. As I reached the scene where Maid Marian dies tragically and Robin Hood is left in the throes of grief, I started to sob. My mother turned towards my brother, the one closest to me in age, demanding, "What did you do to her?" That memory marks one of the first moments of experiencing my feelings through "safe" outlets like books, other characters, lives removed many times over. Neutral places where loss could momentarily be made visible.

My mother occupied a different identity, and as such was not prepared for the ways my siblings and I would face exclusion. When my father joined us in England, he was emotionally unavailable. In survival mode, he was busy making plans for the future. He wouldn't talk of Iran and there was absolutely no speaking in Farsi. Contact with extended family and friends was virtually impossible. It was as if the first seven years of my life had been erased. I thought my father's arrival would offer a bridge back to Iran, the only place I knew as home, but that bridge just wasn't there.

There was no road map explaining how to fit in, so I had

to figure things out on my own. In those early months, I learned two valuable things: how to recognize the invisible power hierarchy around me, and that no one would rescue me from being thrust to the bottom. Not that I didn't keep trying. At that age, I was still resilient.

We spent our second year in England in the city of Birmingham. It took a full year there to upgrade from "outsider" status to making a handful of friends, including ginger-topped Emily and sweet, quiet Claire. I liked our life in Birmingham better than Skellingthorpe. When you're different, living in a small place can be a liability: everyone notices you, but no one really sees you. We'd been more visible *and* invisible in my grandparents' small village. Birmingham was more cosmopolitan, more like Tehran; it offered more diversity and a big-city anonymity, so we blended in more. Yet getting a job was a challenge for my dark-skinned, foreign-born father. Despite his high status in Iran and his British education, my father was frequently unable to get interviews for entry-level accounting jobs. When he did eventually get one of these jobs, at an accounting firm in Birmingham, it was as though the stock market guru had been sent to the metaphorical stockroom.

Though my parents talked about moving to a number of nations where our British citizenship would permit us entry, like many immigrant families we followed the path of least resistance. One of my father's closest friends, Keyvan—one of the original seven sent by the Central Bank of Iran to study accountancy in England—had landed a job with the auditor general's office in Alberta, Canada. One rainy day indistinguishable from any other, Uncle

Keyvan excitedly called my father. "Did you see the ad in the London *Times?*" The Government of Alberta, in the capital city of Edmonton, was hiring. My father applied and was one of the lucky few to be selected for the handful of available positions. So it was that an old friend and a single phone call changed the course of all our lives.

In the spring of 1982, we began preparations to move from the tiny nation that had birthed the Commonwealth, home to some fifty-six million people, to a Canadian province with a similar land mass but a fraction of the population, at just two and a half million. From the Old World to the New. It was a blow to receive the news that we were leaving—again. Before departure, I was allowed to celebrate my birthday early, with a party that would double as a farewell to the friends I had made in Birmingham. Despite the balloons and birthday cake, presents and laughter, it was bittersweet. Emily, Claire, and I promised each other through our tears that we would write often, that we'd be best friends forever. (In girl time, "forever" translates to exactly four months.) I felt numb. England had just started to feel a little bit familiar.

My father flew to Canada before the rest of us to look for a house and get settled. He sent a postcard with a glossy photo of palm trees and a brilliantly red setting sun. To this day, I can't imagine any image further from the reality of the land of winter cold and snow that awaited us in Alberta. England's grey skies had nothing on Canada's long winters.

WE MOVED AT THE very end of May 1982, two days before
my ninth birthday. My first impression of Canada was
made on our way home from the airport, at a 7-Eleven at
the top of our new street, where my father invited each of
us to choose a special present, welcoming us to our new
home. "I want a torch, Daddy," was my plea. I emerged
with a small yellow flashlight. I don't know if I was afraid
of the dark or just liked the colour. Either way, I entered
our modest, corner-lot, split-level house with my new
flashlight in hand, prepared to beam light into whatever
darkness I found.

Uncle Keyvan and his wife, my Auntie Liz, hosted a
second birthday/welcome to Canada party for me at the
local pool. Amidst the balloons and water games it was a
happily boisterous event. They invited a handful of other
Persian families, and I was surrounded by enough familiarity to make the new seem inviting.

I couldn't believe all the swaths of open green space in
my new environment. We could drive a long way without seeing more than a handful of people walking by the
side of the road. How wide the roads were, how big the
houses! Everything in Canada was like looking through
a magnifying glass. We were settled in the middle of the
Prairies, famous for their pancake-flat landscape and endlessly sunny weather. In the height of summer, it would
stay light until 11 p.m., the sky a seductive and impetuous
mistress, changing her dress every half hour from cobalt to
cyan to cerulean, shades of transcendent blue. The prairie
sky, the open land, and the unflinching sun were the backdrop to the rest of my childhood. I was quickly anchored

to the place, finding unconscious respite in the vastness
continually hinting at freedom.

By contrast to the landscape, our neighbourhood had a
boxy, ordered feel to it. It lacked both the old-world charm
of Britain and the contained chaos of Iran. Despite the
township being called Sherwood Park, I couldn't imagine
a Robin Hood figure ever gracing a place like this. But
because it was different, it was also interesting. Most
of the modest houses around us displayed Block Parent
safety signs in their front windows. Schoolchildren acted
as crossing guards. We had to drive everywhere, even to
buy a carton of milk. The glorious exception was the Dairy
Queen a short walk up the street, which delivered a slice
of heaven in a paper cup otherwise known as an Oreo
Blizzard. I was thrilled to have my own bedroom for the
first time since leaving Iran — though I was oblivious to
the fact that the orange shag carpeting was a decade past
its expiration date. And shortly after our arrival, someone
from the local neighbourhood association dropped off a
welcome basket containing, among other things, a tin
of English corned beef. This small gift of a familiar item
seemed such a friendly gesture.

The suburban community of Sherwood Park was one
of the townships hugging the city of Edmonton. Sherwood
Park was loosely middle class, ranging from neighbourhoods with bigger homes on larger lots with more expensive
cars in the driveway to more modest homes like ours on
the other end of the spectrum. Overall, Alberta is a contradictory province. It has the most good-natured people, but
also the most politically conservative. Having been ruled

by right-wing parties for over half a century, the Alberta of
my childhood produced some of Canada's most successful
conservative political figures, including Preston Manning,
Ralph Klein, Ezra Levant, Stockwell Day, and long-time
prime minister Stephen Harper. This brand of conservatism espoused traditional (read: religious) family values and
viewed foreigners with suspicion. New immigrants stood
out; non-white immigrants even more so. People could be
friendly but still look at you suspiciously or put on a polite
face while holding closed the door to the club.

Census data shows that visible-minority immigrants
still made up a relatively small percentage of Canada's total
population in the early 1980s, at just 5 percent. Those who
did arrive tended to cluster in urban centres like Toronto
and Vancouver. There was a large South Asian community in south Edmonton but only a smattering of Indian or
Pakistani immigrants elsewhere in the city. By comparison,
Sherwood Park was a Norman Rockwell painting. Every
teacher, community group leader, politician, and store
clerk I encountered fit the image of middle-class Christian
whiteness. Except us. We were the colour. We were one
of the visible-minority families that made up less than one
percent of that township of about sixty thousand people.
We had the advantage of speaking English, but like most
newcomer families we had very little money with which
to begin our new lives.

Almost immediately after arriving I started school.
Deciding it was better to acclimatize sooner than later, my
parents enrolled me in grade three just a month before the
end of the school year. After a week at home sorting our

boxes, I was dying to get out of the house. Conveniently, the local school, Brentwood Elementary, was only a few minutes' walk from our house. We were given a tour of the school and I liked what I saw. The playground was huge, and the classrooms were double the size of those in Britain. There was a lot of light and colour. With my backpack over my shoulders and wearing a new outfit, including pink leg warmers, I was ready to venture forward. Everything in this new land seemed possible, including happiness.

Into the class of all-white, Canadian-born children I marched—this brown-skinned, curly-haired little girl with a British accent and a bossy, forthright nature. Needless to say, I stood out like a neon crayon in a box of pastel colours. It didn't take more than a couple of weeks for the first flush of hopeful anticipation to fade. The students were initially wary, then openly rejecting: "I don't want to be your partner," "You're weird," "Don't let her sit here." Once it started, it was contagious. Mostly it was kids in my own class and grade, but it dashed my hopes of this new place being an improvement over England. Two years away from the fiery, confident girl I had been in Iran, my resilience levels were low.

It was an immense relief when school ended, and for two short months of summer my brother, sister, and I were free to visit the local pool, explore our neighbourhood on second-hand bikes, and spend hours kicking a soccer ball around in our big backyard. I caught my breath again.

⌣

UNAWARE OF THE SEVERITY of shunning I had already experienced, my parents assumed that a new class and school year would reboot the social dynamics. I was wary but hopeful as well. The beginning of a new term arrives with that "I'm going to conquer, here I come!" mentality, as if, with the right pair of shoes and shiny enough smile, you'll be able to start over.

My grade four teacher was Mrs. Bunny, and her personality matched her moniker. Once again I was the only different-looking child in the class, and while the other children openly mocked me, refused to sit near me, and avoided me on the playground, Mrs. Bunny sat inanely by, unable or unwilling to intervene. Kids graduated from avoiding me to making it so that anyone who touched or spoke to me was contaminated and would be shunned as well. If I reached for a book, no one would touch it afterwards. When the gym teacher assigned me, always the last one standing, to one of the teams, my classmates would jump away with open calls of "Ewww, gross, get away!"

My torment would start with the walk to school, which took me along a short section of forest skirting the edge of the school playground. The trees offered a reprieve from having to walk across the open field in front of the other students, who would ignore me if I was lucky but would more often ridicule my hair or braces or whatever else would score laughter from their friends. But this escape was not without its own hazards. There was a group of boys around my age who also took the forest route, and if they were behind me I inevitably became their target. They would call out, "Paki, hey Paki!" Then, as their voices got closer, "Why do you smell so bad?" The possibility of attack hung in the air. Running wasn't an option as it would only encourage them to chase. Sweating, I would put one foot resolutely in front of the other, trying in vain to block out their taunts and threats, my whole system on high alert.

About halfway through that year a new girl joined our class. I remember the spark of excitement I felt: here, perhaps, was someone who could be a friend. The day started off well. The teacher chose me to show the new girl—another Emily—around during recess. Emily shared my love of books, and we spent the twenty-minute morning recess talking about our favourite characters in the corner of the schoolyard as we watched the other children chatter and play around us. Nancy Drew. Anne of Green Gables. Harriet the Spy. I thought for sure Emily must be a kindred spirit to love the same feisty heroines I did.

"Do you wanna come over to my house after school?" I shyly asked her.

"Yes," she instantly replied, "I'd like that."

I spent the rest of the day planning what snacks I would assemble—definitely something with peanut butter!—to impress her. By the afternoon bell, however, she would no longer speak to me, or make eye contact. She had been poisoned against me by my classmates, who had made it clear to her that I presented a risk to her own nebulous social status.

Other kids came to signify a threat. Learning quickly that there was no place to escape while on school grounds, I lived in a constant state of hyper-vigilance, always ready for fight or flight.

After Emily, the initial flaring of hope for something magical to happen to change my circumstances just disappeared. By the end of that first year in Canada, I no longer let myself believe that I could be liked.

⌐

ON MY FIRST REPORT card in October, my grades were the lowest I'd ever had in my life—Bs and Cs, in a household where only As were acceptable. The Dashtgards, like many new immigrant families, placed a great value on learning. Both my parents were college educated, and they believed that education produced knowledge, and that knowledge was power—the key to climbing the social ladder in one's adopted land, the very currency of belonging.

When I returned home from school that fateful fall day, I entered our kitchen to find my father seated at the table. I'd hoped he'd forgotten what day it was, but of course his first words to me were, "Where's your report card?" I slowly handed it to him, avoiding eye contact. As soon as he'd scanned the report, my father exploded. "You are stupid, good for nothing! Worthless." Crumpling up the piece of white paper with its black marks, he threw it across the room at me. Then he started towards me. "You don't deserve to live here!" he shouted, coming close and stabbing a finger into my chest. I stood frozen, trying to meld my body into the wall behind me. I had no words to explain myself. It was the first time I remember encountering such rage from him.

In retrospect, I can see my father's anger being a mask for his fear, seeing his child in such a vulnerable position.

Perhaps it was also a response to shame, my own outsider status riding too close to his. At the time, I took his reaction as proof that the problem must be me. Why couldn't I please him? I couldn't admit to him what was happening at school. I was terrified he would see in me what the other kids saw. Our script was set: I became desperate to redeem myself and he to eliminate any signs of vulnerability in me. From then on, academic performance (really, performance of any sort) became my perceived path to redemption and the metric of my self-worth.

SOON AFTER THE REPORT-CARD incident I was diagnosed with a bladder infection, which prompted me to pee multiple times during the day. With antibiotics the infection cleared up, but the behaviour didn't change. I was fine during the day, but at night I'd continue to visit the bathroom multiple times. It started to become a ritual. I would count my visits to the bathroom, unable to sleep until I had visited a certain number of times — sometimes six, sometimes nine, occasionally more than twenty-one. It had to be in multiples of three. If I went once, I was guaranteed to go at least twice more. But it wasn't just the frequency of visits that was a problem, it was also the length of time I spent on the toilet: rarely less than thirty minutes, sometimes hours. I couldn't sleep until I felt my bladder was completely empty, or beyond empty, a physically impossible state to achieve.

My bedroom was across the hall from my parents' and

so my nightly trips to the toilet kept my father awake. He responded in much the same way he had after seeing Cs splashed across my first report card: with anger and threats thrown at me night after night, trying to keep me in my room, trying to squelch behaviour he viewed as clearly not "normal." Yet no matter how much he raged at me to stop, I couldn't hold back. I was in the throes of compulsive behaviour. Nighttime found me lying on my bed in the dark, huddled under blankets, silently counting, my body hyper-alert for every creak and whisper until I felt it was safe to go just one more time. Then I would creep down the hallway on tiptoe, praying to be left alone to complete my ritual of release.

These nightly trips became my outlet, and my father's invasion of this space only fed the compulsion. Most of the time he threatened me verbally, but occasionally I was jostled, pushed, or even smacked. Although such disciplinary measures were not uncommon at the time, the impact on me was that the threats from outside the home became amplified by threats inside the home. I became more afraid. In response, I would retreat into my bedroom, feeling trapped and panicked. Regardless of how scared I was, I would just wait on my bed, trembling, until I thought he'd fallen asleep again. I could only sleep when it felt like the right time. I, or some primal part of me, had to be the one to make the call. I needed control. Until that point, I would sit on the toilet, often propping my head on my arms, as I sat watching the seconds tick past midnight, desperate for rest, yet unable to surrender.

The real cost of immigration is the assumption of safety. I no longer felt safe. Even inside my own skin.

THREE
Tundra

FOR THE FIRST FEW years in Canada my mother stayed at home. Her British teaching credentials didn't qualify her to teach in Canada, so she went from assistant-principal of an international school in a major metropolis to housewife. It was nice for us, though not always easy for her, and I never heard her complain. My father worked hard at his new job, his unhappiness only evident in his near-constant anger and growing irritability at home.

Like many new immigrant families, we spent a lot of time, especially in those first few years, happily exploring the land around us: the Prairies and the Rocky Mountains. Not only was everything new and therefore exciting, it was also close at hand. Our family of five would regularly squish into our Chevy Malibu with food for a picnic lunch, hot water in a thermos for tea, and supplies for building a campfire. The kids would fight over who got the window seats (my sister, the youngest, usually lost), who got to pour the first cup of tea, and who would be in charge of building the fire to roast our hotdogs. I excelled at shoving aside my younger siblings to successfully lay the teepee foundation, and best of all, light the match, under my mother's watchful eye. The highlight of these explorations was jumping into whatever bodies of water we found ourselves near. I have memories of diving into many a glacial lake, often the only person willing to brave the cold, gleefully swimming as fast as I could through mineral-infused, gem-coloured waters. Face in turquoise. Flash of evergreen. Speed in body. Water was my home element.

In grade five, my love of water led me to join the local Silver Tide competitive swim club. I began attending swim practice three evenings and at least one morning (6:30 a.m.!) every week. And at least one weekend a month there was some kind of swim competition. I found respite in the quiet buzz that comes from repetitive exercise, the particular fullness of silence underwater, a silence that can bear sound without breaking. After each practice session I felt cleaned out, strong. And I was good at it, which really mattered to me at the time. It was something I could do on my own terms, with minimal interaction with others. Swimming is an extremely solitary sport. Many sports are, but there is something about being immersed in a physical element that separates you from others. When I was in the water, I wasn't brown, or different, or shunned, I was just in motion — another body blurring past.

It was good to have a physical anchor to counterbalance the internal stresses that had become a normal part of my everyday life. Social violence is different than its physical counterpart, harder to observe, more easily transmitted, and ever-present. The level of isolation I felt was so extreme that, as time went on, sometimes it even felt as if negative attention was better than none.

I was in the middle of grade six when one day a blond-haired boy a couple of years younger than me approached me as I was entering the school after recess. He looked me right in the eye, curled his upper lip in a sneer, and spat as hard as he could: a gooey white gob landed on the top of my shoe. I stood frozen to the spot. But in a twisted way I was also relieved. Here was proof that I mattered enough to elicit a strong reaction from someone. It was a sign that I existed.

The highlight of my years at Brentwood Elementary occurred during gym class in that same year. Usually I dreaded gym. Watching classmates choose their team members was a form of social torture, for a short time the pecking order rendered painfully visible. On this day, towards the end of class, as equipment was being disassembled, a group of my peers accidentally dropped one of the metal volleyball poles on my head. As I numbly felt sticky blood trickling down my scalp, my classmates clustered around, thrusting their faces close to mine. Bliss, to experience even a few moments of intimacy through their visible concern. It was the only time I can remember when all eyes on me felt unthreatening.

The only other brown student I remember in my grade was named Rajesh, and he lived a couple of blocks away. There was no solace to be found in each other's company, however, as together we were just more visible in our brownness, or, more accurately, our non-whiteness. In grade six Rajesh won the top prize at our annual school science fair. I remember watching as he accepted his blue ribbon, for a moment catching his eye, both of us unable to look away fast enough. Seeing ourselves reflected in the other's expression was too close for comfort. At least if we kept far apart we could each individually hold on to the pretense of fitting in, or at least protect ourselves from the reminder of how much we didn't. It's striking that the only people whose names I remember from those years are other non-white kids close to me in age: Pia, who was Asian; Rajesh, who was Indian; and Sonia, who was also some kind of Desi (someone of South Asian origin). Clearly my unconscious mind registered them as closest to my clan. I was drowning in white.

The low point of those early years also occurred in my last year at Brentwood Elementary, when my parents were called in for a special meeting with my teacher. I remember standing between my mother and father in the classroom as my teacher tried to illuminate why the other children didn't want to sit near me. "They say that Annahid smells," she explained, and then went on to give credence to my bullies by making their insults into an issue of personal hygiene. "How often is she showering?" she asked.

I watched as my mother responded with another question—"What kind of smell?"—caught between wanting to appease and trying to understand. My father had a defeated look on his face, balancing his own shame with concern for his daughter. Though my father was, in my eyes, an unquestionable paragon of authority, in that elementary school classroom he seemed somehow smaller. The teacher never once made eye contact with me.

I felt the hammer blow of that exchange in my soul. After a thousand cuts, something inside me severed. The soft animal went into hiding, trapped in the frozen tundra. That moment locked in my belief that there was something deeply wrong with me. It was easier to believe the problem was me than to lose faith in the ability of my parents and the adults around me to make things better. What child wants to grow up in a world that seems unfixable?

Soon after the parent-teacher conference on hygiene I was referred to the school counsellor for help. I began attending weekly sessions.

⌒

MY MOTHER SAW OTHERS' poor treatment of me through the lens of childhood bullying, not as a systemic rejection of a brown body in a sea of whiteness. I believe it was too hard for her to acknowledge that what I was experiencing was racism, because then she would be more closely linked to the racial identity of my tormentors than to me, her child.

Similarly, my father didn't want to name "racism," because any association with victimhood meant a drop in social status. The message I was left with, by forces both inside and outside the home, was: "You're the problem. Work harder, be better. Fix yourself, little girl!" The implication was that if I did something differently, the entire social structure might somehow magically shift. I knew even then that wasn't possible.

How does any person or group know they are popular? They measure the distance from where they stand to the farthest outposts. Status comes down to simple mathematics, and we learn to calculate our role in the hierarchy within milliseconds of meeting someone new. I had become the margin, thanklessly securing others' more elevated status.

And the discrimination I experienced and observed wasn't confined to school—it was everywhere. It could be seen in subtle dynamics, like the time we went to a church event for Father's Day and I watched as other parents easily chatted while my dad, despite all his charms, was left on the sidelines, his fixed smile reading as a grimace.

Sometimes it would come out more overtly.

Just before starting my final year of elementary school, in 1984, I went on a Girl Guide camping trip. Guiding was one of the few activities that had been consistent in my life since leaving Iran. I had started as a Brownie in England, then graduated to a Girl Guide in Canada. Every week we'd meet in the school gym, where I learned how to tie knots and sew by hand, filling my sash with badges until all that was missing was the coveted camping badge. To get it, I had to go on the camping trip.

I spent days carefully preparing all my equipment, excited to finally show off my fire-building skills. On the day of the trip, my mom dropped me off after I'd double-checked all my gear, and I waved proudly as I climbed into the minivan. But despite my high expectations, I did not fare well. The Guide leader immediately disliked me. She made a habit of ignoring me, overlooking me when it came time to assign tasks, and openly belittling me in front of the other girls.

One evening, as we were all gathered in the group kitchen to make dinner, I was asked to open a can of beans. I hesitated. The leader looked in my direction with a sneer on her face as she barked, "Don't you know what a can opener looks like?"

The answer was no. I didn't know what a manual can opener looked like because we owned an electric one that my mother had bought through her part-time job in the housewares department at the Hudson's Bay store. I felt myself sweating, unable to find the appropriate words to answer. I desperately didn't want to appear ignorant in front of my fellow Girl Guides.

The leader reached over, pushing me aside, and grabbed the can opener from the drawer in front of me. "Who doesn't know what this is?!" she repeated scornfully, as if I were the stupidest creature on earth.

Despite being one of the few girls who knew how to collect wood and arrange the twigs into both a log cabin and a teepee formation — I had spent a lot of time in nature, after all — at the end of the trip I was the only one who didn't receive my badge. No explanation was given. Apparently, I had the honour of being the first girl to fail a camping trip in the history of Guiding in the province of Alberta. My not-easily-angered mother wrote an assertive letter to the camping trip leader and dropped it off in her mailbox. She then wrote to the regional director. We never received a response from either woman. I left Girl Guides soon after.

An interesting addendum: I didn't remember any of this until my mother reminded me as I was beginning to write this book. So much detail from my childhood remains buried under protective layers of forgetting.

⌒

ONE OF MY WAYS of coping in those early years was to escape into my imagination. I became a daydreamer. Sometimes I would spend whole days between the covers of a book, imagining myself in various idyllic settings.

My favourite real-world place to be was the local library, hidden somewhere among the shelves. Our township library was a wonderful, light-filled, open environment. One of the librarians, Mrs. Schindel, a woman blessed with an abundant halo of honey-coloured hair and a silky voice to match, would roll out a red-carpet welcome whenever I arrived. She always had a smile on her face, and she patiently answered all of my questions, guiding me towards books she thought I might like, such as *Charlotte's Web*, *The Secret Garden*, and anything by L. M. Montgomery. Escaping into an alternate reality through the pages of a book was preferable to raging at the real world I confronted every day. I preferred books where characters acted nobly, and with great love. I found that reassuring.

At home, I was looking for a way to be myself, and to safely express my anger, but I wasn't going to find that in the complicated relationship I now had with my parents, both of whom seemed heavily invested in denial of what was really going on. And so I ended up venting a lot of my frustration on my younger brother, Shahin. Shahin mirrored back to me the parts of myself that I had learned to feel ashamed of. He wanted my attention, but, like most little brothers, he tried to get it with teasing, taunts, and annoying jabs. And that did nothing but remind me of all the cruel provocations I faced out in the world and could not respond to. So Shahin would tease, and I would lash out at him cruelly in return. All siblings fight, but I was trying to inflict damage. Soon, the boy who had once greeted everyone with a happy smile was gone; my brother had learned to shield himself. I had, in effect, helped to pass my own mutilated self-image down the line.

My sister Fariba, on the other hand, was a refuge. She thought the sun rose and set on my shoulders, and from her I felt the rare reflection of unconditional love. When we were little she would knock on my door before bedtime each night, always with a different excuse. I'd entertain her for a bit and then tickle her while exclaiming, "Disperse! Disperse now!" This nightly ritual became our routine and private joke — her tugging at my attention, me teasingly turning her aside with language out of a Jane Austen novel. Using big words, sheltering myself in a place of intellectual superiority, became another sanctuary.

When my brother and I weren't squabbling, my siblings and I were a team. We would sometimes hang out with other kids on our street, but more often we lazed around in our basement playroom, making up games, wrestling with each other, teasing my father about the cherry blossom mural he'd insisted on because it reminded him of

Iran. Even in the 1980s that decor trend did not pass muster.

Saturday mornings were spent in front of the TV watching cartoons: *The Mighty Hercules, Scooby-Doo,* and my personal favourite, *The Smurfs.* Sunday evenings were marked by a very British beans-on-toast supper eaten in pyjamas on the couch. We were allowed one candy each night after dinner, and the three of us would fight like dogs to get to the drawer first to make our pick, like a movie star at Tiffany's selecting a diamond ring for his lover.

Eventually, we were each allowed to choose a small pet. My brother chose a rabbit that bit so hard it drew blood and later (perhaps as an illustration of poetic justice) was eaten by a neighbourhood dog. (Rabbit number two lived longer.) My sister cycled through so many guineas pigs (they have a short lifespan) that I lost count. But I declined the invitation. I didn't want the responsibility of looking after anything else.

We'd gather every couple of weeks with Uncle Keyvan, Auntie Liz, and their boys, marking birthdays, Iranian and Christian cultural celebrations, or just because. The summer when I was twelve we were over at their house one very hot afternoon. I remember their oldest son, Padra (who was a year older than me), taking off his shirt to cool down and taunting me as he pranced around. In a flash, I pulled my own shirt over my head before I had time to think. "Girls can do this too, you know!" I retorted. The part of me that had felt anger years earlier in Iran at the idea of being constrained in a chador when boys would continue to dress comfortably was still there. I knew what fairness was, and I did not hesitate to give it voice.

Padra looked surprised, but he didn't challenge me. In that familial space, he knew I could hold my own.

⌒

MY MATERNAL GRANDMOTHER, Elsie Exton, had followed in our footsteps and immigrated to Canada a year after us, in 1983. My grandfather, Allan, had passed away in England not long before that. An outspoken woman, she came and wrapped us kids in her protective presence like a chinook, a warm prairie wind. I learned how to sew sitting beside her solid bulk. She also taught me how to play Scrabble, using all the seemingly endless two-letter words to best advantage. But mostly she provided a refuge; her apartment was one of the few places I could let go a bit. As I grew older, the first thing I would do when I visited was lie down on the couch to nap. Then we would have tea in china cups that now adorn my kitchen shelves. I remember her regularly chiding me for outbursts of temper by blowing patience into the top of my head (counting slowly from one to ten). As she grew older she became hard of hearing, so I had to speak slowly and enunciate more clearly. The lessons in patience continued as I learned to repeat things for the second... or fifth time. Just as my sister became an unconditionally loving presence for me, my grandmother was of a similar ilk on the other end of the age spectrum.

I also made one, best friend; I was happy to embrace quality over quantity. Every week my mother took my siblings and me to Trinity Baptist Church. One Sunday I looked across the aisle to meet the eyes of a girl my age named Caroline. As we left the service we gravitated towards each other like metal filings to a magnet, linked by our fragile status as newbies in the church community. By the end of that first service, I felt confident enough to tentatively ask her, "Do you want to come over to my house for a sleepover?"

It took her only a moment to matter-of-factly respond, "Okay."

Caroline slept many a night beside my bed, though I more often slept sandwiched between her and her sister at their home on an acreage outside of Sherwood Park. It was the beginning of a lifelong friendship marked by hours on the phone (as only teenage girls can manage), clothes swapping, and countless summer camp adventures. Years later, Caroline was the one to scrape the hair back from my temples as she helped style my unruly locks in preparation for my marriage ceremony. Although my Persian background was little referenced in our friendship, she helped fan the embers of the girl I had been.

Around the same time I met Caroline, my best friend from my childhood days in Iran sent me a letter. Mehrnaz had lived down the road from our marble-built mansion in Tehran. One of the few memories I have left from those times is of sleeping over at her house, and her mother giving us both a cup of warm milk with a spoonful of sugar before bed—liquid comfort. We wrote back and forth a couple of times until she sent me a letter filled with anti-Western sentiment. She praised the Ayatollah Khomeini, talked about studying the Quran in school, and then went on to denounce the TV shows, movies, and books that she assumed I was consuming. The insinuation was that I was lost as a Westerner, inferior somehow.

I didn't laugh it off; I couldn't put it into perspective. How dare she judge *me*? I felt furious as well as helpless. In retrospect, I see her as a stand-in for the girl I had been. I was angry that I wasn't allowed to be *her* any longer, furious that that girl no longer existed because the Iran I knew had radically changed since our departure, and outraged because the Persian girl I used to be best friends with was also now rejecting me.

As an adult I have since reconnected with Mehrnaz. She is a journalist and interpreter now working in the United States for the *Washington Post* and BBC World News. She is no longer the girl she used to be either.

⌐

IN THE SUMMER OF 1985, after graduating from elementary school, I attended my first week-long overnight camp run by the City of Edmonton. The days were filled with activities, and at night we slept in tents around a campfire surrounded by teenage staff. The nights were especially challenging because I still needed to make numerous trips to the toilet. Each time, I had to climb out of my tent, walk across the patch of grass towards the fire, and ask to be escorted down the forest path.

On the last evening of the trip I had to go pee, but I had already gone to the outhouse twice. I was frozen with shame at the thought of requesting to go again. Yet the more I suppressed it, the stronger I felt the urge to go.

The dark shadows that surrounded the campfire began to take on mythic proportions. They were guards and I was in a prison cell. If I ventured out again, those young bodies in the darkness, whom I was forced to depend on while there, would laugh at me and think I was damaged. I couldn't—wouldn't—invite that experience again, so I was left sweating inside my tent, hands clenched and heart racing. After more than two hours of staring out through the tent flap into the darkness, in my panic I finally gave way to a desperate last resort. Careful not to wake my tent mate, I seized a nearby garbage bag that had held my sleeping bag and clumsily peed into it. Terror, yes. Shame, profound. But I also felt something akin to protection. Like an animal primitively marking its territory, I was claiming a safe place to exist.

As trapped as I felt, I also experienced in that moment the ability to rally on my own behalf. Looking back, it was a tipping point.

Soon afterwards, after more than five years of having been the ostracized outsider at school but maintaining silence at home, I spoke up. A letter arrived that summer containing information about the junior high school I was to attend. Going there meant that I would continue with the same cohort of kids from my elementary school. I remember sitting after dinner with a parent on either side, begging, as tears streaked down each cheek, "Please don't send me there. Please!" I knew for certain that I couldn't win against the curl of a lip, the turn of a body as I approached, the insidious cloaked contempt. And I also knew that I couldn't go on—something had to change. It was the first time I had let myself cry openly on my own behalf in front of anyone since we had left Iran. As the sobs came, I bent over at the waist. I couldn't hold it all together any longer. Although at the time it felt like weakness, I realize it was a part of me stepping forward to advocate for myself. It was a plea to my parents for help. And this time it was answered. My mother wrote a letter to our district superintendent, with the result that I was placed in a different middle school for grades seven to nine. Hallelujah!

⌒

MORE THAN THREE DECADES later, when I was pregnant with my first child, I decided to go back and visit Brentwood Elementary as a way of making peace with the preadolescent part of my childhood. As I walked through the front doors of the school and down the main hallway, catching sight of the black-and-white photos of my younger self, I noticed a deep exhaustion start to creep through my entire body. I passed by the school office, and the administrator—a middle-aged woman who could have been a transplant from the past—called me in.

"Can I ask why you're here?" she said.

"I was a student here many years ago," I responded. Then, looking for validation—still!—I went on, "I was bullied here as a child." I considered using the word "racism" but opted to omit it as I didn't want to offend her. Her facial expression didn't change. "Hopefully," I ploughed on, feigning a lightness I didn't feel, "things have changed since then."

I saw her gaze harden, then her eyes dropped down to the desk surface, her silence a tacit signal that I was dismissed.

I was surprised by the immediate wave of rejection that washed over me, followed by an intense rage. I felt swept away from my own body, and I sank into the seat directly outside her office. In her micro-response lay the entirety of my childhood. It was the same pattern: implicit blame that somehow I was the one at fault. How hard would it have been for her to simply say, "I'm sorry that happened to you"? My difference still unconsciously registered to her as a threat.

I felt bone-tired, so much so that I couldn't imagine walking back to my car. With eyes closed, I pictured my body sinking down through the floor, past each subsequent layer of dirt, rock, and lava, so that I could finally come to rest deep in the earth's core. I hadn't entered the school feeling that way. The heaviness was a kind of reflex or muscle memory, evidence that childhood had been a punishing place to live — correction: a punishing place to survive.

FOUR

Mixed-Race Misfits

IN THE FALL OF 1985—the same year the Iran-Iraq War reached its midpoint, Michael Jackson and Lionel Ritchie wrote "We Are the World," and *Back to the Future* came out— I started attending Clover Bar Junior High School on the other side of Sherwood Park. During the shoulder seasons (September and October, and from April to the end of the school year), I'd bike there in forty-five minutes, and during winter I'd spend an equivalent time on the bus. The school was closer to my grandmother's apartment than our own house, so a side benefit of attending Clover Bar was that I got to improve my Scrabble skills. By grade six I had mastered the addiction-to-perfection mode and was able to manufacture the requisite A grades, so I was placed in the gifted stream, where it was safe, encouraged even, to be smart. Although the move didn't eradicate the more subtle forms of discrimination, it skimmed the daily dose of overt hatred off the plate.

Even though we had little money for new clothes, I loved dressing up. I believed that if I could just find the right outfit maybe I'd unlock the door to belonging. In one of my standard outfits—blue pinstriped polyester pants, red acrylic sweater, and gelled hair set like a square helmet on my head—I looked like an unfashionable version of Melanie Griffith in the hit film *Working Girl*. I may not have been trendy, but I remained blissfully unaware.

Except when it came to my hair. It was not my crowning glory, and I knew it. No one, but no one, knew how to cut wild, curly Persian hair, and if I left it untamed I'd look as if I'd just stuck my finger in an electrical socket. I remember going to the mall with Caroline to get a haircut; she left looking like she was from Venus, and I looked like an alien from some planet way out of this solar system. It was easier to tamp my hair down with gels and sprays, but that also invited social censure. If we were jumping on the trampoline in gym class, the other girls' hair would billow out gracefully with each jump. My hair wouldn't move. Not a single inch. My attempts at flying were choreographed to the background music of teenage girls twittering. Either it was too unruly or too repressed—an externalization of how I felt all the time. Although the rejection during these middle years wasn't as overt, it was still like being surrounded by an invisible force field I couldn't break through, no matter how hard I tried.

From grade seven until the end of high school, Caroline and I belonged to a Baptist church youth group that organized weekly adventures, including mini-golf, rollerblading, and visits to the West Edmonton Mall. These outings were the highlights of my teen years. The group gave me my first experience of real friendship post-Iran. Having a shared set of values created an island of safety where I could relax. Although my family were still very much "others" adrift in our community, the church group offered a lifeline. While people might not accept me, Jesus did. I didn't feel that the church was taking advantage of my neediness, or trying to brainwash me. Christianity allowed me to feel a connection to a part of my consciousness that sat outside the present moment, larger than me and what I was experiencing. When I prayed, I felt more expansive. It was comforting to know that there was some experience beyond what I felt on a day-to-day basis. It was like being tethered to a hot-air balloon that could lift me above the fray in moments when I needed to get perspective, allowing me to glimpse other possibilities, perhaps even future selves.

AS I GREW INTO my teens, the conflicting, invisible undercurrents in our household provided more emotional pressure. The language of love was uttered through conflict: competition, blame, retaliation, recrimination, insult, yelling, sometimes screaming, and occasionally silence — all played out against a backdrop of shame. Power and love are codependent forces, and love in the shadow of parents who were stripped of their social and personal power became an unreliable beast. Present but injured.

The household tone was set by my father, and to a lesser extent also by me. At a young age I became conscious of the dynamics of power: how to identify it, who possessed it, and later how to attain it. I learned that anger was an expression of power, and so it became my go-to emotion. Anger became both my sword and my shield.

My father was a powerful dictator at home, yet I was painfully aware that if he accompanied me to any social event outside of the home he was immediately tagged as lower rank because of his skin colour, accent, and overzealous body language. We may as well have had a neon light flashing above our heads saying, "We don't belong here! We don't belong here!" I felt simultaneously protective and ashamed of him. I hated seeing people underestimate or avoid him, but at the same time I wished he didn't have to have such a thick accent or be quite so loud in public places. By virtue of her gender and conflict-avoidant personality, my mother had less influence inside our home, yet in the outside world she carried more racial and cultural status. Socially, she blended in with the dominant group, and being out with her made our brownness somewhat more palatable.

To survive, my father forced all visible signs of foreignness into the closet. We all paid a price for that decision. He directed his anger mostly towards the dominant cultural (European) and religious (Christian) markers in our new community. Once, as we were almost out the door, he forced us to stay back from attending a St. Patrick's Day party at our local pool. "Why participate in another 'Western' holiday when no other culture's landmarks are recognized?" he cried. I was furious at being denied the opportunity to participate in something social, especially when I could not understand the reason.

His fury often felt random. On another occasion, he blew up about the *Anne of Green Gables* books I was reading, insisting that they were "reinforcing the wrong ideas." His unvoiced fear was that we would grow up as "white kids" with no connection to Persian culture, or, by extension, to him. Yet his fear of the family being further branded as outsiders meant that we lost any fluency in Farsi, we had no grounding in cultural traditions like *Nowruz* apart from attending the annual celebration, and we had no sense of the Shia Islamic tradition that our father had grown up in—we never once set foot in a mosque after leaving Iran.

In fact, religion became a lightning rod for the household power divide. My father's rejection of Islam meant that we didn't continue to celebrate the *Eid* holidays in the same way that cultural Christians will celebrate Christmas and Easter. Yet the more he disowned his upbringing, the stronger the ghost of Islamic culture became in our household, as he fought against Christian influences to protect a tradition he never acknowledged openly in any way.

My mother went in the opposite direction, openly practising her religion in our newly adopted country. Maintaining her Christianity had been a way of asserting her identity when she moved to Iran—we kids were all raised in the Christian faith—and in Canada she had the additional benefit of a wide community of support. My mother thus became the target for my father's rage at losing his social status: her whiteness, her British-ness, her Christianity were all part of the invisible cloak of power she was able to wear in Canada. She was a victim of my father's aggression, and my father was a victim of social

violence: sexism versus racism. They both struggled with
external forces that reflected back to them an unworthy
and inadequate self-image.

For years I could see only my mother's suffering.
Emotional abuse is easily visible. It took me until early
adulthood to recognize the extent of my father's struggles.
Systemic violence like racism is less visible because it occurs
on a much broader scale, requiring a wide lens trained on
the whole of society. I was twenty-three when I came across
a confidential file from my father's time with the office of
the auditor general of Alberta. It revealed that sometime
during those early years after immigrating my father had
filed a claim of racism against his employer, citing racial
prejudice as a reason for being held back from a promotion
that was his due. I was shocked. He had never once mentioned it at home. And he wasn't alone. An Iranian relative
of ours in the United States completed a two-year master's
degree only to receive a failing F grade on his final paper.
Unbeknownst to him, his thesis supervisor was the regional
director of the Ku Klux Klan.

My father rose from extreme poverty to become auditor
general of Iran, only to face racial discrimination on the
other side of the ocean in the lower ranks of a provincial
government office. He went from making the rules in Iran
(social privilege) to being a racial minority in Canada unable
to deviate from a single social norm (oppression).

Imagine forgetting the polite Western greeting of
extending a hand and defaulting instead to leaning in to
kiss someone three times back and forth on both cheeks.
In 1980s Alberta such an action was tantamount to social

suicide. Decades later, when I asked him if he thought about Iran after being forced to leave, my father's response, after an uncharacteristic moment of hesitation, was simply, "Those first years I missed Iran at least 50 percent of the time—all the opportunities I had." He too was pushed to the margins in this new country, and we all became collateral damage as he raged to regain territory within the home we shared.

COMING HOME WITH MY mom from Sunday church services was one of the worst times of the week. We'd say grace before eating a traditional British lunch of roast beef with potatoes, Yorkshire pudding, gravy, and some kind of limp vegetable, followed by pie, always served with perfectly smooth yellow Bird's custard (a very worthy British export). The meal was tasteful, the ambience less so. Meals like this brought the battle lines into focus, each meal another skirmish in the long-running war. My father would begin by lobbing a grenade towards Christianity, starting with a deceptively mild inquiry about the subject of the sermon. My mother would always treat his question seriously, as if he might be won over if given enough information, thus lighting the fuse. I would sit silently at the edge of the table, praying that this time my mother wouldn't take the bait. Yet, it was the same every time—the ruder his questions and remarks, the more detail she offered. She would attempt to justify her beliefs, while he would attempt to tear them to pieces (I see now that for him they represented the epitome of WASP privilege). I always jumped to her defence, and these meals would typically end with at least one family member in tears while my father and I were left going at it.

I became a scrapper. Like my father in temperament, I would take him on, feeling it was my role to defend the rest of our family. I learned from him how to mould anger into sharp verbal weapons and to hurl them across the table at my opponent. He would goad me, attack what I was saying, and then chide me for overreacting. There was no "right" response—I was either being pushed further or criticized for going too far. We found intimacy in this dance of wills that took place on an almost daily basis. My father would pick on a different family member for some innocuous issue, such as my mother not cooking dinner the right way, my brother not finishing his homework, or my sister not listening. Then the volume of my father's voice would rise along with the spectre of encroaching violence. I learned to step into the breach and yell back at him, protecting mother, brother, and sister by pushing him away. He was a bully, and he became the bully I could fight. Perhaps channelling all that anger helped me; it became a way to keep the fire burning inside. It was easier to fight each other than to acknowledge the bars of the cultural prison we were caught inside.

BEING MIXED RACE — caught between the identities of British and Persian, Christian and Muslim, white and brown skin—meant inheriting a fragmented sense of self. There was no tribe that reflected me back to myself completely, no place where belonging was an unspoken presumption. Each situation required its own decoding so I could figure out which part of myself to showcase, which tricks to pull out to encourage acceptance. My mixed-race identity created a constant feeling that if I could just lose ten or twenty pounds off my personality I'd finally be in the club.

One of the most significant signposts of Iranian culture is *ta'aroof*-ing, a complex social dance that goes back and forth following an expression of unconditional generosity, often establishing social rank. Ten people knock on the door at midnight, and they are invited in, with the host *ta'aroof*-ing that they simply must stay and eat. The would-be guests decline the invitation; they couldn't possibly impose. Back and forth it goes, with each side becoming more insistent until a mutual understanding is reached based on an implicit understanding of each party's limits. In Canada, people always took the *ta'aroof*-ing at face value, and my dad got into hot water numerous times in our early years as a result. On one occasion he invited another five-person family on holiday with us (fine enough), except they were also expecting to hitch a ride in our Chevy station wagon (not so fine). Right up until the very last minute, my father continued trying to come up with a way to fit them in, including stowing a couple of us away in the trunk. I love this part of Persian culture — the over-the-top generosity — and as an adult, I still find myself *ta'aroof*-ing until I realize I'm in the middle of an offer I know I won't be able to follow through on. You can take the girl out of Iran, but you can't take Iran out of the girl, I figure.

Iranians deliberately exaggerate their feelings and opinions all the time. And they are always, always late. Even after Dad set up his own accounting firm, he would regularly arrive at least an hour late for client appointments, sometimes half a day! He'd apologize profusely, and then repeat the behaviour again the next time. This is another habit I picked up from him, though I've got myself down to fifteen minutes (most of the time). If I arrive late for a Persian cultural event no one bats an eyelash.

Canada is the opposite: modelled on British culture, punctuality is associated with trustworthiness. It is often the least emotionally expressive person in a group who holds the most social rank. And while Iranian culture is modelled on relationships, everything a bit messy and overlapping, Canadian culture is systematized and very boundaried. Chatting politely to white folks in any social setting was completely different from the constant noisy squabbling among Iranian friends and family members. At Persian gatherings I usually ate a lot more: being on the losing end of a *ta'aroof* meant that I had a lot of unwanted food heaped on my plate! By contrast, at Canadian events I would often get subtle questioning glances if I went for second helpings. As time went on, I became hyper-focused on pleasing others in whatever context I found myself, often at the cost of my own feelings, needs, and boundaries. I learned to code-switch: mastering the art of shifting gears between the implicit rules governing the different cultural zones I moved through.

We would dip our feet back into Persian culture about once a year at the *Nowruz* gathering every spring equinox.

My father was president of the Alberta Iranian Association for a number of years, affording us some degree of social status, although it was complicated by our mixed background. At an event one year, my little sister, Fariba, was the headlining act. She danced her six-year-old faltering ballet steps with a row of tutu-clad men behind her mimicking her every movement. I remember laughter exploding in the room, temporarily shocking my sister, then buoying her movements across the stage. Such moments were the heart of communal connection at events like that, temporarily filling the empty spaces inside. With all the other kids, we'd spend hours playing hide-and-seek, gorging ourselves on stolen plates of food from tables groaning under the weight of it all. Yet to dig deeper than superficial camaraderie often meant hitting a wall.

Most of the time, especially as I got older, chatting with peers and other adults meant engaging in awkward, stilted conversation. On top of the fact that we weren't full-blooded Persians, we didn't speak the language. I would be asked over and over again, *"Haleh shomeh chetori?"* or "How are you?" When I couldn't respond in Farsi, the conversation was rather quickly terminated, often with a look of pity crossing the other person's face. Even as an adult, regardless of being born in and spending a considerable chunk of my childhood in Iran, I lag far behind Canadian-born Farsi speakers in the stakes of cultural credibility.

Language is the key to acceptance, and being without it meant that we were outsiders in our own community. Many immigrant communities police their own boundaries (who is in and who is out) more strongly than the dominant culture, one of the impacts of systemic discrimination, an after-effect of communal loss. Threatened from the outside, exile communities often become more protective of what is familiar, their ties back to home. A circling-the-wagons kind of response. It was painful to experience such cultural familiarity and yet to feel at arm's-length from it at the same time—like seeing a place I used to live now trapped in a snow globe that I could look at, turn over in my hand, but would forever remain external to. For this reason, as an adult I rarely attend Persian cultural events. It's too painful to feel like an outsider in my community of origin.

⌒

AT THE OTHER END of the spectrum were our more regular doses of white, Christian culture through regular Sunday attendance at the Trinity Baptist Church. This world mirrored the broader society we lived in, and I desperately wanted to blend in. In 1985, soon after I started junior high, my Mamanbozourg came to stay with us for a few months. She spoke no English and couldn't leave the house without my mother or father accompanying her. She gave me a pair of solid gold pine cone earrings—my most valuable possession. I treasured them, proudly wearing them to school with an awful gold acrylic sweater I borrowed from my mother. The earrings were stunning, almost making the sweater a passable clothing choice.

As a Shia Muslim, my Mamanbozourg practised *nemaz* (Islamic prayer) five times a day on a rectangular piece of carpet placed next to her bed. Yet she also attended the

Baptist church services with us every week. God is God, except when God isn't. Religion is, after all, subject to human dynamics. At church, she was treated with the sort of shallow civility that allows people to feel they've been supportive while staying clear of a meaningful relationship. "How are you? Good? Good to hear!" End of conversation. But I didn't want to spend time with her at church either. Church was somewhere I experienced some degree of social acceptance, and I didn't want that to be compromised.

Early on, during one Sunday at our regular service, she accepted the Communion cup and wafers as they were passed down the aisle. I was furious with her, afraid what others would think of us letting this "foreigner" and non-believer engage in such a deeply Christian ritual. "Why does she have to do this?" I whispered to my mother. Why couldn't I have a grandmother who looked like one of the Golden Girls, who opened doors rather than making them harder to open?

For many years, we were the only non-white children in the entire congregation of approximately three hundred. From my perspective, it looked as though my mother was trying to atone for our outsider status through her enthusiastic interactions with other church members. Watching her eagerly engaging in conversation, jumping to complete the other person's sentence, laughing too quickly and too often—it looked like overcompensating. I despised it. What was she compensating for? The social niceties extended to my mother and us turned my stomach; I was convinced they were nothing more than rituals of engagement that mimicked acceptance but really reflected an unspoken pecking order. It was exhausting. I didn't know how to turn off my awareness of the hierarchy in any room I walked into, and wherever we went I knew we'd never reach anywhere near the top tier.

My father's favourite joke during my adolescent years involved God and gingerbread men. With the full power of his charm he'd start off, "God was hungry, so he put his first batch of gingerbread men into the oven. But he left them too long and they got burned, so he had to throw them out. The second batch he didn't leave in long enough. They were uncooked, so he had to throw them out as well. The third batch were golden brown—just right!"

Without any framework for understanding racism at the time, I knew there was something not quite right about this joke, but I couldn't help smiling at his boisterous telling. It was the only time my father openly revelled in his—our— brownness, one of the few times I got to feel that perhaps the skin we were in wasn't such a bad thing. Though over time I started to chastise him for telling the joke, I'd simultaneously relish the undertones of pride in his voice.

The closest thing we had to a regular community in our newly adopted country was a group of five other immigrant families whom we met with every couple of months. Some of the kids were fully Persian and others were mixed-race, half-Iranian like ourselves. These gatherings were the primary cultural antidotes to being otherwise fully immersed in small-town Canadian culture. However, even in that multiracial setting, belonging was a difficult dance. We kids would hang out together during the visits, but not outside of them. Rather than bringing us together through the immediacy of a shared culture, our mutual struggle to assimilate into Canadian society made us uncomfortable mirrors for each other's outsider status. I call it the first-generation-immigrant-brown-kid shuffle. Years later, after moving to Toronto, I met one of the other group members my age, Mohammed, for a drink. He talked to me of meditating for a couple of hours every day to keep his depression at bay. White, conservative, small-town Canada was not a hospitable environment for any of us.

⌐

IN 1987 — AROUND the same time Alex Keaton started college on *Family Ties* and Jo and Blair were still at odds on *The Facts of Life* — I started grade nine, my last year of junior high school. It was a time of flavoured lip gloss, learning how to properly use a tampon, and spending long, fruitless hours in front of the mirror. That pivotal year of transition from junior high to high school was also marked by my father's announcement that my Auntie Fereshteh, Uncle Shadfar, and two young cousins had finally been approved for immigration and would be staying with us in Sherwood Park.

Staying behind in Iran had been challenging for them. My uncle was a site engineer working for the Iranian Oil Company, travelling to different refineries around southern Iran. The new Islamic regime, inexperienced in the business of governing, took shortcuts with even basic safety measures at the plants he worked in. Why not let the atomization column run a few degrees hotter than usual if it meant faster oil supply? Immune to feedback, the Iranian government often promoted young American-educated students into management roles. My uncle's years of experience counted for nothing.

Meanwhile, my Auntie Fereshteh was left behind in Tehran to look after their two children. She and my cousin Shideh, just a couple of years younger than me, were forced to wear the chador in public, in an environment where everywhere watched everyone else, and no one was ever sure who might snitch to the authorities if one didn't comply. Panopticon justice.

Like my Mamanbozourg, my relatives spoke no English, but there were a lot more of them. It meant that at all times someone in the house was being left out of the conversation. They stayed with us for six months, adding more voltage to the live wires of power and identity running through our household, before moving into a rental home of their own. It was hard to experience more exclusion in my home environment.

For a couple weeks after they arrived I went to stay at my grandmother's house so they would have more room to settle in. Although it was a relief to be away, I also felt the distance. Like any teenager, I wanted attention from my parents, but more than most, I needed it to address the deeper scars of inadequacy. In that year of transition, I resented my relatives for their intrusion into our lives. But most of my animosity came from unconscious internalized racism. Their outsider status was too close to my own. I couldn't risk my tenuous visibility being jeopardized by more brown people, particularly people who barely spoke the language. I wanted to understand what was being said in Farsi, to feel a part of the breeze of Persian culture that had come into the house, but at the same time I wanted to hold myself apart from any differences that might be viewed as "less than" in my part of the world.

My sense of self was schizophrenic. I was marked by skin colour as being of Persian descent yet desired the higher rank that came with my mother's white skin. My personality was largely formed by my early years growing up in Iran, and yet I tried to stifle those strong tendencies — I wanted to fit in as a soft-spoken Canadian. Being close to my Persian relatives intensified the ambivalence, all the unprocessed shame, towards the part of myself I had placed in exile.

I hadn't always felt this way. My father's other sister, Auntie Mahin, had emigrated to Minnesota around the same time we'd left Iran, and one summer she and her husband, Uncle Noori, and their two girls, Nassim and Nedda, had travelled north for a two-week vacation. We'd rented a camper van to tour the Rocky Mountains for a few days. Although these cousins were also brown, because they had been in North America as long as we had they had assimilated. My cousin Nassim, just a year younger, introduced me to Madonna's hit single "Like a Virgin." We'd play the song over and over again, taking turns with an imaginary mic in hand, relishing the freedom to contort our bodies in impossible ways. Eventually we'd keel over, howling with laughter. To this day, that song transports me back to a short period of time when I got to feel like the cool older cousin.

AT THE BEGINNING OF my grade nine year, on top of all
the social pressures to fit in, I felt a driving need to compensate for the family influx and any lingering signs of
being a foreigner. My name was the first and most obvious
place to start. Anahid is the name of the goddess of water
in ancient Persian (Zoroastrian) mythology. Names are
among the strongest anchors to culture — the mix of con-
sonants, vowels, and syllables reflecting the pace, rhythm,
and heartbeat of the people they represent. In Nigeria, names
are partly sung. Indigenous names often reflect the land a
tribe is based on. Persian names are proud, languorous, trib-
utes to pagan goddesses, ancient kings, and religious leaders.
Mine felt like one of the few threads connecting me back to
what I remembered of my country of origin. Every so often I
would hear my father tell the story of my deep-rooted love of
water, of holding my wriggling toddler body over a backyard
fountain as I delightedly splashed around. Before he knew it,
I'd launched out of his grip to slide head first into the basin.
Each time he'd finish on a laugh, ending with the punchline,
"And I've never been able to pull her away from it since!" I
relished that story. Proof my name belonged to me. Water
goddess. Ocean spirit. Yet it was also a stumbling block to
acceptance in my new land. Its constant mispronunciation
became the early trigger warning that I wouldn't fit in, sending the internal message "Prepare to abort."

Sitting in class at the beginning of that year, I listened to
the teacher perform what felt like the millionth hatchet job
on my name. *"An-NAY-hide,"* she painstakingly recited with

a puzzled frown, eliciting sniggers from the class. *Damn it!* I thought. *This. Will. Not. Happen. Again.* Popular jock Kim Kadash looked at me from across the aisle with pity in her eyes, her body already shrinking away from me.

"No," I heard some part of me reply to the teacher, "my name is Anna."

My inner resilience once again came to the rescue. For the next fourteen years, I was Anna Dashtgard. I did my best to sever the Persian goddess and all her attendant power from my consciousness.

At that time I was still swimming competitively with the local Silver Tide Swim Club. We travelled often for swim meets to even smaller, whiter towns across the province, and everywhere we went we were billeted by the host team's families. Every trip felt like a test—I never knew what environment I would end up in or what degree of acceptance I would find. Looking back, the travel, the uncertainty, the moving into someone else's home, even temporarily, were all elements that too closely mirrored what I had gone through in the move to Canada, and not in a comfortable way. My nervous system would slip into even higher gear, and sleeping beside my teammates in someone's dark, unfamiliar basement made nighttime trips to the toilet even more clandestine. I never slept enough on those trips, and then I had to get up and compete in my race categories the next day.

Partway through that year, I attended the provincial championships a day's drive away in Calgary. This was the biggest competition of the year and we had been building up to it all season. I was the leading contender in my age category to break the provincial record for the sport's most prestigious category, the 100-metre front crawl. On the day of the event, heart racing and body clad in my favourite too-tight all-black swimsuit, I lined up on the starting block ready to power myself off. My swim coaches and teammates lined the sides of the pool, while the stands were filled with spectators cheering loudly. The whistle was blown and I dove into the water, moving forward strongly, leading my heat, when all of a sudden I lost my breath. My lungs felt like a balloon suddenly jabbed with a pin as the air swooshed out. Suffocating, I pulled up short, gasping. Panic and then shame swept through me in quick succession over this very public loss of control. I dipped my head back into the water, plowing on despite the feeling of drowning, until the same thing happened again on the next length. Quitting was not an option. Desperately I kept moving, one arm after the other slicing through liquid resistance, carrying me forward as I struggled to breathe, until finally I touched the pool's edge. For a moment I floated there, grasping the edge and panting in relief, the only body left in the water. Everyone, everything was silent.

I was profoundly shaken that my usual bravado had faltered. Betrayed by my own body. Publicly, I wanted to pretend it had never happened, although inside I was afraid something was seriously wrong. I hauled myself out of the pool and slowly walked over to my swim coach, "Kathy with a K." I was shivering, both scared and embarrassed, wrapped in an inner cloak of self-loathing. Kathy didn't look up until I was right in front of her. She swept her gaze slowly from my feet up to my eyes, a look of disgust on her face as she issued curt instructions. "Go dry off. We'll talk about this later."

As I walked away I was unable to stop the tremors that swept through my body. But I didn't cry then, or afterwards. I never cried. I was too numb to feel anything close to grief. I wonder if there wasn't also an underlying determination to protect what I had left to protect: my real emotions, my innermost self. They never got to see *her*.

After the event, there was no further mention of what happened, just a noticeable harshness of tone in practice thereafter, a pulling back of attention, as though I was to blame for having a panic attack at age thirteen. That was my last swim competition. I quit the club shortly afterwards. Looking back, I associate the lopping off of part of my name with the loss of breath in that race. There is always a price paid for fragmentation.

⌒

A YEAR LATER, in the break between junior high and high school, my Mamanbozourg came back to live with us. She had been diagnosed with lung cancer and the doctors had given her only a few months to live. She stayed with us — cared for by my mother on top of her new full-time job teaching English as a Second Language — until she had to go into the palliative care unit at the downtown Edmonton General Hospital. Right up until she went into hospital she would still get up and do *nemaz* beside her bed five times a day, sometimes the journey down to her prayer mat taking as long as the prayer itself. I didn't register it at the time but her determination stuck with me. She was a fighter too.

In Persian culture there is a belief that you should withhold the truth of someone's diagnosis, particularly if it's bad news, as it may affect the outcome. There is a risk that the person might give up altogether. This led to the peculiar situation of visiting Mamanbozourg in hospital but not being able to say aloud words like "cancer," "death," "pain," or "illness." I never bought it, though. I think my Mamanbozourg knew full well what was happening but played her part in the scripted cultural dance. She knew it would make her family—especially her son (my dad) and daughter (my aunt)—feel better. Active denial protected and sugar-coated the time she had left.

Shortly before her death she accepted Jesus into her heart. Or so my mother later told me. I didn't know what to make of it at the time. Yes, I had been ashamed of her Muslim-ness, but it also felt wrong to hear that she had watered it down or given it up. Later I saw it as proof of the power that the dominant culture exerts on parts of ourselves that are different or stand out. It is always easier to conform, and I believe she did so out of fear. She was in a hospital surrounded by people who spoke a different language, where the only religious support available was Christian. Or perhaps at that point she just saw that all paths lead to the same place anyway, so why quibble between Muhammad or Jesus?

Her funeral was held on a cold, grey day, and as we stood around her grave listening to the words of the Christian preacher, all I could think was, *Where are those gold pine cone earrings she gave me?* I never did find them. Like my Persian grandmother's stories, the ones I never got to ask for or hear—about her own mother who made vats of wine each year with Shiraz grapes but never touched a drop, how she coped with marriage at age thirteen, how she managed to raise six children almost single-handedly, and, most important, what it felt like to die far away from the place she was born—they were gone.

FIVE

Body Battle

IN THE FALL OF 1988 I started grade ten at Salisbury Composite High School, part of the International Baccalaureate (IB) program, a challenging academic curriculum that encourages rigorous inquiry and a broad international focus. Many of the students in the class were immigrant kids, geeks, and misfits. I wasn't considered beautiful or popular, but I was smart, and I fit in with this group of outliers. This time Rajesh (from elementary school) and I were in the same class, our proximity to one another no longer such a liability. That group of twenty-five with whom I spent every day over a three-year period gave me a taste of regular friendship and community. We were like a nerdy version of *The Breakfast Club*.

Socially, I was finally able to relax a little. We goofed off, dissected frogs and pigs together, and played summer games of flag football and baseball. I had my first alcoholic drink with them and cycled through class crushes. In that small pond, I was one of the cool ones for a change. And I was able to hone my nascent organizing skills. Many of our social gatherings were initiated or coordinated by me. I made things happen.

The first year of high school marked both my eight-year anniversary in Canada and the end of the seemingly endless Iran-Iraq War. Neither would have registered if the principal hadn't called me into his office to ask, "Are you hearing any bad comments? You know, because of being *Eye-RAY-nian?*" It was the right move, but because he was poking a part of me completely dormant at the time, I only felt embarrassed to be singled out and couldn't exit fast enough.

Overall, the experience of finding somewhere that I fit in, along with my father's grand dreams for me—he regularly referred to me becoming prime minister of Canada one day—gave me confidence to get involved in other ways. As punitive as my dad could be, his actions were largely motivated by his high expectations for us. His ability to paint a future where there were no barriers to success rubbed off. This was one of his greatest gifts to me.

Over the course of my high school years I was elected to student council as the public relations representative, which involved writing a biweekly column for the local community newspaper. I was nominated to the township's Student Advisory Board and started our school's first Amnesty International chapter. I was curious about most things; my growing brain was absorbing stories and information. Like most adolescents, I was trying to make sense of the world around me. In retrospect, I was also trying to gain mastery over it as early as I could.

Like so many high school girls, I was hyper-aware of my looks, my body shape, and their effect on my social status—in short, I was fully trapped in the meat-grinder of obsession with body image that befalls so many in Western culture. For non-white girls, the pressure to meet the standards can be even greater. The dominant image of the tall, skinny supermodel was a goal that was simply unattainable for me. It is a strange feeling to inhabit something you have learned to reject; most of the time I felt as though my body was vacated property that I was merely squatting in. I didn't know how to live in something that had been shunned by so many around me, a body that was not reflected in any beauty standard in the new society I was part of.

Being a brown girl in a white girl's world meant that I was stuck in a special kind of purgatory: the more I tried to emulate beauty standards by controlling my body's various messy appetites (in myriad punishing ways), the more it pulled me in the other direction. My body began to fill out, I started menstruating, and I saw acne flourishing across my face—all changes that I hadn't asked for, all making me feel increasingly out of control. Periods were really painful, and if I used acne cream on my face the pimples turned into angry red boils. Skipping breakfast meant that I'd be gobbling down fries at lunch, and then my thighs would grow even larger. The worst, however, was the excess body hair; it was like wearing fluorescent paint that wouldn't scrub off. Sure, it showed up in the places where I could appreciate it, such as longer eyelashes, but those little benefits were nothing in comparison to the volcano of unwanted hair erupting on the rest of my body. I shaved, waxed, and bleached, and then did it all over again...to no avail. Sideburns, gorilla arms, knuckle hair. I had it everywhere, the mark of the untameable, uncultured female. Now I was at war with my body.

It was also a time of experiencing the first confusing waves of desire, always for the cool (seeming) guys. My first celebrity crush was Michael Douglas, after I saw the film *Romancing the Stone*. It was a longing I could feel palpably, painfully, because I knew already that men like him (white and successful) would never want a woman who looked like me.

I remember my all-the-way-through-high-school crush, Richard, trying to tear his gaze away from my hairy arm as I turned to him one afternoon during math class. This was the first of many white-boy infatuations in which I fantasized that if I could transplant my personality into a different gene pool I might have a chance. Unrequited love is addictive. Looking back, I think I subconsciously believed that if I could win the favour of the smart white guy, I'd gain citizenship in the land of acceptance. I'd be safe; I'd be "in."

My first romantic relationship underscored this belief. It was 1989 and I was close to finishing grade ten. At the behest of my father I had joined the Junior Achievement Club that year and met Jason, a tall, gawky, Christian white guy. He came over on Valentine's Day with a box of chocolates and gave me my first tongue-filled kiss outside my front door. Gross. I went out with him a couple of times after that until he stopped calling. He only ever spent time with me alone. I never met any of his friends. I didn't even really like him, but more than that, I didn't like feeling that he had rejected me. Though my experience was, in retrospect, typical of what many teenagers go through in their early relationships, the lesson I took away was that I had to be different. I thought that I just needed to work harder and hide more of myself.

On top of a distorted body image, the conservative Christian teachings I had absorbed portrayed the female body as a site of sin, not pleasure. "Masturbation" was a dirty word, and outside of a (very) basic sex education seminar in junior high, I had little access to knowledge of what felt good, let alone a sense that I was allowed to feel good. It wasn't until the middle of high school that I discovered if I rubbed myself against the chair, something magical happened. Good girls, or at least girls who wanted to be accepted, did not speak of such things. In Persian culture, women's bodies are openly and frequently commented on—my aunt would grab a handful of my waistline after a large family dinner and loudly proclaim to the packed room, "Here is fat!" But that is not so very different from any other culture in the world. Nowhere do women have the right to their own bodies as much as men do.

IN 1990, THE SUMMER before my last year of high school, we went on a family vacation, travelling from our home in the middle of Alberta all the way south along the western U.S. coast to Tijuana, Mexico. I was heading into *the* performance year, with applications to university due in a few months, and I was already starting to feel the pressure. Failure—meaning anything less than a fleet of As and acceptancē into top-rated academic programs—was not an option. And that trip pushed me over an edge.

My father had finally left the auditor general's office that year to start his own accounting business, in the process leaving behind his name, Jamshid, in favour of an anglicized version, Jim. He was under a lot of pressure too. And the plan for the trip called for the whole family to share a one- or two-bedroom hotel room, so we were around each other all the time, which meant there was no escape from his criticisms of everything, from what I was wearing to how much I was eating and the right way to get rid of pimples.

The hardest part of being in such close proximity to my father was the feeling that I couldn't freely access the bathroom at night. Compulsion is inner desperation. Repetitive behaviour is a form of self-soothing. As the trip wore on, my nervous system just kept amping up, and I grew more and more anxious as night approached. I'd often stay awake until I suspected my father was asleep, feeling that only then could I visit the toilet as often as I wished. It was a momentary freedom, though the following day would be hard to get through on persistent lack of sleep.

At this time, my father was on another health kick, pressuring us kids about the merits of being fit and losing weight. It was the latest of numerous fads my father initiated over the years, all of which I suspect were meant to turn us into something we inherently were not: white, skinny "Brady Bunch" kids. A spoonful of peanut butter and honey was pushed at us each morning to boost energy. We were forced to swallow gallons of some awful-tasting brown herbal concoction marketed as all the nutrition we'd ever need in one bottle (a colleague of my dad's had invested in a pyramid marketing scheme). A daily dose of orange juice was hailed as a cure for zits. On it went. It wasn't that each individual trend was bad in and of itself, it was more that the fervour with which my father embraced them left no room for us to say no; our strength of character was measured by how quickly we jumped on board. If I refused, it meant that I didn't want to better myself.

Always in a struggle against my unwanted weight, that summer I embarked on my own personal improvement program. At the start of our trip, I loudly declared that I was going to lose seven kilograms (or fifteen pounds) before school began. Fine in theory, difficult in practice. I started off eating breakfast and then going all day without lunch or dinner. The problem with that plan was that my body (traitor!) needed feeding every four or five hours, and by evening I was panting for food. But my father was so impressed by my willpower that he lauded it extravagantly and held me up as an example to my younger siblings. Basking in his pride, I continued to control my food intake during the day, but I started binge-eating in the evenings when I lost the battle. I did lose the weight, but not in a sustainable way, and when I returned to school I received lots of compliments, which only affirmed the destructive behaviour.

For girls, being skinny equals social status: the less you weigh, the more you are entitled to confidence. I couldn't

change the colour of my skin, but perhaps I could change
the shape of my body. In exchange for a boost in self-esteem
that lasted a couple of months, I gained a messed-up relationship to appetite that lasted far beyond high school. It
was another time when I lost the ability to trust my own
signals, even ones as simple as hungry/not hungry.

⌐

MY FINAL YEAR OF high school was a tug-of-war between
hitting academic targets and enhancing my physical appearance. Self-worth and looks continued to be increasingly
intertwined. All the girls vied for attention from boys (at
that time, in that school, anyone who was gay remained
closeted). Desperate to maintain my weight loss, and with
no swim team available, I joined our high school's inaugural girls' rugby team. We spent two months practising at
least twice a week. Our coach had played rugby abroad,
and he was the father of one of the girls on the team. He
was tough, and short on praise. It was a coaching style that
worked for our team of adolescent girls—we all fell into
line competing for his approval.

Our first game was on home turf. In the first half hour,
I got hit repeatedly in the same shoulder. The third time it
happened my shoulder gave way and dislocated. An ambu-
lance was called; I was taken to the hospital and knocked
out with a morphine injection so they could reset it. When
I returned to practice two days later with my arm in a sling
and updated my coach on what had happened, he squinted
at me with a combination of disbelief and contempt as he

declared, "There is no way you dislocated your shoulder. I've seen players do that. That's not what happened!"

I stared back at him, dumbfounded. It was the middle-aged white man versus the teenaged brown girl: What could *I* possibly know? Prevaricating, I mumbled back, "Well, maybe they got it wrong." Then, in the face of his stony silence, I said, "Sorry."

I quit the team. Not one of my teammates expressed any sympathy, then or afterwards. Once again, what I lost was trust in myself, belief that my experience mattered, and the ability to know my own boundaries. I lost the ability to calibrate to the right setting in relationships: I either over-exerted or distanced myself. I learned to distrust simply being present. On top of that, for the next fifteen years I suffered shoulder dislocations on a regular basis, once while swimming lengths in a pool, sometimes because of nothing more than twisting the wrong way in bed.

Given the context I was in, and the subtle as well as overt bias I was subjected to, I started to question whether success was available to me, fearing how much my identity and background were perhaps a liability. In that final year of high school, a friend and I had both applied for a full scholarship that could be used at any university in the country. Grades, parental finances, and an essay documenting evidence of overcoming hardship were the key requirements. Around Christmas I was over at her house after school one day when the mail arrived with a letter indicating that she had been awarded the scholarship. When I received my own letter, it turned out that I had not. I knew my grades were higher than hers, and that her parents earned more money, which meant the essay must have been the deciding factor. When I asked what topic she'd chosen, she said she had written about her experience of moving from northern Alberta to Sherwood Park a year earlier. By contrast, I had written about my family's immigration to Canada from Iran. Although I was happy for her (she was my friend, after all) I was also frustrated and a little jealous. I couldn't help feeling that my foreignness had worked against me. I didn't understand why, despite working so hard all the time, I always seemed to lose out. My anxiety over getting perfect grades increased. Good simply wasn't good enough.

My focus on getting high grades increased a thousand-fold. I felt as though I was carrying the weight of generations, not just my immediate family, on my back. It was performance time, and I had to get it right. For all of us. As much as I was looking forward to taking my next steps out in the world, I was also scared. On an unconscious level, I associated change with chaos. Underneath it all was the terror that if I failed, something really bad would happen.

⌒

AT THIS POINT, I certainly wasn't about to join another team sport, and that meant that I was getting almost no exercise. Plus, I spent almost every night studying until the wee hours and I wasn't getting enough sleep. Often, breakfast would be a cup of instant coffee and a Tylenol — caffeine and a painkiller. I was still in the starve-binge-starve-binge cycle I'd picked up during summer vacation, and by the midpoint of senior year I'd gained nine kilograms (twenty pounds) on my 160-centimetre (five-foot-four) frame. I went from one extreme at the beginning of the year to the other by the end.

My changed appearance did not help my peace of mind. It pushed social acceptance even further away. Subconsciously I also needed another way of coping with the waves of panic threatening to capsize the take-no-prisoners ship I was sailing. Final exams were approaching and I was beginning to freak out. Food was the most readily available source of comfort. It was easy to eat feelings I couldn't name. Food and feeling became intertwined. Food became a proxy for the unconditional love I was starving for. But I couldn't let it stick around, because then I compromised what I most desired: social acceptance and belonging. I was in a double-bind.

I don't remember exactly how it started but halfway through that year I started binging on food and then making myself throw it up. I had found another way to empty out uncomfortable feelings, because the nighttime toilet ritual was no longer enough. A typical evening would find me eating a full dinner of Persian lamb stew and rice. Then I'd bring muffins up to my desk to eat while studying. One tasted good. Why not two? After the muffins I'd reach for a bag of cookies or chips. Then ice cream. It felt so comforting to let myself get really stuffed, like a hug from the inside. No more feeling, just numbness. By 10 p.m., I'd be filled with the opposite feelings. I'd start to feel gross, ugly, dark, shameful. What was wrong with me? Where was my control? I learned to gulp down water—liquids helped force everything out more easily. I'd make my way to the bathroom, caught up in a spell of internal loathing, and then, thinking dark thoughts and sticking a fork or toothbrush in the back of my throat, I would expel it all. I could undo the spell, just like that.

Purging was such an addictive behaviour. It felt like the ultimate cleansing ritual, a kind of baptism that was totally under my control. Each time I emptied my stomach I felt more inviolable, thinner, and "good"—whatever that meant—until the bad feelings resurfaced, and then I'd be caught up again. A journal entry from this time captures the deep yearning I felt for absolution, and how what I felt about my body reflected how I felt about myself: "My stomach is a round ball, a separate entity. What comfort to imagine a knife slashing into the roundness of it, levelling my belly to a flat, beautiful, strong surface." Desperation, satiation, punishment, and purification. Such was the cycle I got caught up in.

Sometimes I would binge just so I could experience the emptying out afterwards. I have since read about religious acts of self-punishment meant to bring one closer to a divine state—I had found my own. It started as a way to control my body size but it served a much deeper purpose: each time, I created a brand new self, with no mistakes or impurities. Like a white girl—or at least my perception of what it would be like to inhabit a body like the ones I saw in images all around me. It seemed as though to be happy you had to be thin, blond, and pale-skinned. I knew rationally I'd never be that, so I found a way to expunge the shame of not measuring up. In retrospect, it wasn't about wanting to be white or thin, but wanting the same access to belonging.

It seemed as though all the girls around me were closer to the finish line, and I had to control my differences, my messiness, to make up the distance.

I tried not eating, but that wasn't possible. If I stayed empty or hungry for too long I'd start feeling panicked. And then I'd binge even more heavily, usually on sweet things—the dopamine hit was an instant high—and I'd feel even better after ridding myself of it all. I had choreographed my own enough/not enough dance, and now I was like the girl in the fairy tale with the red shoes who was unable to stop moving. For the next decade I wore the shoes of this addiction, rarely able to find rest, at most going a few days without purging, at worst vomiting multiple times a day.

ONE NIGHT DURING THE early days of this behaviour, as final exams were imminent, I overheard my parents in their bedroom across the hall having a conversation about me. It was late at night, but I was often the last one up in the house, and I had ears like a bat's. My mother was expressing worry over my bulimic behaviour and advocating for external psychological support (as she had many years earlier when the toilet ritual began). My father, in typical fashion, became angry and dismissive. The more she attempted to persuade him, the more he derided me. Any sign of vulnerability in me was a reflection of his own. I heard him exclaim, "If she wants to keep doing this, she can leave this house and go live by herself! I don't want her here."

Even though, by this time, I was more than well acquainted with my father's blustering, and I told myself that underneath it all he loved me, this was too much. I was floundering. His rejection locked in the belief that I was unlovable, and the attendant idea that to have a chance at belonging I had to be competent, in control, and never, at all costs, show vulnerability. I had inherited two settings in relationships: invincible Teflon Woman, all superficial confidence, and under her strong exterior, Sponge Girl, with deep underlying insecurities and a need to be constantly filled up.

I graduated high school in 1991 and launched into the world in a state of mild yet chronic depression that I was unable to recognize for many years. I never told any doctor about my bulimia: I'd lost faith that those in positions of power might be able to understand me, never mind help me. I thought it was all up to me. I rejected feedback that would force me to rely on any form of external support. The depression was hard to recognize as it was overlaid by a mania to go faster, do more, fight harder. My antennae were attuned to pick up signals of rejection, broader social injustices. I was a master at recognizing the suffering of others, but not my own. Add a fiery temperament and a history of being the rescuer, and my path towards activism was well paved.

PART II

REBELLION

You do not have to be good.
You do not have to walk on your knees
for a hundred miles through the desert,
 repenting.
You only have to let the soft animal of
 your body
 love what it loves.

— MARY OLIVER, "WILD GEESE"

SIX

Losing My Religion

MR. PEZEM, MY HIGH school English teacher, told my mother that literature was my strong suit. No surprise. Disappearing into a maze of words was like visiting my internally located second home. Yet when the time came to choose a career path, I was still caught up in trying to please my father, so I followed the one leading farthest away from what I loved: business instead of literature, status over art. I was well aware of the gold-star professions that many immigrant parents pressured their kids into, careers that guaranteed stability and financial success: doctor, lawyer, engineer. Corporate something-or-other seemed like a decent runner-up. My dad's advice was to make money, then make a difference—a common yet unfortunate fallacy. In the fall of 1991 I travelled from Sherwood Park, Alberta, to Kingston, Ontario. Queen's University School of Business had a reputation for being one of the hardest-won academic

placements in the country. And I had been accepted, so how
could I not go?

I tried not to think about the arguments that had played
out at home about this decision. My father pushed me to
attend; I think he wanted to see his own sacrifices pay off,
and to ensure his children earned the kind of status that
would protect us from all the indignities he'd had to suffer.
My mother was worried about the extra debt brought on
by travel and accommodation costs; my dad was still in the
throes of starting his business (in its first year he earned
less than eight thousand dollars) and money was tight.
When they both finally agreed that I should accept, I felt
it was because they saw me as my family's investment in
a better future.

The exclusive business faculty at Queen's was filled with
extremely privileged, well-dressed white kids who liked to
drink—a lot. During frosh week, I was quickly introduced
to the ritualistic drinking games, to the long-standing
(mostly) friendly competition with the purple-jacketed
engineers, and to the concept of nepotism. More than one
wide-eyed blond freshman shared a story that first week
about getting in because of parental connections, despite
having grades well below the standard.

Until that point in time, my father had been the most
dominant influence in my life. But being away from home
opened my eyes to the fundamental ways in which I was
different from him. Money didn't motivate me, and studying spreadsheets made me want to pass out with boredom.
As the year wore on, I relied more heavily on prayer and
Jesus to get through days I had little passion for and a social

hierarchy that had once again positioned me at the bottom. That first year at Queen's unmoored me. I thought it would be liberating to be so far from home, and yet, away from everything familiar, I started spinning out. The paradox of freedom is that it's experienced in the context of limits. Without a sense of boundaries, I started free-falling.

I lived in residence at Chown Hall, in a coveted single room. Along with most of the other girls in my residence, I'd go to the common room on Thursday nights to watch even richer white kids living their incredibly vacuous lives on *Beverly Hills 90210*, then all the rage. Sharing my floor were Tracey, a whippet-thin, tall white girl who had spent the previous few years modelling in Japan (what impressed me most was that she was able to resist an unopened Mars bar on her dresser for the entire freshman year! I yearned to be her); Elaine, who struggled with depression, and with whom I'd talk late into the night trying to resolve all her unresolvable issues (pain management outsourced); and Shalini, one of a handful of other non-white girls I remember meeting during my time at Queen's, though we never once talked about our ethnicity together (shared internalized racism). These women became a kind of disjointed family for me, yet they were not enough to keep me grounded.

⌒

FROSH WEEK INTRODUCED ME to the sole friend I made in my faculty, Amanda. She had spiky blond hair, and though she was short she compensated with a bulldog personality.

She ate with great gusto and never dissected calorie-counts or dissed her body like most of the other girls. I liked her forthrightness, her get-it-done-at-all-costs attitude. But others didn't, especially some of the male students.

Halfway through our first year she walked out of her room in a co-ed dorm to find a picture crudely tacked to her door. It was a black-and-white, finely detailed image of a vagina with the word "cunt" scrawled across it. This happened twice more over the next three months, and Amanda became increasingly agitated each time. She decided to take the case to the university harassment committee, on which I was the recently appointed student representative.

Amanda came in to voice her concerns. What I remember most is the power that shrouded those of us in the room, mostly older white men (I was one of the few exceptions). Like a modern-day set of *The Crucible*, we sat on one side of the table facing Amanda as she struggled to plead her case. And I do mean plead, as her story was met with the predictable dismissal and minimization: "Come on, this is just a bunch of guys having fun"; "You're taking it too seriously! Have they ever touched you?"; "Did you do anything to provoke it?" This was also the year that Queen's found itself in the spotlight after signs were seen hanging from male dorm rooms with the counter-phrase "No Means Yes!" to the "No Means No" campaign against sexual assault.

I wish I could say I was an ally to Amanda. The truth is that I was wishy-washy in my support, caught between acting from my intuitive adherence to a feminist philosophy (though I had no framework for it at the time) in order to back my friend and sucking up to those with the power. I didn't want to tarnish my own image in any way, to invoke the marginalization that I felt at subtle levels pretty much all the time I was there. Uneducated about the dynamics of race, gender, and power, I had no way to put any of what I was experiencing into a broader context. The result was that I let Amanda down. The guys in her dorm got off easily, a mere slap on the wrist. She was angry with me, justifiably, for not arguing her case more strongly. Sadly, I lost her friendship. And the whole incident sent me further into emotional confusion and turmoil.

As the year went on, my bulimia worsened. I started staying up later and later, having an even more difficult time surrendering to slumber, pulling all-nighters for no good reason and then sleeping far into the day. I knew I had to keep up my grades, or in my parents' eyes the year would have been a failure, the money wasted. I spent a lot of that year locked in one of the residence bathrooms caught in my own cycle of bingeing and purging. As final exams approached, I slipped into an altered state. Very little of what I was eating stayed down. The stress accumulated so that I remained awake three nights in a row studying for a psychology exam. Just a year earlier I had written the International Baccalaureate exams, each four hours long and requiring encyclopaedic knowledge. In comparison, that first-year psych multiple-choice test was the training-wheel version.

And I cheated. Such opportunities were rampant and openly discussed in the ethics-optional School of Business. I had never cheated before, and have never cheated since, and I'm certainly not proud of it. Ironically, getting the answers to a handful of questions was more trouble than it was worth, and I got a worse grade than if I'd just relied on my own knowledge. It was a testament to how panicked I felt, so completely out of my depth. I felt lost in that sea of whiteness and privilege, like flotsam on the ocean, ready to be picked off at any moment.

⟋

I CAME BACK TO Alberta for the summer of 1992 following that first year at Queen's, realizing that, as imperfect as my family was, I missed them. And they needed me. My younger brother and sister were in high school and junior high respectively, and they were struggling in different ways with similar challenges around identity and belonging. My sister had trouble leaving the room after our nightly "Disperse! Disperse now!" ritual. My brother was uncommunicative and surly. The fault lines in my parents' marriage were also deepening, the family structure slowly falling apart. As the protector, I couldn't leave again. Living three provinces and a four-hour flight away for another three years meant that I would miss all the important transitions.

I wasn't thrilled about returning to Alberta—it was better than where I'd been, but that wasn't saying much. That summer I quickly landed a job at a daycare in Sherwood Park. I enjoyed being with kids—it was a welcome break from academia. Plus, I needed income to pay off some of the debt from my year away.

The daycare operator was a white woman, and she ran a strictly regulated program. About halfway through the summer she called me over. "Did you take some crackers from the cupboard?" she asked. I explained that I had—a couple here and there—because I wasn't aware that access to the food was restricted. It was clear to me, though, that this wasn't a conversation, it was an ambush; a tiny composite of flour and water was overriding hours of carefully built relationships with children and other staff.

My mom picked me up from work that day. I explained what had happened, and she downplayed it. She was trying to present the other woman's perspective, but in that moment what I needed was someone to take my side for once and say that I had not done anything wrong. By the time we got home I was screaming at the top of my lungs, enraged with the daycare boss, another uncaring white woman, and furious at my mother for her inability to see that this was a pattern—that her daughter did not have the luxury of blending in the same way she did, that I had never fit in. Alberta wasn't home to me; it felt like a holding pen for ongoing betrayal.

I quit my job at the daycare. Leaving was the only way I knew how to cope. I really needed to fight—on my own behalf—but the time for that hadn't yet arrived.

Towards the end of that summer I arranged a last-minute transfer to the University of Alberta, where I would major in psychology with a minor in English, subjects closer to my heart. I successfully applied for a student loan, which, in combination with a part-time job, meant that I could cover the costs of my own education. Even though it felt somewhat like a step backwards, the transfer to Alberta was also a relief because it meant I would be studying what I wanted without feeling financially and emotionally beholden to my parents. My mother was relieved to have me closer to home; my father was silently supportive. Although neither of them addressed the situation directly, they were aware that I wasn't thriving at Queen's and were pleased to have the prodigal daughter return home.

I moved into an apartment near the university with a friend who had been in the IB program with me in high school. I didn't really want to—it wasn't an easy friendship—but, as I did in most of my relationships, I deferred to my friend's wishes. Huan was Filipino, the son of immigrant parents, and he was both academically and artistically gifted. He was ahead of his peers, reading Camille Paglia for fun, buying high-end designer clothes, advising me on all dress- and dating-related matters. "You can't wear that!" was a common refrain. He was charming, yet extremely controlling. Looking back, it was a friendship bound as much by experiences of exclusion in a white-dominated, small-town context as it was by shared interests.

When I moved in with Huan at age nineteen, about to start my second year of university, I was still a virgin—a fact I attribute to a combination of my Christian beliefs and a childhood hangover of low self-esteem. We had a best friend in common, Phil, who I was secretly in love with. On weekends, Huan, Phil, and I started frequenting Buddy's, an underground but popular gay club in town. It was a thrilling few months when it felt as if we were collectively pushing a cultural edge. In the early 1990s police raids were still a possibility, threatening the world inside the club, which was dominated by six-foot-something drag queens, buffed and hairless gay men of every background, and costumes that wouldn't have looked out of place in a Bollywood dance number. I was the token "fag hag." It was a natural role, as I felt a kinship in the scene of cultural outsiders. You'd think the penny might have dropped as to what was going on with Huan and Phil, but this was Alberta in the 1990s, and in many ways I was still a small-town girl.

After a small party one night at our apartment, a male friend told me that he had given Huan a blowjob in his bedroom next door to mine. Huan and Phil both came out to me shortly thereafter, cracking my world wide open. At that time, a few years before the courage of Ellen DeGeneres, coming out was still a revolutionary act—no one else I knew identified as anything other than heterosexual. Their revelation immediately cut a hole in the middle of my Christian safety net. I couldn't reconcile my belief in an all-loving God with one who would reject some people simply for having a different sexual preference. Caught between the religious security I had clung to since childhood and the bone-deep knowledge of what it felt like to be an outcast, I was in crisis.

Desperate for someone to help me reconcile Huan's disclosure with my core beliefs, I confided his secret to my old friend Caroline when we were talking on the phone. I thought it was safer to talk to someone outside of our circle of friends, but Huan happened to overhear me and went ballistic. He started questioning me, then threatening, and finally he shut me out completely. "Who were you speaking to?" he asked. "How could you betray me? What kind of person are you? If I hear you mention this to anyone else, I will kick you out of this apartment. You don't exist to me any more." It was only later that I began to understand his justifiable terror at being found out, magnifying my mistake to mythic proportions.

In the short term, I lost both Huan and Phil as friends, and my relationship with Caroline became a distant one. I couldn't shift my beliefs fast enough for Huan, and I had shifted them too far outside the Christian framework for Caroline. In addition, I faced an emotionally difficult situation. Huan would either openly deride me or ignore me completely. In stepping into his vulnerability as a victim, he transferred the face of the aggressor to me. I've since learned that this happens at every level, victim and perpetrator roles recycling moment to moment, sometimes generation to generation, century to century. Unresolved pain searches for an easy place to land. It was like living with a variation of my father, only without the tempering ingredient of love.

Nevertheless, I struggled in isolation between heart and head, lived experience and church dictates, terrified to face rejection either way. It was a time of inner revolution, the end result being that I broke up with God. Not able to swallow the idea of heaven as an exclusive club for straight people, I turned away from Christianity, the only self-loving reflection I possessed. Without this core belief system, I lost my release valve for all the unprocessed emotions roiling just under the surface. A king tide of self-loathing washed over me, taking with it any sense that I mattered or belonged anywhere.

⌐

LOOKING FOR AFFIRMATION, I turned to sex. It wasn't a conscious choice. Since I was already acquainted with food addiction and I was scared of getting addicted to drugs (of losing control), sex was the most readily available distraction. It allowed me to feel something, anything really — to fill up on love (or the fast-food version of it: lust). I started going to straight bars on the weekends, mostly with my friend Lisa, a petite Asian woman with straight black hair that reached almost to her waist. Lisa was drop-dead gorgeous and had heads swivelling in her direction wherever we went. I was her bigger-thighed, less-polished, still hairy sidekick. We revelled in the attention that came our way when we danced sexily together. As we were frequently the only non-white girls in the bar, we were often cast as the "exotic fantasy" of the mostly white crowds. Somewhere mid-evening we'd gravitate towards male partners and make-out sessions.

One night like any other, I left the bar with a man called Darren. He was a tousle-haired blond, part of the local rugby club, and he had a slight Australian accent that only increased his appeal. He secured my easily won affections by telling me, "You're one of the best kissers I've ever had." I felt as though I'd been awarded the Nobel Prize for sexiness. I invited him back to my apartment, unsure whether Huan was in his room next door or not. It wouldn't have mattered anyway as we weren't on speaking terms by then.

Darren led me right into the bedroom, bypassing any pretense of food or drink. It wasn't until we were on the bed, with things quickly progressing, that I realized this was "it."

"No," I protested. "No, I don't think this is a good idea."

Darren pressed ahead. He'd had it easy so far—how could he possibly weigh all my "no"s against all the strong "yes" signals he'd been receiving all night? Except that they were there, floating in the silence, not tiger-roar "no"s but not butterfly "no"s either. They went ignored.

Later that night, after Darren left, I took myself to the University of Alberta Hospital emergency department to get the morning-after pill. It was 4 a.m. in the fall of 1993, and I found myself being asked by a young, white, male doctor, "What's your sexual history?" "Is this the first time you're taking this pill?" and the clincher, "Are you going to make a habit of it?" He spoke professionally, his voice devoid of emotion but carrying an undertone of censure. (How entitled men must feel to comment so casually on women's bodies!)

For a week after the assault, I obsessed over whether or not he'd call, but then Darren invited me out for dinner. I dressed carefully in metallic-gold flats, a tucked in white shirt, and some light makeup. I thought at least if he liked me it would help justify his behaviour. He took me to a twenty-four-hour diner near my apartment. I ordered a burger, fries, and vanilla milkshake, surprising myself in the process—the vanilla milkshake seemed excessive, something I'd never ordered before. When it arrived, I stretched out my hand to pull it towards me but my body had other ideas and I inadvertently spilled the white liquid across the table into Darren's lap. He looked embarrassed to be with me. I felt my stomach drop. As our meal stumbled to a close soon afterwards, Darren grudgingly asked, "So, are we okay now?"

When I looked confused, he explained that some of the guys on his rugby team had advised him during a locker room chat that there might be repercussions for having sex without consent, especially with a virgin. The meal wasn't a date. It was a bribe.

I felt suddenly nauseated. Here I was in the middle of yet another moment of being asked to ignore, excuse, or deny someone's abusive behaviour towards me. But instead of saying "Fuck you, asshole!" I did what I had always done. I dissociated, over-eagerly assuaging his fears, laughing away any notion of transgression, playing the good girl because I didn't know who else to be.

THE DESPERATE HUNGER FOR affirmation that had led me towards Darren didn't disappear. But rather than continuing down that path, I decided to funnel my time and energy into the kind of laudable pursuits for which I had no trouble getting recognition. Over the next year, I ran for and won an elected position on the Academic Governing Council of the university, got a part-time job as volunteer coordinator for the student council executive, and was part of a group that set up an alternative women's sorority, kOr. During this time, the extroverted part of me that loved being around people really got to stretch her muscles. I found out that I was exceptionally good at organizing and inspiring others. Despite how I may have felt inside, I could stand in front of a crowd, speak powerfully on an issue, and *move* people. And it made me feel good. It was a glimmer of hope that perhaps having strong emotions wasn't a liability but something I could use in an external role. I began to think that perhaps I had a desirable ability after all.

I also began to regain my footing academically. I took courses in neuroscience, abnormal psychology, sociology, political science, English literature, drama, and history. The purpose of a humanities degree is to study a broad range of paradigms offering insight into humanity. It was like carrying around a camera trained on human beings and being able to zoom around, in and out, capturing new perspectives on familiar scenes. A humanities degree is not easy, nor is it dispensable; for me, it was foundational. Although I pushed myself hard, I was thriving intellectually.

I continued, with new vigour, to make sense of my own life thus far. The courses I took drilled deep into the theoretical side of things, laying out personal motivations as well as systemic factors influencing human behaviour. I would then go to my office and write a speech for an upcoming student event. Yet in neither world—academia or activism—did I feel my experience was truly reflected. Experiences of revolution, immigration, racism, and belonging, if addressed at all, were so abstractly presented that it was hard to locate myself in the picture. I was reading Hemingway, Freud, and Durkheim, all Western-born white writers. Meanwhile, all my professors and the faculty staff I interacted with shared the same homogeneous background. I thought I was the same as the white Canadian-born peers I was surrounded by, even though other parts of me knew that wasn't the case. It was the marginalized parts of myself that were searching for representation, pushing for me to make space for them. But I had no framework to see them in, and so my body paid the price for the continuing denial of all these aspects of myself. I spent days in my head, and nights vomiting it all out, in an attempt to re-enter my body, to reintegrate.

I couldn't have identified this at the time, but I came to be interested in how the personal intersects with the political. What was the connective tissue between neuroscience and political science, between psychology and sociology? During these years, I found the question I was to wrestle with my entire career: Is social change motivated from the inside out by shifts in consciousness, or from the outside in by broad-scale political change? And if neither of these models applies, then how does social change happen? How do we create inclusive communities in which everyone experiences belonging as a fundamental right? It turns out I would discover an answer to those questions, but not for a couple more decades. Being of mixed race had implicitly taught me that multiple frameworks, or ways of looking at the world, could exist simultaneously, and the work—the magic—was to be found in the overlap.

IN THE SUMMER OF 1995, before my last year of university, I funnelled my unmet longings into a long-term relationship. I got a job in the geriatric ward of the Edmonton General Hospital doing research into private care homes. One of the social workers on the hiring committee remembered my Mamanbozourg from the time she'd spent on the palliative care unit years earlier, mitigating the fact that I'd arrived for the interview a few minutes late and somewhat dishevelled with a long run up my newly purchased nylons. The other person on the committee, Nancy, who became a lifelong friend, had a dream about me the night after my interview. How can we ever know fully the myriad reasons we are pulled to one place instead of another?

I met Omar early in my new position, my first official job in a big institution. He was one of the pharmacists. Eight years older and Indian by nationality, he was an Ismaili Muslim, though not actively practising, who had immigrated to Canada by way of Kenya. He asked me out for dinner one night, and we quickly became a couple. Part of what drew us together was our shared history of being racial minorities. His way of coping with immigration and the racism that followed was to become a hyper-perfectionist. He applied it everywhere. Shoes were lined up neatly in the foyer of his home, jeans carefully creased. Not a chair or hair was ever out of place. At first it didn't bother me that he straightened up my shoes after I'd left them on the mat, or that he'd shift the chair back into position after I'd sat in it. His mother would cook dinner for us at least twice a week. Most Friday nights we'd go out to eat pizza and fattoush salad at a local Lebanese diner. For my birthday he paid off my Visa bill.

I moved on from my part-time summer position researching private care homes to a year-long part-time job of larger scope organizing a series of events in 1996 to mark the General Hospital's one-hundredth anniversary. The main project was a health promotion program for school-children with exhibits covering the history of health care, interactive displays on the human body, and a visit to one of the geriatric units in the hospital. I designed and led the whole program, and by the end of the year we'd had close to a thousand children go through free of charge. It was the first time I had fully stepped into a community organizing role.

Towards the end of the year, as I approached gradua-tion and was simultaneously unfurling my wings through work at the hospital, I started feeling suffocated in the pre-dictable order of my relationship with Omar. I remember sitting down to yet another dinner prepared by his mother, the three of us watching TV together in the living room, feeling the familiar urge to scream. It was a cozy prison I had locked myself into. As much as I felt comforted by his presence, I couldn't stand feeling so controlled. I struggled internally: the needy part of me wanted to hold on to him as a lifeline, while a more mature me was searching for the eject button. But I couldn't break up with him. I didn't trust that I'd be okay if I did.

As I was working at the hospital and also finishing my degree part-time, the struggle in my parents' marriage intensified. They had recently moved from our childhood home into a rental property; it was part of a plan hatched by my dad to sell the house, wait for property values to drop, and then invest in something bigger and better. The rest of us were skeptical about the wisdom of this decision, and my mother was reluctant at best. I hated going to visit that house. There wasn't enough light, there was too much grey, and it had too many walls—exactly like the emotional atmosphere inside. My brother and sister—now in grade twelve and grade nine respectively—were both stuck living there.

Shortly after they moved in, I got a call late one night from my sister while I was studying in my new, seedy apartment (cheap trumped pretty at that point). She'd had an accident and needed a ride to the hospital. It was one of the few evenings when my parents had gone out together and no one else was home. Omar wasn't available either. I jumped into my second-hand K-car, relieved when the engine started immediately, and madly drove the twenty minutes to Sherwood Park.

Returning to my dungeon space a few hours later after seeing my sister safely back home, I turned on the fluorescent light beside the shower. I always had a hot bath or shower before bed; it usually calmed me. In this place, a basement room in a sub-divided house, the shower head was bizarrely stuck above a concrete pathway connecting the front door to the apartment proper. I stood under the stream of water, feet numb on the cold surface, unable to halt the waves of negative thoughts crashing through my head. Various versions of mental self-flagellation, worry about my sister and family, anxiety about my relationship with Omar—all leading to the same place of feeling desperate, unlovable, and deeply alone. I shivered into pyjamas as the tap dripped into the deafening silence. It struck me that this was how I felt in my life, trapped in a space between the outside world and my inner sanctum, neither fully in one or the other.

Getting out of the shower, I walked into the kitchen and steadily ate my way through the sugary desserts I'd bought on the way home, and then made myself throw it all up. Only then did I feel able to slow down the mental torture train. I didn't have any answers, but what I felt most strongly was an urge to escape my life and everyone in it. I started turning over possibilities. It had to be far enough away that I could drown out all voices but my own. I wanted to be alone so that I didn't have to feel responsible for anyone else. And I had to be able to feel in control, so non-English-speaking countries were out. After a few weeks of ruminating, I decided I'd travel back to one of the places of my ancestry, the fair Isle of Britannia.

IN JUNE 1996 I was twenty-three, I had just graduated, and my contract at the hospital was at an end—it was the perfect time to go on a backpacking trip to revisit half of my ancestry. After all, I hadn't left North America since arriving fourteen years earlier.

I visited my grandparents' cottage in Skellingthorpe, my first landing place after Iran. I laid eyes on the tree my grandfather Allan Exton's ashes were buried underneath. I walked through the nearby woods, remembering the magic they had held for me as a child. I could still hear the whispering of the trees, imagine the toadstools as tiny troll houses, and catch a glimpse of a fairy queen's face in the occasional sighting of a ladybird. I visited family members, and tried to ignore the "benign" racism that I was supposedly exempt from. "There are so many Paki immigrants moving in and overtaking England," one relative remarked. I began to feel grateful to have landed in Canada.

While away, I realized that I needed to break things off with Omar. When my feelings were no longer clouded by desperate need I was a different, saner person. Although I didn't realize it at the time, relationships for me were another form of addiction. It wasn't the person I wanted so much as the high of feeling desired, and the more I had to work for it, the more hooked I was. If I didn't have to earn love, it lost its appeal. Travelling alone was wonderful because the only opinion I had to listen to was mine, and finally the background noise was turned down enough that I could actually hear it.

After a couple of months of travel, which saw me partying at secret raves in London, visiting Loch Ness and the Isle of Skye, and walking what felt like more distance than I'd covered in my entire life up to that point, I made my way to Ireland for the final leg of the trip. I travelled by bus from Dublin to Galway, from the east side of the country to the west. I was already in love with Ireland, with the magic realism so interwoven into Irish culture, the storytelling and music hinting at deeper waters, older times. Ireland felt like a kind of spiritual home, a different, more earthy kind of spirituality than the narrower Christian traditions I had grown up with. It reminded me of Iran. It was also an introduction to the feminine face of God: intuitive, emotional, and connected to the body—themes I would later return to in more depth.

At that point it had been raining for a few days, and as we were driving past the endlessly green rolling hills, the sun decided to pay a visit. In the distance, I could see her gently parting the greyish storm clouds, insisting on her place to shine, lighting up the landscape with her brilliance. As many a poet has eloquently described, for a few minutes, all that was green turned to gold. It was the first time I could recall, since early childhood, that I felt genuinely and purely happy, where being in my own body in that place and time, simply and transcendently, was enough. In the time alone, I found the freedom to just be myself.

When I returned to Canada after four months abroad, I was ready for a bigger canvas to paint on.

SEVEN

Political Awakening

I RETURNED TO ALBERTA in early fall 1996, a few months before the spring provincial election in which Progressive Conservative Party leader Ralph Klein was campaigning to form the government once again. His austerity measures—significantly decreased funding for public services and social assistance—were part of a rollout of extreme economic conservatism sweeping global democracies. During my two years working in the hospital I had witnessed first-hand the human fallout from massive cuts to health care. The atmosphere in the hospital cafeteria had radically shifted over the few months before my departure: loud chatter had given way to quiet whispers, with heads bent over tables around the room; there was a palpable anxiety over what jobs might last the week, and what would happen to vulnerable patients in care.

Politics can seem like a faraway sport, until there

is extreme change in a short period of time, and then it becomes the taste in the back of everyone's throat they can't get rid of—a mixture of bitterness, powerlessness, and grief. In a province where the Progressive Conservative Party had been in power for more than forty years, a steady stream of cutbacks to already thinly spread public services had created a crisis for many.

I landed a day job developing a smoking cessation program for youth at a health care centre while working weekend nights at a group home. In both places I was able to see up close the myriad obstacles affecting young lives: poverty, racism, learning challenges. With drastic cuts being made to services helping them overcome these unasked-for barriers, how those young people would navigate the future was, quite frankly, unimaginable. A young Indigenous man at the group home, Frank, described overt racism as a part of his daily experience since he was small. He told me how he had joined a well-known gang in the city because it was the only place he experienced a feeling of belonging. He was about to move out of the group home to live on his own for the first time, and was unsure whether he'd be able to access social support grants. I was furious on his behalf. What kind of government supports the privileged but leaves vulnerable young people to fend for themselves? What would happen to Frank at this important fork in the road?

After hearing me rail against the cutbacks for the umpteenth time, my friend Nancy suggested that I get involved in the upcoming election with the leftist New Democratic Party, run by the only female party leader in the country at the time, Pam Barrett (known in political circles as "Mighty Mouse"). I was ready to do *something*. I was tired of feeling so powerless. I thought that playing a part in the creation of political change might bring more personal happiness.

It was late 1996 when my political career started in an east-end dive bar over a beer with Pam's right-hand man, Brian. I walked in wearing a T-shirt, long navy-blue seersucker skirt, and Doc Martens boots, more than fifteen minutes late. Brian didn't blink—he seemed like the kind of guy it would be hard to rattle. With lank hair framing his face, kind brown eyes, and a drooping moustache, he looked kind of like a cross between a trucker coming off a forty-eight-hour shift and an eager social worker. I was searching for a place to belong, to feel useful, and Brian somehow saw past my youthful appearance and recognized that I was somebody who could get stuff done.

By the spring of 1997, I was in charge of coordinating all the volunteers for the campaign in Pam's provincial riding. The job required a mix of PR and people skills and involved recruiting, orienting, and managing the hundred-plus volunteers involved in the campaign. Larry, our campaign manager, would lay out the week's plans, and I was responsible for finding on-the-ground people to make sure the work got done. The last election in 1993 had left the New Democrats without a single seat in the legislature, so there was a lot riding on our efforts.

The campaign was a personal turning point. It was electrifying. I had found a place to apply my organizing superpowers to make a positive impact. Larry had been flown in from Ontario along with a good number of our motley yet competent crew, many of them seasoned staff organizers. I felt completely at home, surrounded by a team of salt-of-the-earth union folks who said whatever was on their minds and often used pretty colourful language in doing so. It was exhilarating to be in a genuine and collaborative environment. By day, the singular focus was on the campaign. At night we would often go out for drinks and a few games of pool.

I felt on fire with the energy that comes with falling in love for the first time — heady, undiscerning, and all-encompassing. It was the early dating stage of my relationship with activism, with the ability to rally people to make a difference. In activism I found a legitimate space and direction in which I could channel my underlying feelings of anger and rage. Finally, my inner rebel could take centre stage. I felt in charge for once. The vacuum of identity created by my renunciation of Christian teachings was filled with a markedly left political ideology.

Pam Barrett won her seat in the March 1997 election in a landslide, and she, with one of the first visible minority candidates ever elected, Raj Pannu (a.k.a. "Raj Against the Machine"), put the New Democrats back into the Alberta legislature. Watching Pam walk through a crowd of supporters in an east-end hotel on election night to the accompaniment of Queen's "We Will Rock You" was awesome. Anything felt possible — it was as if we were on the brink of a new world. Brian immediately hired me as part of Pam's team, and I began working alongside him as an office assistant. There I was, age twenty-three, behind a desk on the ground floor of the Alberta Legislature Building sandwiched between Pam's office and Raj's, a couple of floors below Premier Ralph Klein's.

Working for a progressive party back in action with only two elected representatives felt like being asked to save all the passengers on the *Titanic* with only one lifeboat. A tidal wave of need hit the office within days: mothers cut off social assistance with more than one child to feed, workers injured on the job and getting screwed in their compensation claims, people on waiting lists for more than a year for basic health services. Those were just the tip of the iceberg.

The feeling of winning, of being on top of the world, lasted only a couple of months beyond the all-night victory party. I was introduced to suffering on a much broader scale. Although I was used to being flooded with my own feelings of anger and despair, I wasn't prepared for the intensity of facing those emotions in others, or confronting the labyrinth of systemically unfair conditions in which rescuing everyone was an impossibility. I felt responsible for every person who called, each issue that was raised. The waves of feeling overwhelmed once again threatened to capsize my ship.

⌒

I WORKED IN THE main Legislature Building and exercised in the windowless gym in the basement. Sometimes I'd be puffing and panting on the treadmill next to Premier Ralph Klein himself. I'd surreptitiously try to get a read on his incline and speed, satisfied to know I could beat him—somewhere. That bubble of superiority quickly burst, however, when I returned to our small office.

Despite our modest political role — the NDP's two elected members represented just 3 percent of seats in the legislature — I was flourishing in my new position. I liked being at the centre of power, part of a team that was influencing systemic change, even if it was an uphill battle. The intensely male environment also brought with it a budding awareness of identity politics. I had been used to relying on my intellect alone, but now I started to notice how my body signalled rank before I even opened my mouth. I found myself invited out for coffee by different male members of the legislature as well as men in the media. This kind of attention was as exciting as it was new. For the first time I had feedback that directly challenged my perception of myself as "ugly." Yet at the same time my attractiveness seemed to have an inverse relationship to my being taken seriously. I felt a new tension between looks and brains; playing up one immediately undermined the other. As an introduction to feminism it was a perfect storm, the first gateway I passed through on my way to understand other systemic forms of power.

⌒

A COUPLE OF YEARS earlier, the fourth United Nations World Conference on the Status of Women had been held in Beijing, China, producing the key global policy document on gender equality, known as the Beijing Platform for Action, that is still used as a baseline today. One of our caucus advisory members, Jenene, had attended the conference. She was on fire about it, and over the course of that year she filled me in on the status of women around the globe, lighting a similar feminist fire in me.

I confided in Jenene about the sexist dynamics I was experiencing in the workplace. She helped me put my experiences into context and label them for what they were. On her recommendation I picked up Naomi Wolf's *The Beauty Myth* and started reading about preteen girls losing their sense of self, the sheer magnitude of female body hatred that fuels the multi-billion-dollar beauty industry, and the staggering proportion of North American women who have been affected by sexual assault (nearly 25 percent). I was angered by the injustice of what I was reading and couldn't understand why more women, as well as men, weren't speaking out.

At this time, my awareness of race was secondary, mostly because I was still defaulting to being white, meaning that any connection to the Persian part of my identity was lying dormant. I occupied the exotic role—different enough to capture attention and fill quotas for racial diversity, but not so foreign (read: dark) that I pushed discomfort buttons. It was only when incidents of overt racism occurred that I became aware of my own racialized identity. At one point Raj Pannu was speaking in the legislature about stopping the privatization of health care and he was interrupted by a white Progressive Conservative Party member who dismissed him abruptly with "Go back where you came from!" I was enraged, shocked that things like that could still happen, especially in the heart of government. Such incidents brought up intense memories of my childhood.

⌐

LIKE MANY ON THE left, I fell into believing that economic and class issues were primary—that if we could only fix the economy it would automatically take care of racial, gender, and other forms of inequity. I was looking for a way to make the biggest difference for the greatest number of people, to make the tent as big as possible. I needed an origin story for the forms of suffering I was being called on to eradicate for single mothers, Indigenous youth, worker's compensation applicants, and more. What was the root cause?

One day, over a lunch of greasy burgers and fries, seasoned union organizer Eugene Plawiuk taught me the basics of the global economy. He explained how cuts happening to public services were a trickle-down effect from a global economic system that favoured the interests of big business at the expense of public good. For example, the 1994 North American Free Trade Agreement included an investor-state clause that for the first time allowed corporations to sue governments directly over any laws that interfered in their profit margins, even if the laws were there to protect the public. Under this statute, in 1997 the Canadian government had to backtrack on a ban of MMT (a toxic gasoline additive) and pay its manufacturer, Ethyl Corporation, U.S. $13 million in compensation. And this was only one of the vehicles facilitating a transfer of power from democratically elected governments to appointed trade bureaucrats and corporate CEOs. Others included a veritable alphabet soup of global economic institutions, like the IMF (International Monetary Fund), WB (World Bank),

WTO (World Trade Organization), and trade agreements such as the MAI (Multilateral Agreement on Investment). This was a light bulb moment for me. I came to believe that if we could expose the source of economic injustice, we could stem the tide pushing the privatization of public services, and perhaps reduce the number of people suffering because the public would have full sovereignty once again over their own governments. The many-headed Hydra of international trade became the monster I could fight.

The perspective on power offered to me by political activism was a way of seeing patterns across the board. It was a telescopic lens on the world, affirming that indeed there were larger systems of injustice operating beyond individual control. How people were treated on the basis of their gender, race, or class wasn't arbitrary and it wasn't personal. For the first time, I was introduced to the liberating idea that perhaps the problem didn't lie with me but with broken systems that were much larger in scope. I now had a scaffolding on which to hang the hardships I saw happening around me, and it was a heady seduction to believe that all problems could be interpreted and therefore solved using this singular view of the world.

French philosopher Michel Foucault once commented that the significant choice we have to make every day is to determine which is the main danger. At that time, the OECD (Organisation for Economic Co-operation and Development) was secretively negotiating an agreement among its members, the MAI, that would create a body of investment laws (going beyond the investor-state clause) granting corporations the right to engage in financial transactions with no regard for a nation's democratically passed laws and policies designed to protect the public good. This seemed to be the greatest danger.

In Alberta, where the possibility of allowing private health clinics was being discussed in the legislature, the threat of American HMOS (private, U.S.-based Health Maintenance Organizations) using the MAI to poke holes in our public health system was a very real possibility. In fact, the Progressive Conservative government's ongoing cuts to public health care seemed a nefarious attempt to pave the way to just this very outcome. Until this point, trade deals had generally been discussed between government officials and corporate representatives in closed-door meetings (non-profit groups that represented broader public interests weren't invited to the table). With the Multilateral Agreement on Investment, for the first time the curtain had been pulled back to reveal the ugly reality of backroom dealings. It was shocking to witness the scope of public services and access to natural resources that governments were offering up for corporate consumption.

From my position working in the legislature, I spearheaded a committee — made up of people from different non-governmental organizations (NGOS), a couple of union representatives, and some prominent local activists — to raise awareness and organize against the MAI. Scott was one of the first people I talked to, one of the few connections who happened to be the same age as me. At the time, he was working for the Centre for International Affairs, a small NGO. He was also an anarchist, so electoral politics weren't necessarily his thing. From the beginning, we hit it off over what we had in common: a dry sense of humour and a revolutionary zeal for justice. It didn't hurt that I found him cute. He fell into my "smart white boy" crush category.

The two of us took responsibility for most of the committee planning. I didn't realize it at the time, but what I was doing was creating a foundation of relationships that would enable me to successfully organize things in the city—the people on that committee represented the nexus of progressive networks in our region. The fifteen of us met weekly to try to get our heads around the MAI's complex language and analysis; the draft text of the agreement had been leaked on the internet in early 1997 and its ramifications were just becoming evident. I learned so much from the diverse viewpoints around that campaign planning table—it was my first exposure to the nuts and bolts of creating broad-scale political change. The feeling of making something happen was empowering.

I spent my evenings in a similar way, with a group of activist friends planning, writing, and designing educational materials to raise awareness. There was some overlap in the cast of characters, but the major difference between the daytime and evening gatherings was what we imbibed. Daytime: coffee. Evening: beer. Scott silk-screened T-shirts in his basement closet. I helped write and print educational pamphlets. Others made buttons, knitted socks, and painted signs. We were fired up with creative ways to spread the word about the threat to democracy posed by the MAI. I remember many a frigid Saturday morning spent accosting people at the local farmers' market trying to offload various of these items.

One night, after a political talk from a visiting South American scholar, Scott and I were biking home while playfully debating the pros and cons of pushing for change through the electoral system versus social movements (our favourite topic). A classic crisp but cold fall evening, the stars shone brightly above our heads as our voices pierced the stillness. As we were about to part ways at the High Level Bridge, Scott spontaneously turned back and called, "I'm so glad we're friends! In forty years we'll look back on this time and reminisce about all that shit we did, the revolution we started!" His spontaneous acknowledgement of our friendship and prognosis for its longevity warmed my heart all the way home. I felt a part of something that seemed bigger than all of us.

⌒

BECAUSE I BELIEVED IN what we were doing I was able to access a powerful sense of confidence. I didn't feel any self-doubt or inadequacy when I was in "Supergirl" mode. I had found my voice; I felt infallible. On the flip side, however, the role I was playing was dangerously similar to the one I'd played growing up in my family. I felt responsible for any form of suffering I came across and I took the approach, "I got this, I got you. Let's fight it." There is a limit to what one person can do. I had found both purpose and tribe, but, like a car careening downhill without brakes, I was entering a personal danger zone.

I didn't know how to care for myself properly. On a deeper level, I didn't believe I was worthy of it. While working out in the gym one day I dislocated my shoulder yet again. After a half-day spent in the hospital emergency room, still dozy from the lingering effects of morphine and with my arm in a sling, I returned to work in the middle of the night. To go home to an empty apartment and face the mountain of feelings crashing inside of me was too intimidating. I just kept going.

At one point, I did try seeking professional support. My friend Nancy referred me to a local psychologist, Julia. She appeared to be in her early fifties, with shoulder-length bleached-blond hair, pearl earrings, and what looked like a crocodile skin purse. Julia suggested Eye Movement Desensitization and Reprocessing therapy (EMDR), a technique for working with stressful situations from the past. I remember sitting on the table as she tapped away on my cheekbones, trying to access feelings that wouldn't surface. Her face kept getting more rigid as she tried to encourage me to feel something. I felt as though I was failing therapy.

In one of our sessions she leaned towards me and whispered, "It seems like you have a lot of anger." Perhaps I would have been open to reflecting if I hadn't heard an undercurrent of censure in her tone. I immediately felt a responsive flood of shame. In response, I stuttered, "I don't think so, no more than usual."

But it was true. I look back now and see clearly how anger was the layer of dust coating my entire personality at that time, so ubiquitous it was invisible. Middle-class liberalism gives anger a bad rap but it's what helped me to survive, to step out of myself and take up space in the world. For me, anger was the antidote to shame. Although it no longer rules me, anger still arises in moments when some boundary has been overstepped, inviting me to renegotiate connection, either with myself or in relationship to the world around me. Anger can be a wake-up call to injustice, a midwife to change. At the time, though, I couldn't see it in myself, and I certainly couldn't access it in the face of judgement from someone I already felt could not relate to my background.

When Julia started a group for women with eating disorders, I signed up, thinking it would be easier to open up in shared company. I was wrong. I was the only non-white woman, the youngest, and the newest to therapy. In every way I felt like the odd woman out. Each session we engaged in a different activity designed to access our emotions: drawing, making plasticine figures, and, once, interpretive dance. There was a woman in the group, Amelia, who struggled with anorexia nervosa. A retired figure skater, she was thin and tall, blond and beautiful, in a delicate, porcelain way. There was an air of fragility about her. I secretly resented her as I wanted to have her body, the option of her passivity. During our movement-based session, I blundered through my routine, feeling like the ugly duckling in a room full of swans. Julia nodded at me as I sat down in silence after my turn. Amelia stood after me and executed a ballet routine so flawless it seemed rehearsed. After she had finished, Julia jumped to her feet, clapping. "Bravo!" she called. "That was beautiful. Well done!" And then again, "Well done!" as if we hadn't all heard her the first time.

It was the last straw. Although I felt empathy for Amelia, I also felt a fierce jealousy, and a familiar feeling of despair that I couldn't do therapy in a way that would meet Julia's expectations, never mind garner her praise. It seemed to be yet another place where what and who were considered desirable was coloured by bias. I couldn't continue therapy with someone who, in my mind, had become part of the problem. That was the end of my attempts to seek out help for the next few years. I felt I was better off on my own.

⌒

WHILE WORKING FOR THE NDP caucus I led the opposition to the first proposed private health clinic in the province by rallying public dissent. In those days, organizing an opposition campaign involved putting up posters around town, placing ads in newspapers, launching an email initiative, and good old-fashioned getting on the phone to all the right people. The day when the bill came up for debate, people filled the upper levels of the legislature, spilling into the foyer and outside the doors. I think I surprised everyone at work. When I went for it, I really went for it.

The issues I was working on as part of my day job with the NDP often meshed with my activism. I used work time to continue organizing awareness of the dangers of the MAI, building up towards a rally we planned for early spring 1998 outside the Legislature Building. Roughly five hundred people attended that first rally, a big turnout in Alberta, especially for an obscure trade agreement no one had heard anything about. It was a major organizing coup. We had arranged for internationally renowned activist Maude Barlow to attend as the main speaker. I stood at the microphone leading the crowd in chanting "Ain't no power like the power of the people, 'cause the power of the people don't stop!" As the chanting died down, Maude approached the podium. She was in her early fifties, with a shoulder-length bob, a casual, sexy presence, and the eyes of a hawk. As she took the microphone from me she laid her hand over mine for a couple of moments. It took me by surprise. Caring, especially touch of any kind, formed little part of activist culture. The warmth continued to spread up my arm for minutes afterwards. That one small act of physical kindness shone brightly against a backdrop of endless verbal analysis and critique.

A couple of months later when I got a call from Ottawa asking if I'd like to be trade campaigner for Maude's organization, the Council of Canadians, spearheading a national campaign against the MAI, I didn't hesitate to accept. I agreed for many reasons, one of them being that Maude had already won my heart. It seems a universal desire when young to work for someone you want to be when you grow up. I felt special to have been singled out.

In 1998 campaigns against the MAI were springing up in other cities across Canada and around the world. That "something" I felt part of that night with my friend Scott was a swelling movement of people standing up to monopolistic economic powers to say, "No. Enough!" Organizing mass protest campaigns is among the oldest of traditions in pushing for political change, yet it never feels old when you're caught up in the tide. For me, it was electrifying to be part of a historical moment, to feel a blinding hope that widespread fairness and equity might be within reach for our generation if we just pushed hard enough. My role as an activist coincided with the birth of the anti–corporate globalization movement that started with the pushback against the MAI and eventually shifted the turn-of-the-millennium zeitgeist. I may have been in a dysfunctional relationship with the work itself but I was head over heels in love with all of it. I was also rediscovering the Annahid who had been left behind in Iran—I could be as loud, assertive, and brash as I wished with no need to ever hold back.

EIGHT

The Big Leagues

WHEN I ARRIVED IN Ottawa in May 1998 I hit the ground
running. I felt as though I'd made it to the big leagues
almost overnight. My first task, even before settling into
my new office, was to make a presentation to the Ottawa
City Council about the impact of the MAI on local governments. I had spent more than eight hours on foot for
three days searching for an apartment while simultaneously
attempting to translate my knowledge of a complex trade
agreement from popular pamphlet writing into a policy
brief without a single word of guidance.

Arriving at City Hall slightly nauseated and sweating,
I was thrust in front of a microphone in the council cham-
ber full of mostly white, older male faces with expressions
ranging from boredom to a mild lack of interest. It was like
being thrown in the deep end without a life jacket. As this
was my first moment in the spotlight, I knew I couldn't

afford to show any vulnerability. I delivered a fifteen-minute spiel on the trickle-down impacts of the MAI on municipal governments. Someone asked a question about water rights. I gave an answer, and then I was ushered out, stage left. I didn't allow myself time to soak in the fact that I'd carried it off successfully enough, and solely on my own merits. Looking back, it was brave to jump in like that as a twenty-five-year-old young woman. At the time, it simply didn't occur to me to ask for help.

Ironically, it was harder to find a sense of community on the national stage, where most people were professional change-makers. The capital was marked by a hyper-competitive, male-dominated, WASP culture that was reflected in the non-profit sector as well. There was very little diversity; downtown Ottawa was even more ethnically homogeneous than Edmonton.

I quickly learned that the NGO pecking order was determined by which Ultimate Frisbee team you belonged to. I didn't play. Gradually, though, I connected with a group of peers who worked for other NGOs and we'd spend nights playing pool, attending various political events, or hanging out at the home of Elizabeth May (now federal Green Party leader), where at least a couple of them were always staying.

For the Council of Canadians, I was in charge of coordinating the efforts of sixty national organizations—all the national unions and NGOs such as Oxfam, Greenpeace, and Amnesty International—collectively called the Coalition Against the MAI. After much debate, the strategy adopted by the coalition was to launch a cross-country public inquiry. The idea was that an assorted group of high-profile

Canadians—including environmentalist David Suzuki, author Margaret Atwood, and president of the Canadian Auto Workers union Buzz Hargrove—would tour across the country to hear presentations from citizens representing different sectors of civil society. My job involved organizing and travelling to each of the events, as well as documenting the input for a final report to be released as part of the public lobby effort.

The high-pressure stakes of helming a nationwide campaign involving more than fifteen thousand Canadians was electrifying. I loved the intensity of meeting with national decision-makers and giving my everything to work that felt so deeply purposeful. On any given day I was juggling meetings with media representatives such as CBC TV national political correspondent Keith Boag, having lunch with a *Globe and Mail* reporter, and speaking about the MAI to groups ranging in size from thirty to over three hundred. Despite having no formal training in leadership, communications, or public speaking, and an uphill learning curve in a city where the stakes were significantly higher than in Edmonton, I was able to absorb enough information to not just survive but thrive. In this way, my childhood served me well. I knew how to adapt quickly to new situations, to scan, absorb, and jump in. Sometimes I'd have to pinch myself to be sure I'd actually landed in the epicentre of national politics and this was not just a dream.

Travelling to each of the cities for the public inquiry was amazing. I was thrilled with this opportunity to learn about Canada in a way no textbook could match. I saw the view from St. John's Harbour in Newfoundland, and from

ghost towns across that province I heard the heartbreak-
ing tales of people who had lost jobs because of industry
heading south for cheaper labour. I experienced cosmopolitan Toronto for the first time — so many people, so much
colour! In Vancouver, I touched the ocean flanking Canada's
western shoulder and learned the challenges involved in
protecting sources of fresh water from corporate attempts
to buy the rights.

In every province I visited, I was invited to sit at the
regional dinner table to hear the insider scoop from a diverse
array of voices — from fishermen, lawyers, grandmothers,
public sector workers, students, Indigenous leaders, and
business folks. Hearing their stories as I travelled across
the changing landscape from coast to coast deepened my
relationship to my adopted home. No longer were the provinces and their capitals part of an old geography lesson; now
they were faces and places I felt intimately connected to.

Travelling with all the high-profile public figures also
proved to be a lesson in the dynamics of rank and power.
As a young activist, I was looking to be inspired by warm,
relational, and grounded qualities in the people who had
been chosen to embody the vision we espoused. And
sometimes I was. I was part of eye-opening, perspective-
shifting conversations about issues such as collective action,
environmental change, and parliamentary strategy. Yet as
powerful and positive as they could be when in front of
audiences of any size, behind the scenes some of the same
people were entitled, abrupt, demanding. At one of the
events on the east coast, a particularly well-known union
leader turned down an invitation for dinner, snapping, "No,

I never socialize while I'm working. I'll take care of myself."
An understandable sentiment, though delivered in what felt
like an unnecessarily harsh manner—the polar opposite to
the Persian tradition of *ta'aroof*-ing! I stood there blinking
in surprise.

The campaign exposed me to the reality of how leadership roles can so easily divorce us from our humanity,
regardless of how progressive our politics might be. I was
introduced in a very real way to the gap between "talk"
and "walk," intention and action, private and public selves.
It was my first taste of disillusionment. I started to wonder
if politics alone was enough to bring about fairness and
justice. My relationships with people in positions of power
marked the first crack in my relationship with activism. It
was also my first glimpse of other identity gaps that were
starting to become visible.

One of our campaign stops was in Edmonton, and I
knew my father would be attending the event. He didn't
understand my choice of career: "campaign organizer" was
not on his list of reputable professions. However, he understood power, and being on stage, talking to the media, and
travelling across the country were signs that I was doing
something important. That night I was on stage with
Maude Barlow, Tony Clarke (of the Canadian Conference
of Catholic Bishops), and another couple of panellists. My
dad joined us for dinner after the event. I was acutely conscious of brokering connection between my white bosses
on the one side and my father on the other, the only other
brown person at the table. I wanted them to notice him, to
afford him status, to bridge the white professional world I

had become a part of and the personal one where I hid any signs of feeling different. The way power often works is that if you cater enough to the interests of those higher in the social hierarchy you may be graced with that person's attention, but don't ever assume they think you are on the same level as them. Maude greeted my father with "Hello" and "How are you?" shaking hands briefly before turning away. Tony talked mostly to me.

Neither of them realized what a cultural slight it was to ignore an elder, to prioritize my youth over my dad's age. No one asked my father a single question—he who had occupied a much higher rank in his own country. I sweated profusely throughout the dinner, unsure how to bridge the gulf, wanting my father to be given cues of respect that he would recognize. I knew their slight wasn't intentional but that didn't lessen the impact. It was another moment of having to choose a role: the good, white-seeming girl or the uncomfortable brown one desperate to broker equal treatment. Fragmentation was the only reality I knew.

A few months into my contract I encountered some squatters, mostly Indigenous activists, who had taken over a jutting piece of land along the Ottawa River that was visible from the Parliament Buildings. They started offering regular ceremonies at the site, which fittingly became known as Turtle Island. I started gravitating there more often, tired of dealing with all the power hierarchies in the city, none of which would place a young female activist of colour anywhere near the top.

Most evenings a fire was lit, and a handful of us sat overlooking the still waters of the river, watching the flames keep the darkness at bay. My body now occupied many privileged spaces: Parliament Hill committees, lunch with national media staff, meetings with leaders of powerful national organizations. Yet the part that sat on Turtle Island was none of those people. She was the child who had found a way through the tent flap to sit at the fire with the big people and feel some warmth.

⌒

SIX MONTHS INTO THE campaign we hit activist pay dirt. Because of the sheer unexpected force of global opposition to the MAI it was defeated in October 1998. Our grassroots campaign in Canada, alongside others around the globe, had exerted enough pressure that a powerful transnational institution, the OECD, had changed its course. Victory! It was a heady moment, marked by a warm feeling of common cause and international camaraderie. I stood with the other staff in the boardroom of the Council of Canadians on Slater Street, listening as Maude offered a toast, followed by cheering and clapping, smiles on all our faces, hugs and high-fives all around. A midday champagne moment.

I also remember the moment because the guy I liked, Neil, a long-haired environmental activist from Nova Scotia, a kind of a better-looking John Lennon, had joined us for the victory toast. He worked for the Sierra Club, which was headed by Elizabeth May at the time; he was one of the guys living at her place. We'd arrived in Ottawa at around the same time and met at some political event. I met most people that way. He was my romantic catnip — the slightly nerdy, slightly artsy, "don't give a damn" white boys; the ones I perceived to be out of reach.

I called him a couple of weeks after the breakthrough victory, still on a high, mistaking victory in one area for possibility in another. It was after 10 p.m., and I was calling to confess that I liked him, as if it weren't obvious. The few beats of silence on the other end of the line gave me my answer. He was a nice guy, but I think my intensity scared him off. That seemed the way with guys like him. Most of the men I dated were initially drawn to my public persona but would start slowly pulling away from the turbulence (read: desperation) underneath.

And if they didn't start pulling away, I did. Always a closet romantic, I fantasized a lot about love, but there was no way I could sustain intimacy. The few times I dated guys who were totally into me, the more they showed their devotion the more it turned me off. One of the last guys I dated in Ottawa, Aron (British ex-army), travelled across the country to find me after I left. Ugh. Ironically, when neediness was directed towards me I couldn't stomach it. I felt something approaching contempt, a reflection of how I felt towards the needy — hungry — part of myself.

⌒

THOUGH THE MAI HAD been defeated we nevertheless finished our cross-country tour. Most of my work then involved summarizing the findings from the public inquiries, writing them up in a report, and starting to do the groundwork for what would come next. The sense of achievement didn't last long—the clauses in the MAI that offered corporations unprecedented power over democratically elected governments merely popped up in other places. Yet it was also true that the MAI was the match that sparked the slow kindling of displeasure with an untouchable corporate power that was broadening the gap between the very wealthy and the rest of society. There was momentum happening, and it meant more learning, more strategizing.

As rewarding as the work was, it also took a toll on me. I was now digesting the reality of climate change and the likelihood that entire cities would one day be under water, displacing millions of people. Or reading of labour abuses half a world away that resulted in the deaths of women in a fire, as they were locked in a room to work. Or watching children picking through garbage piles in countries where most of the natural resources were funnelled to American corporations. Margaret Atwood once wrote, "The facts of this world seen clearly / are seen through tears." It felt that way. I still didn't have a sense of personal boundaries so I continued to absorb and feel responsible for the now global level of suffering I faced. Underneath it all, I struggled with imposter syndrome, running fast and then faster to prevent people from somehow seeing the real, flawed me.

On the personal front, I was fielding regular calls from family members who were in crisis around my parents' impending divorce. I would get calls, often daily. As the eldest, and as the protector, I also felt responsible for each one of them. Soon after the MAI defeat, my brother came out to visit me. I raised the topic of our childhood for the first time. We sat beside each other in my narrow living room

on an Ikea futon in front of the flickering TV screen, and I
placed a tentative hand on his back as I sobbed, "I'm sorry, I'm
so, so sorry." He glanced awkwardly down, unable to make
eye contact with me. I was clumsily trying to right the past,
sorry that I had been a bully to him, sorry that I wasn't able
to save him from his own bullies, sorry that I had stopped
seeing my brother, even temporarily, as anything other than
kin. Like Gretel with Hansel, I was trying to follow the bread
crumbs taking us back to some place like home.

The combination of personal and professional pressures
slowly was starting to become too much. I felt simultaneously overwhelmed by how much I was shouldering and
guilty for not doing more. To cope, I was bingeing and
purging almost every night. I would wake up with an ideal
script for what I would eat and how much exercise I'd get
that day, and if I didn't follow through I'd berate myself
and compensate by forcing up whatever I'd swallowed. I
would starve myself for a while, trying to be the good girl,
then fall prey once again to my inner rebel, determined to
get her needs met at any cost. Then I made myself pay the
price for her neediness. Focusing attention on the size and
shape of my body offered a false sense of control at a time
when I felt little of it in my external surroundings. Our
bodies often become the site where we play out our inner
drama, and mine had become a battlefield.

Continuing to ignore my body's cries to slow down
and *feel* meant that the physical symptoms simply amped
up. There was only so much feeling I could stuff down on
top of a system that was already overwhelmed. By early
1999, eight months into my contract, I developed what's

called "urge incontinence." At moments during the day, when experiencing a spike of adrenaline, I would feel a sudden and urgent need to urinate, and out it would come, often before I could make it to the bathroom. Sometimes it would mean some minor dampness; other times I'd need to change my whole outfit. I was in a high-voltage role in a body that was already emotionally saturated.

In spring 1999, after we'd wrapped up the MAI inquiry, I accompanied Maude to Parliament to present our report findings to the Standing Committee on International Trade. I remember orange juice and plates of manufactured pastries, a kind of carbohydrate rainbow spread across a pressed white tablecloth. I don't recall the identities of those present. Food represented safety, faces threat.

I was so nervous (terrified, in fact) about providing expert advice to a group of Canada's top lawmakers that my system went into overdrive. This group of elected federal members of Parliament represented the ultimate gatekeepers to acceptance. What if I choked?

Maude ran through a twenty-minute spiel, and I finished off with a ten-minute campaign recap and "what's next" summary. I did my part well enough—I always did. When I needed to, I could perform, but I often had to dissociate to get the job done. As we left the building I had to excuse myself and run into a side alleyway when I felt the urge to urinate turn into a warm trickle inside my panties. I bent over double, forcing the Kegel muscles controlling the bladder to lock into place, shame coursing through my every cell. One minute I'd felt as though I was near the top of the ladder, and the next I was lying face down underneath it. At the time, I felt as though my body was betraying me with its weakness, rather than calling to me with deeper wisdom I could benefit from listening to.

⌣

MY CONTRACT WAS COMING up for renewal in May 1999, and even though I wasn't sure if it was what I wanted—I still didn't know what that was—I was anticipating that my job would become a permanent position. Then, towards the end of my term, I found out that my contract would not be renewed.

Even though it may have been for the best, at the time it felt like another betrayal. I had given up home and health to take the job, only to feel that I was once again disposable. Maude took me out for lunch, all smiles and gratitude. I suffered the familiar need to play along, when in truth I felt hurt considering how much I had given and how little I felt seen in return.

My last hurrah with the Council of Canadians was attending the "NAFTA at Ten" conference in Montreal. In a hotel ballroom with close to a thousand politicians, bureaucrats, and assorted business people, I experienced the first wave of relief knowing that I was no longer confined to that world. I started feeling the first stirrings of a desire not just to be visible, but to occupy a role where I also had the freedom to be myself.

Where could I go next? I didn't feel a sense of belonging anywhere, and I was certain the answer was not back in Alberta. With my sister out of the house attending university in Montreal and my brother working in Calgary, my parents' differences finally overcame any motivation they had left to stay bonded together in marriage, making divorce imminent. I didn't want to be around for the dissolution. It was devastating for our whole family. Though there had been considerable conflict in our household there had also been love, connection, and sometimes even joy. What history I was connected to I was losing. It made me realize how much of our past is stored in memories of the small things: the way we'd all tease my dad for wearing a toque when he was sick; the family-sized plastic thermos of tea that came with us whenever we ventured more than a dozen blocks away from home; the way we always sat in the same spots around the dinner table. These were the little rituals that represented home.

I knew if I went back I'd get caught in the middle of things, and I had no emotional or mental space left. I really wanted to escape, to be like Jack climbing the beanstalk to a different world, but finding a place of quiet retreat without spending a lot of money I didn't have was going to be challenging. After surveying some different options, I decided to leave Ottawa and go somewhere that could offer me the most peace. I applied to work at a bed and breakfast on Galiano Island, one of the Gulf Islands west of Vancouver, through a program called Worldwide Opportunities on Organic Farms (or wwoof, as it is informally known — not a particularly helpful acronym). I was accepted, and in June 1999 I packed up my necessary belongings, invested in a magenta Mountain Equipment Co-op anorak, and high-tailed it west.

Arriving on the island in a green mist, tall evergreens towering above me, I felt something unfurl as I hitchhiked (the main method of transportation on the island) to my destination. The island's unfamiliarity was liberating; its beauty was breathtaking. I found myself at an oceanfront B&B run by two hippies with the requisite Sanskrit names: Kali and Nandeep.

While seemingly a breeding ground for white hippies (during my entire stay I met only one other person of colour), like many of the islands off the west coast, Galiano was also a hotbed of creativity. The house itself was a charming four-storey complex overlooking the Pacific Ocean. It was decorated with massive canvases painted by Kali, and Tibetan singing bowls of every shape and size. Sunlight streamed into rooms surrounded by glass. The food was always fresh and plentiful.

After swimming in blue ocean waters every day I would retire to the bathtub centred halfway up the cliff, pour in bubble bath, and sink back to soak under a blue sky surrounded by wildflower blooms on every side. Water was a balm for me.

My time on Galiano Island also offered inspiring glimpses into a wide array of spiritual and artistic practices. I encountered guests who practised reflexology, palmistry, and astrology, alongside island residents who made a living as herbalists, painters, and photographers. The binding vision in this part of the world was not global justice but self-actualization. For the first time in my life, my right brain got to wake up and really play.

I started writing, painting, and learning about chakras,

meditation, and energy medicine: other ways of seeing the world beyond the political reality I'd lived in for the last four years. To live surrounded by these things that were so foreign to my immigrant upbringing yet felt intuitively nurturing connected me back to that place of contented happiness I had experienced while travelling alone across Ireland. I couldn't inhabit the feeling for long, but I started dipping my feet in more regularly.

Galiano was an opportunity to reconnect with the spiritual seeker I had lost touch with since abandoning my religion. It was a part of myself I'd felt I had to push aside to inhabit the political realm. As a young brown woman, the emotionally intuitive part of who I was seemed like a liability. If I couldn't occupy leadership in a way that resembled the mostly white men around me—hyper-rational, serious, disembodied—then I felt I must somehow be lacking. Although I never felt at home on the island, a deeper part of me thawed out there and started jostling for more expression.

⌐

WHILE LIVING ON GALIANO I took a filmmaking course at the Gulf Islands Film and Television School (GIFTS). We were divided into groups of four to make a short documentary film in one week. Our team's short film, *Bread*, about the commercialization of centuries-old artisanal practices, was subsequently accepted into a handful of film festivals.

At the end of the course we held a celebratory barbecue, where I met a fellow traveller who became a lifelong soul sister, Rachel Johnston. Rachel and I gravitated towards each other immediately. She is, coincidentally, the daughter of OECD president Donald Johnston, whom I had encountered in my days with the Council of Canadians. We shared an interest in preserving democratic rights, and we were both in our mid-twenties and looking for a way forward, though we couldn't have articulated that at the time. Following on the success of *Bread*, I sold Rachel on a scheme to make a documentary about the protests in Seattle against the World Trade Organization that would be taking place in November 1999. Although I hadn't made plans to go, I couldn't stay away from the biggest activist gathering of my generation. I had to be there. I had enjoyed a taste of slowing down during my time on the island, but I was ready to get back into the world. I was still awash in so many overwhelming emotions, and I dealt with them the same way I always did: by going to work and taking action.

Excited by the possibility of making a documentary to educate the broader public about the issues at stake, I withdrew all my personal savings and got some seed funding from a couple of organizations I'd worked with as part of the Coalition Against the MAI. I took a ferry to Victoria and bought a new handheld digital camera with a microphone. I'd never owned anything that expensive. It seemed like a big gesture, but I sensed something big was coming. The night before we drove down to Seattle, I tossed and turned in bed with anticipation. At 3 a.m. I had a glass of warm milk. At 4:30 a.m. I checked on my new camera. And at 6 a.m. I got dressed. I could feel in the hum of energy surging through my nervous system that the storm brewing south of the border was going to be a turning point in my life. I was right.

⌒

THE WTO WAS SEEN as the most powerful of global economic institutions, and so their annual meeting in Seattle became a symbolic target for anti-globalization protestors. As the site of the coming-out party for the anti–corporate globalization movement, it was *the* place to be for any activist in North America, if not globally. Over 100,000 people flooded the city over a three-day period. Rachel, I, and one other project partner from the island, Dima, travelled down on the first day, ready to do whatever it took to get the story of Seattle on film. I planned to leverage my connections, as well as my ability to move across boundaries, to access international and local-level organizers, boardroom and street activists, peaceful protesters and anarchists, to tell a story that would help the broader public understand why we were in the streets protesting—our version of the free trade story. Soon after arriving in the city we were directed to a massive warehouse complex just outside the downtown core that served as a hub for protesters. The level of organization was astonishing.

The Direct Action Network (DAN) space was filled floor to ceiling with handmade puppets in the form of turtles, money men, and the planet, all painted in bright, eye-catching colours with attention to the finest detail—the turtles represented the WTO ruling that protections for turtles in the U.S. Endangered Species Act were discriminatory against other countries, the money men were caricatures of entitled CEOs, and the planet was symbolic of the reason we were all there. Each puppet would have required many days of careful construction. In another corner sat signs of various sizes displaying slogans, alongside tables set up to make more. There were stations directing people towards accommodation, food, and educational events. The space hummed with youthful vigour and smelled faintly of sweat, paint, and turmeric. Collective anticipation created a buzz that was almost visible in the humid air, the throbbing energy of a new movement being born. I instantly felt my tribe multiply.

The Seattle protests really set the blueprint for other actions across the globe over the following two years, wherever international trade and economic meetings occurred. The first day always saw the sanctioned march endorsed by a wide range of NGOs—in particular the trade unions, who brought out the largest number of people—and a diverse array of people representing various countries and causes. Global trade issues brought together a truly international gathering. There were the burly unionists, environmentalists carrying animal puppets aloft above the crowd, radical cheerleaders with sassy lyrics, balaclava-clad members of the anarchist black bloc, and even Buddhist monks meditating along the sides of the street. Most of them left the city after the march.

The hardcore protesters stayed on—most of them white, leftist college students in their twenties. There was very little colour in large part because the issues were abstract, involving institutions and concepts many people had never heard of, never mind decoded sufficiently to understand their impact. It took great effort to translate a term like "investor-state" so that people could readily understand it the same way they understood more tangible issues such as food shortages or police violence against people of colour. Opposition to free trade had started as a conversation among those who worked in global non-profits and unions, but it was led by students with access to university courses on political theory and economics.

Over the three days of the Seattle protests, strategy meetings were held each evening in the warehouse space. Activists had pre-organized into hubs of about fifteen people called "affinity groups," with one nominated spokesperson per hub. Each spokesperson sat in the nightly council meeting alongside hundreds of others to debate and vote on the next day's strategies. It was an impressive exercise in participatory democracy. The day after the formal march, protesters scattered across the city in their affinity groups, enacting strategies voted on the night before. There were standoffs with riot police, marches in various parts of the city, and singing that could be heard from blocks away.

Throughout all of this, Rachel, Dima, and I tracked down, or happened upon, public figures to interview, such as Body Shop founder Anita Roddick (whom I ran into in a coffee shop as we ducked in to avoid the clouds of tear gas), Michael Moore (whom we saw sitting at a bar having a beer after speaking at a big event), and Vandana Shiva, biodiversity champion. The rest of the time we split up to get different footage. I preferred the freedom to follow my own lead anyway. I roamed the city with my camera, capturing people's faces — the contrast between a hard-set mouth and the telltale twitch of eyes as a seated twenty-something woman held her ground in front of a helmeted riot officer carrying a baton, taser, and firearm. I wanted to tell the David and Goliath story of what it took to stand up for one's beliefs in the face of monolithic state power. The movement had grown far beyond the terms of a single trade agreement. We were facing a world where the wars of the next century were predicted to be fought over access to fresh water. While we marched, the world's major water corporations were manipulating various WTO agreements in order to be able to bottle and ship water from developing nations to people in the first world, while in those same countries one in nine people lacked safe drinking water. And this was only one thread in the woven blanket of what was at stake in those complex economic deals. When I stood back to look at the bigger picture, it seemed we were the only sane ones in a world gone mad.

The images broadcast into people's living rooms during the "Battle of Seattle" shook many in privileged Western nations: "How could that peaceful coastal city be turned into a war zone?" was the question of the day. When I was frequently asked afterwards, often with disdain, "How did it get so violent?" or "Did you get hurt?" or "What were you there for?" I found it hard to describe the images and stories that I was left with, only some of which I was able to record. It was like being on the front lines of a battle for a more peaceful and collective future, the stakes of which only a few seemed aware of.

I remember standing in the packed warehouse at the

nightly council meeting looking on as my peers debated the next day's actions, believing for the first time that a shift in the balance of power was truly possible, not only *in* my generation but created *by* my generation. Is this not every generation's job — to improve the legacy handed to them? To imagine more? To leave their mark?

My own response to this question was to co-edit a fifteen-minute video and teachers' guide called *Bye Buy World: The Battle of Seattle* that told the story of the movement I had become a part of. Our little creation was picked up by a distributor and sold to organizations, libraries, and universities around the globe. I felt so proud. I had found a way to leave my mark.

NINE

Protest, Rinse, Repeat

AFTER SURVIVING THE THREAT of Y2K as one millennium ticked over to the next, I relocated to Vancouver for a couple of months to help distribute our Seattle film. We initially set up a documentary video collective called RADAR — a palindromic acronym of our names, Rachel, Annahid, Dima, Annahid, Rachel. Unfortunately, none of us was in a place in our lives where we had the time, energy, or skills to create a successful business. Vancouver was also isolating. As much as I appreciated the oceanic landscape, the city was too racially homogeneous. There were large Persian, Asian, and South Asian populations, but they were largely segregated from the very white downtown core. When I spoke with people working in various organizations about the need for more diverse representation, I was often met with blank stares or silence. In awareness of equity issues, the scene out west was a quarter century behind what I had encountered in the east. I wasn't willing to be the token brown girl all over again, shaking the tree of homogeneity. I needed to see myself reflected in the people around me, to be part of a community where diversity was celebrated rather than something I had to convince people had merit.

In March, I got a call from the Toronto-based Centre for Social Justice, a well-established NGO, asking if I wanted an educational coordinator position. The chance to be in Toronto was as appealing as the job itself. By spring I found myself planted in Toronto's west end. If Vancouver was a woman with a beautiful face but little substance, Toronto was all substance with flashes of beauty. The city felt gritty, diverse in every sense of the word, and full of surprises. It was the first place I'd lived where walking any of the downtown streets felt like an adventure — neighbourhood grocery stores, graffiti-covered walls, and cool clothing boutiques. Soon after arriving, I got my hair cut short at Coupe Bizarre, and had my left ear triple-pierced at a downtown studio where the walls were painted a perfect midnight black.

The first time I stepped on the subway I felt my whole body exhale a deep sigh of relief. Here were as many brown and black bodies as white. In some neighbourhoods recent immigrants outnumbered Canadian-born residents; Chinatown was located just a few blocks away from the financial district; Greektown bordered on a Muslim enclave situated beside the city's largest mosque. Toronto was a working experiment in inclusion. I fell in love, and, more important, I felt safe. It was the first time in my adult life that I felt fully relaxed in public spaces, surrounded by people who looked like me. Though I didn't know it at the time, it was the perfect base for the inclusion work that would, in a decade's time, become my bread and butter.

⌒

DURING THE NEXT COUPLE of years, a domino effect of sorts occurred as anti-globalization protests were organized around the world, from Washington to Doha to Melbourne, wherever major economic meetings took place. Although I attended the protests of my own volition, I often had organizational support of some kind, be it time off work or coverage of transportation costs. There was little separation between what I did in my work hours at the Centre for Social Justice and my personal time: both were spent organizing and advancing the cause. My activism and identity became one and the same.

The major protests in which I played a role included: Washington, April 2000 (International Monetary Fund/ World Bank); Windsor, June 2000 (Organization of American States); Montreal, October 2000 (G20); Quebec City, April 2001 (Free Trade Area of the Americas); and Kananaskis, June 2001 (G8). Over time, the anti-globalization protests became increasingly polarized, with state police forces on one side and mostly youthful faces on the other. In Washington, D.C., soon after Seattle, I saw actors Susan Sarandon and Tim Robbins wander by. The movement had gained some mainstream cred. It had become cool to rebel.

There were also moments of grace amidst the violence, such as when I gathered with other protesters in

Washington outside the local jail the day after a mass arrest of six hundred had taken place. People were spread across the lawn playing drums, waving signs, a scattered few slowly hoisting huge puppets above their heads. It was a bright cacophony of sound and colour. Slowly the group started forming an impromptu line, shuffling in formation one after the other in a kind of snake dance, moving to the tempo of the drumbeat. As I joined in, my hands gripped by those of strangers, I remember a feeling of peace washing over me. I reached up to brush a dampness off my cheeks and realized tears were streaming down my face. I had found an ablution of sorts.

However, putting myself through the rinse-repeat cycle of attending a protest every three months became difficult. I found it harder and harder to wash away the accumulated barrage of emotion left over from each multi-day stint in the streets sucking in tear gas, barely escaping harm, watching riot police beat young protesters with no provocation, all while the mainstream media turned away. I always travelled alone, moving in and out of spaces, preferring freedom of movement and relying solely on intuition to stay out of danger. I was cavalier in the risks that I took.

During the protests I always placed myself right near the front lines, inches away from police weaponry and the possibility of violence. Risk management wasn't part of my skill set. I justified this behaviour with a leftist politic that was all about individual sacrifice for collective benefit. But the reality was that I took risks because my body was still in a numbed-out state. Even though I was working for the common good, I didn't believe in my own goodness.

My actions were based on a belief that my body wasn't worth caring for. I often went way beyond my safe zone into dangerous territory where I could have been seriously hurt, because my childhood, and then my adult years as an activist, had desensitized me to distress. Because I had damped down fear for so many years, it was useless as an early-warning sign. I only felt it when I was in extreme situations.

At one point, when I was walking back to headquarters in the middle of a protest, I remember being stopped on a side street by three police officers in riot gear. They climbed down from an armoured tank parked smack dab in the middle of the street. Luckily, I was carrying my ID. One after the other they interrogated me about where I was staying and what I was there for. When I told them my name was "Anna" they questioned me about the "Annahid" on my ID: what it meant, where I was born. I'd been interrogated this way before, but always when I was surrounded by peers. This time I was isolated, and I felt that their quiet intimidation carried a very different threat. I was a young, racialized woman alone on a street with three tall, white men with guns and a fully armoured tank. I knew enough by then about the dark side of state power—how some people with status can hurt other people behind the scenes without reason or accountability. Although the incident itself lasted only a few minutes it shook me, and its impact reverberated far beyond that. Being born in Iran meant that although I took risks, I consciously avoided being arrested. I knew my body didn't carry the same privileges as many of my white, North American–born peers.

Each protest meant that I was piling more fear onto a stockpile of still unresolved feelings. As much as I thrived on feeling like I was part of a meaningful push for change, my nervous system was switched to continual high alert. Relief was still found primarily through a regular cycle of bingeing and purging. Although I had many acquaintances in Toronto, I had few close friends. If I wasn't working or committed to some event, I'd be at home. It was easier to stay wrapped in my own cocoon than to risk socializing with others. Intimate exchanges with people triggered too much anxiety. Big audiences I could deal with; personal connection was way tougher. I hated feeling the needy part of me surface, desperate for acceptance. It was easier not to go there, to keep myself distant and above the fray. Though I longed for connection, I kept myself in the role of lone wolf.

I remember leaving one multi-day protest, still shocked at the brute physical strength of state forces cracking down on their young citizens exercising their basic democratic right to freedom of assembly and expression. I was travelling back to Toronto from New York and it was close to midnight when I stood on the train platform alone, facing the familiar stirrings of panic. Catching sight of a pay phone I collect-called my mother and sister in quick succession, and found neither of them available. Finally, in desperation, I called my brother. Shahin was a certified geologist working for Talisman Energy in Calgary. He worked in one of the heartlands of big corporate power in Canada, and we'd had many an ideological battle because of this. He was my opposite in many ways, quick to draw his boundaries, often holding his emotions close to his chest. I didn't expect much support from him, but I needed to hear a familiar voice. Shahin picked up the phone on the second ring, his voice slightly groggy as he accepted all charges for the call. A verbal dam burst, and I started babbling an incoherent narrative of the preceding days. He listened, not once interrupting.

To my great surprise, when I finally paused, he said, "Annahid. We need you out there doing what you're doing. I'm proud of you." To know that he could see me in a moment of need, and support me in it, was healing for me and for our relationship. It calmed me down enough to figure out my plan for getting home.

Months later, when protests against the G8 took place in Kananaskis, near his home, Shahin was the singular voice behind corporate walls arguing the cause of the protesters. My brother might not have agreed with my politics, but he did have my back. It was proof that there was more support available to me than perhaps I allowed myself to see.

IN DECEMBER 2000, I got a call from the executive director of the Council of Canadians, Peter Julian (later a member of Parliament), offering me a job coordinating another national coalition on trade issues, this one called the Common Front on the WTO (CFWTO). It was a network of roughly sixty national organizations, charities, and unions — many of which had been part of the anti-MAI coalition — this time focused on a different trade agreement, but with similar issues at stake. I was honoured to be headhunted, seduced once again by the fact that they wanted me.

Trade issues were still where all the hype was at, so I let myself be pulled once again to the epicentre of activist organizing, like a moth drawn towards a raging bonfire. I didn't stop to examine why I needed more intensity, to wonder where all the desperate urgency was coming from, or why anger was still such a dominant emotion for me. I just kept moving closer and closer to the fire, external need matching inner desperation. I was hostage to the part of me that, yes, was looking for ways to create the biggest social impact but also, on an unconscious level, was driven by the need for greater visibility and voice — my childhood self wanting to reclaim what was taken away so early on.

Earlier that year I had started working with a shiatsu bodyworker, a therapist who was trying to help me heal in a way that would integrate body and mind. When I told her about the job offer, she advised me in the strongest terms possible not to take it, telling me point-blank, "This isn't a good idea. Your body is very stressed. How are you going to manage?" In our sessions (which I was invariably late for) she would vainly try to draw attention to my clenched muscles, locked diaphragm, overwhelming nausea, or frozen shoulder as proof of this. I heard what she was saying but I wasn't ready to listen.

After accepting the position, I returned home to celebrate the Christmas holidays with my family in Edmonton. One morning I woke up to find that I had wet the bed. At age twenty-seven. Even I could see that my body was madly trying to tell me, "No. Enough." Yet I wasn't able to respond to the cues, to properly slow down. Politics felt like a warrior sport; there was no room for any expression of vulnerability, compassion, or intuition. I had to marginalize many parts of myself to exist in that world, which left me in an ocean of unshed tears that would leak out only when I was knocked out, in a state of complete exhaustion.

⌐

A BIG FOCUS OF my new job, which started in January 2001, was organizing an event to take place during the Free Trade Area of the Americas (FTAA) gathering beginning on April 20, 2001, building up to our campaign launch in September of that same year. The FTAA was a proposed intercontinental trade agreement that would bring together North and South American trade and finance ministers in Quebec City. Their meeting provided another opportunity to protest the corporate-led free trade agenda. By the time April rolled around, I was in the middle of organizing cross-country through my day job; locally, on my own time, I was busy as a volunteer for the Toronto Mobilization for Global Justice (or Mob4Glob), a local offshoot of the Direct Action Network that had formed to organize the Seattle protest. DAN was the movement's organizing infrastructure.

Bridging the gap between institutionally driven national-level organizing and local volunteer-led efforts was challenging. Although they were both different faces of the same movement, broadly speaking, their approaches were vastly different, like ballroom dancing versus hip-hop.

National organizations are motivated by long-term impacts, have slower turnaround, and weigh countless political factors before acting, while local activist groups are more focused on short-term goals, employing down-and-dirty tactics. Frontline groups like Mob4Glob also tend to be made up of younger activists, more radical in vision and strategy, and are thus viewed with wariness by leaders of national groups.

Informally, part of my role was mediating between the two, relaying to national groups what was happening on the ground and who (plus the what and why) to support, and relating to local activists why organizational leadership couldn't get behind certain of their recommendations. It was a constant tightrope walk: I had too much rank to be fully accepted as a peer by the local activists, and not enough rank to carry weight at the national coalition table.

I was a spokesperson for the anti-globalization movement, regularly speaking about the issues of the day in front of audiences across the country, doing media interviews for TV, print, and radio, and leading chants at protest events. I checked every box: I had a foot in local and national circles, I was old enough to speak with experience but still young enough not to be seen as a threat (I was twenty-seven at the time), and I was passionate yet not offensive in my delivery. It was a heady role. I was the centre of attention, the one sought out after the formal program had ended, surrounded by people eager for a chance to connect. I got to enter movement spaces as the popular one for a change.

However, becoming a public figure was also isolating. As much as it was affirming, it quickly became uncomfortable to be placed on a pedestal, facing praise or criticism unrelated to who I really was. The damaged girl in me craved the status brought by my new position and at the same time distrusted such easy acceptance.

During this period, I made a couple of appearances on feminist organizer Judy Rebick's CBC TV show, *Straight From the Hip*, one of them alongside former prime minister Kim Campbell. I showed up in tight, stretchy black pants and a casual long-sleeved turquoise T-shirt, my hair twisted into tiny cones all over my head. By contrast, Ms. Campbell was in a well-tailored black suit, her blond hair perfectly coiffed. The topic of conversation was Bill Clinton's affair with Monica Lewinsky. At that point I was too overwhelmed organizing for Quebec City to have a strong opinion on the Clinton-Lewinsky affair one way or the other, yet I was invited to take the leftist position of criticizing his abuse of power. Afterwards, Judy asked me, "What happened to you? Where was your passion?" I didn't have a response. The interview was fine, but my trademark zeal was missing. I was losing myself again under the pressures of the role.

I didn't know that saying no to appearances, to requests to speak, or to anything else was an option. I couldn't access any healthy boundaries because I still unconsciously felt that I wasn't entitled to look after my own needs. The shame from childhood, of being different, of being brown, coloured my view of myself so completely that even in the midst of my most powerful activist days I felt that I wasn't doing enough, *wasn't* enough.

Being mixed race complicated things further. It meant that I could pass as credible enough (read: white) to speak publicly and educate, and also that I was different enough (read: brown) to challenge the homogeneous whiteness of the movement. I was "diverse" enough to be photographed for promotional materials, but was asked to swallow the lack of commitment to supporting diversity beyond such token gestures. I was becoming increasingly conscious of the many invisible manifestations of racism, but this awareness continued to be subverted under the leftist idea that economic justice would automatically bring about racial justice as well. I was starting to question that assumption.

BEFORE THE SHOWDOWN IN Quebec City between politicians and protesters, our Toronto Mob4Glob activist group started seeing new faces appear, like one clean-cut man in his thirties dressed in scuffed jeans, flannel shirt and vest, and the cleanest combat boots I'd ever seen. He had the right costume, but it was missing the telltale signs of wear. Something felt off. On top of that, my home phone number started to click and crackle strangely in the middle of both work and personal calls, and other activists were being stopped by police at random times during the day and asked strange questions about what they were doing and where they were going.

During the workday I was busy organizing speakers for our coalition's event in Quebec City, and making sure the thousands of postcards, video presentations, and other materials arrived on time, while during the evenings and on weekends I was organizing direct-action strategies, transportation, and legal support for Mob4Glob. Tens of thousands of protesters were expected to arrive in Quebec City just as the government put the finishing touches on a three-metre-high (nine-foot-high) fence to keep them out of the downtown core where elected officials would be meeting. It was an astounding metaphor for the lack of public transparency that characterized all these gatherings.

I travelled to Quebec City with Paul, a relatively new boyfriend. A couple of months earlier I had spoken on a panel for the Canadian Media Guild at the Château Laurier Hotel in Ottawa. Paul had approached me afterwards asking for a sound bite; a freelance journalist, he'd been hired as an event reporter. And so our flirtation began. I left my number for him at the front desk on checkout. On one of our first dates, at a trendy west-end restaurant in Toronto, a woman walked up to us and commented, "I just have to say, you two look like the happiest couple!"

Paul was also a supporter of the Conservative Party, a "Red Tory," and what were at first charming ideological differences at the start of our courtship became more entrenched when we hit the ground in Quebec City. I was outside the fence perimeter leading protest efforts while Paul was let inside each day to get the official government take on the protests. His response to the whole situation was detached and intellectual, whereas mine was primal and deeply emotional. It was a great idea to be there together in theory, but sadly not so much in practice.

Quebec City drew not just the usual activists and trade union folks but concerned citizens who had never attended a protest before, including parents with children, artists,

filmmakers, and teenagers. The anti-globalization movement had reached its zenith. Despite this turnout, there
was an unprecedented escalation of police violence, and
on average one canister of tear gas was sprayed into the
midst of largely peaceful crowds every two minutes over
a forty-eight-hour period.

Activists had divided the city into green, yellow, and
red zones that supposedly corresponded to different levels
of risk for protesters: green signalled little risk of police
response, yellow meant an intermediate risk, and red zones
were high risk because they were closest to the fence perimeter. Within a couple of hours, police were volleying
tear gas and rubber bullets into crowds of protesters even
in green zones where parents were marching with children
on their shoulders and wide-eyed youth out of school for
the day were wandering around. The many people who had
bused into the city with the promise of a peaceful march
instead experienced a war zone. Anticipating this, my friend
Scott from Edmonton staged a guerilla action that involved
a giant wooden catapult about 2.5 metres (8 feet) in length
that sent teddy bears flying over the perimeter fence. It
was awesome. The images of teddy bears flying one way
as rubber bullets were fired the other kind of said it all.

In the afternoon of the first day, just after the big march,
I found myself on a side street—Avenue Ste. Geneviève—
with riot police stretched out in rows behind the fence,
regular police in front of it, and seated protesters filling the
small cul-de-sac all the way back to the main street. After
a few minutes someone started humming a well-known
protest tune, and soon other voices joined in harmony. It

was at this moment that the police decided they needed to clear the space. There was no traffic, nobody blocking an intersection, no obvious reason for the police to flex their muscles. Ten regular police officers retreated behind the fence only to be replaced by sixty other cops in full riot gear. One of them issued a warning from a black cylinder, some high-tech version of a megaphone. I swallowed an unexpected giggle—he looked and sounded like Darth Vader.

The protestors held their ground. Another warning was issued. At this point the singing stopped and was replaced by a thrum of tension almost audible in the too-abrupt silence. As I started to retreat to the back of the street, I caught sight of two students, Matt and Connie, who were part of a group I had met a couple of months prior when I visited their university to give a speech on why it was important to come to Quebec City. Here they were, right in the front row, arms linked. The riot police issued their last warning and started marching slowly forward, spraying tear gas directly into the faces below them. A second wave of assault involved swinging batons over their shoulders and bringing them down onto the backs, legs, and shoulders of the young people struggling to stay seated. Without thinking I threw myself on top of Matt and Connie, screaming, "Come with me!"

"No!" they hoarsely shouted. "We came here for this. We want to stand our ground."

I could feel the police shoving at my back as I began to choke, unable to breathe through clouds of tear gas.

"I'm with you," I screamed, and then I squeezed their

shoulders briefly before I proceeded to push, shove, and crawl my way towards the end of the street, gasping for breath, tears streaming from my burning eyes. Once I reached the main thoroughfare I sank to the ground and started sobbing as volunteer medics, other protesters, and police passed by in some kind of macabre choreography. The feeling of powerlessness to protect my kin was all too familiar, and past meshed with present, bringing me to my knees on the uneven cobblestones.

Alone that night, I passed under a bridge, watching as a large group of activists started breaking apart old furniture, grabbing fence posts and whatever else was close at hand, tossing the pieces onto a large bonfire. It was already dark and the figures were hooded, as though this were some kind of early Hallowe'en party. At one point someone started to beat a rhythm with a broken chair leg on the metal fence perimeter. Another joined in, banging on the bottom of a garbage drum. Others started to dance around the edge of the fire as I observed from the sidelines, feeling their rage, trauma, and anger move through my own body. My peers, who had risked their safety for an ideal, who had faced unexpected and unrelenting brutality, who had encountered the failed promise of our democratic system, needed an outlet for their despair.

The next morning I hobbled my way into the CBC building to be interviewed for a national program that would be heard by millions of Canadians. In a voice almost gone from sucking in too much tear gas, I croaked out words about peaceful direct action being an important tactic when governments weren't responding to other approaches. I spoke of the overreaction on the part of police, of watching friends, allies, and colleagues getting hit with rubber bullets and tear gas, rinsing their blinded eyes with water from plastic bottles, and of watching riot police wrenching supine bodies off the ground to twist arms behind backs in arrest. I finished, squeezing out the words from a brain reeling from exhaustion and chemical gas, "But this is how change has always happened—through people brave enough to put their bodies on the line for what they believe. One foot in front of the other, one step at a time." Clichéd, idealistic words, but also true. And spoken that morning in the lost voice of my twenty-seven-year-old self, they seemed somehow prophetic.

⌣

THROUGHOUT MY TWENTIES I gave everything I had to political activism. The success of any movement is always hard to measure in the moment; the societal impact takes a long time to assess because of the sheer number of people involved. We represented the early adopters of capitalist fatigue, and we soon dragged the rest of society along. A month after Quebec City I was walking down Queen Street in Toronto when I caught a glimpse of the trendy Diesel storefront window display with a collection of mannequins dressed in full-on protest gear: ripped jeans, combat boots, shirts with mock slogans on them, and bandanas worn across the forehead and over the mouth. I stood there slack-jawed in astonishment. I couldn't believe they had co-opted what people wore in the streets protesting unrestrained corporate power to sell their own corporate brand! I came to realize it was an early sign of our growing mainstream influence.

Of course, there was much left undone in terms of enforcing ethical standards on our global capitalist system. Some claimed the anti–corporate globalization movement was made up of too many disparate groups with too many different agendas to have a central message. Some argued that the movement got cut off at the knees before widespread change could actually be made into law. Others thought it was too young, too white, and too homogeneous to have large-scale impact.

Looking back, even though I was burnt out and despairing at the time, I know that we changed things. *I* changed things. The anti–corporate globalization movement introduced the notion of corporate social responsibility and suspicion of unethical "profit-at-any-cost" motivations that are now part of popular culture. We put a spotlight on the corporate outsourcing of manufacturing jobs to places like China, placing greater value on "local" because of the often fairer production standards. We laid the groundwork for the tipping point for environmental awareness that continues to this day. We blew the whistle on large agribusiness and water corporations stripping resources from poor communities in the global south, so that now every time I see a bag of ethically sourced coffee beans sold in a big box grocery store, I silently raise my fist in solidarity. For a couple of years, as the global clock ticked from one millennium to the next, we had people looking up from their day-to-day choices to imagine a more fairly constructed society and what was possible if we collectively pressured even one company to do things differently. We altered perception of corporate intentions from benignly neutral to potentially Machiavellian. We shifted the Spiritus Mundi.

I didn't step forward just to have an impact. I became involved in the movement because at the time it seemed the only path to address the suffering I saw around me — and within me. Activism gave me a wider lens on global injustice and the space to do something about it. It gave me countless lessons in collective power as an antidote to the powerlessness that can often be accepted as the status quo in the face of creeping destruction. I was lucky. As complicated as it was, it was one of few communities that would allow a young brown woman to shine in a leadership role. I came of age during the anti-globalization movement at the turn of the millennium, and though I left somewhat bloodied and bruised, I will forever be grateful for the opportunities it gave me to roar.

TEN

Wounded Warrior

SAVING THE WORLD WAS a relationship of passion, requiring fidelity and obsession. At least that's how it felt for me at that time. Everything I did was framed in terms of the better society that would come into existence after certain actions or policy changes or shifts in government took place. There was never any time for the here and now. Everything that happened at the individual level was overshadowed by a focus on collective oppression. Taking time for a coffee, sharing personal experiences, was not really a part of the culture. The famous line attributed to Emma Goldman, "If I can't dance, I don't want to be part of your revolution," was oft quoted but seemed to miss the mark. Time for laughter, celebration, or fun was so rare it was like a unicorn sighting. More often, activist culture was defined by stress, tension, and endless critiques, of the world and of each other. It felt as though we were at war not just with our opponents but also with a gentler way of being within and among ourselves. Stopping for any length of time might bring on an onslaught of too many feelings that we were not equipped to handle.

After Quebec City, I started to free-fall. That June, Paul and I went on holiday together out west. I arranged for us to travel to Galiano Island, hoping that the familiar west coast beauty would offer some peace. In the week we were there I got my period. Like a tidal wave washing through me — ferocious, crippling, and extremely painful — it left no energy in its wake. I'd never experienced anything like it, to the point where I considered going to the hospital. I later found out that tear gas can have a lasting effect on menstruation, resulting in excessive bleeding, cramping, and clotting. I had all three.

My relationship with Paul was still new, and I wasn't in the right space to express my needs, or completely understand them myself. I asked a lot of him in roundabout ways, and criticized him when he wasn't able to understand or respond to my mixed messages. That week together on Galiano Island marked a turning point in our relationship, and not for the better.

A couple of months after returning to Toronto I was offered the opportunity to travel to Genoa, Italy, to attend the protests against the twenty-seventh meeting of the G8 and report back to coalition partners on what I learned. Organizing around the globe was rapidly escalating, and groups within the movement were trying to assess the ramifications for our plans on home soil. I was on the third floor of a downtown mall on a Friday evening, standing at a pay phone opposite the public bathrooms, speaking to my contact at a national union, who trilled, "Good news, Annahid! Go ahead and book your ticket. We'll take care of the costs."

What should have been invigorating news instead had the opposite effect. I felt the life suddenly drain from my body, the familiar spiky urge to pee. There was no more rescuer-energy left. The thought of placing myself once again in a chaotic situation with the promise of escalating violence was completely and utterly overwhelming. My mind and body were now truly in different countries, the former plowing ahead and the latter screaming messages to slow down. In the days following, I couldn't bring myself to make the plane booking. Usually I could get by on will-power, but like a soft drink left out too long on a hot day, I had no fizz left in me. As it turns out, the Genoa protests (July 18–22, 2001) drew a quarter of a million people and marked the first occasion of a protester being shot and killed by the police. Years later, the European Court of Human Rights would rule that the over-the-top violence of the police during the summit — in particular an attack on pro-testers that the court described as causing "severe physical and psychological suffering" — amounted to torture.

The news coming out of Genoa hit close to home. It was too easy to imagine one of the rubber bullets that had struck me and numerous of my friends and allies as real. Sitting in my home office I called Paul to tell him what had happened. He offered words of sympathy that dropped into what felt like a bottomless black hole. I needed more; I wanted it differently said. I wondered if he "got it." Hanging up the phone I felt restless, desperate, and full of emotions that I couldn't name or control. I called him again, then again, and still again, over six times in a one-hour period. I didn't realize the depth of the emotional desperation I was experiencing, and what I was able to see I didn't know what to do with. I really needed my activist community to mourn with, but we didn't know how to do that with each other. This was before self-care became more consciously a part of activist DNA.

⌒

THAT SUMMER, AFTER MONTHS of planning, the national WTO coalition I was working for finally launched its campaign against the General Agreement on Tariffs and Trade (GATT). Two caravans, one from the east coast and one from the west, started travelling city to city to raise awareness and mobilize people towards a national day of action that fall. I was the point-person for activists travelling on the caravans, and I had to troubleshoot everything from interpersonal conflicts and event logistics to setting up interviews with the media. The behind-the-curtain coalition politics were draining.

In reality, it was a coalition in name only — a few national organizations like the Council of Canadians, the Canadian Labour Congress, the Canadian Union of Public Employees, the Canadian Federation of Students, and the Canadian Auto Workers decided strategy in the name of the more than sixty signatory organizations. Contacting people to pitch in resources to make the campaign happen was challenging. It meant handling egos, dealing with differences over strategy, and more often than not following up with someone who had promised to do something but didn't. I was back to having to go through the whole chain of command. Nothing felt easy at this point, and I was irritated by every energy-draining obstacle.

I travelled to Ottawa for the campaign kickoff that June. We had a press scrum on Parliament Hill and I delivered my spiel to the national media standing next to Ken Georgetti, then president of the Canadian Labour Congress, Maude, and a couple of other prominent national leaders. I nailed my message in front of the TV cameras, and the launch was by all accounts a success. The story was carried on all the national news broadcasts that evening.

⌒

AS FALL 2001 APPROACHED our campaign was in full swing. The two caravans were close to arriving in Ottawa. We had tens of thousands of campaign flyers, handbooks, postcards, and videos produced and distributed. Petitions had been signed, and the media had been alerted to our designated national day of action: September 13, 2001.

Two days before our key campaign date, with events planned across the country and a press conference scheduled on Parliament Hill, I was called down to my neighbour's apartment to watch as planes flew into the World Trade Center buildings in New York City. I felt shock, then sadness over the senseless loss of lives. But I had no idea how much of a game-changer that moment would prove to be.

September 11 not only shifted the international political landscape, it changed the direction of my work entirely, altering my identity and sense of who I was in the world.

Overnight, being an activist was equated with being a terrorist, and exercising one's civil liberties—especially protesting in public—was seen not as a democratic right but as a public threat.

The morning after 9/11, David, our communications guy, called me up and said, "Look at our campaign logo. What does it remind you of?"

All of our campaign materials featured a logo showing two people shining a flashlight up at the giant letters "WTO." It was meant to play on the secretive yet threatening nature of the trade agreement we were opposing.

"Uh, I dunno," I responded, not especially quick on the uptake that morning.

"Well," he replied, "I hate to say it, but it looks like two kids setting off a bomb."

"Come on!" I snorted. "Anyone can see that's a flashlight in their hands."

But as I looked closer, I got what he was saying. The flashlight aiming up at the letters "WTO" could indeed have been mistaken for another, more violent image.

All our months of coordinated efforts, planning, and caravan travels went down the toilet. Not only was the central campaign message derailed, but relationships among coalition partners, between coalition members and grassroots activists, and between the movement and society in general all started to unravel. The whole tent came crashing down. Buzz Hargrove, president of the Canadian Auto

Workers union, reneged on participating in our national day of action in November and publicly called for the plans to be cancelled. His comments fed directly into public fears by linking anti-globalization protesters to terrorism. I immediately called his direct line and left a voicemail, furious with him for betraying the movement and for turning his back on the young people left to face the prejudice of an angry public wanting to lay blame somewhere. I never heard back from him. My attempts to connect with Maude were also brushed aside. Their responses were an echo from childhood: elders in positions of responsibility turning away when most needed. Activism is a community in which relationships are measured by their utility. Mentorship was not part of the culture, and progressive organizations had a reputation for eating their young. Despite being a face for the movement, I felt completely ostracized.

⌒

BY THE FALL OF 2001 I had been churning away at the lack of diversity in the movement for several years. In my role as coalition coordinator I had reached out to groups such as the Canadian Arab Federation, the Chinese Canadian National Council, and the Muslim Canadian Congress and not a single NGO or union leader had followed up. Coalition leadership was 99 percent white. There was a lot of talk about diversity but no walk. Not even a step.

With this in mind, I felt that 9/11 was an opportunity to build relationships with communities of colour facing the brunt of the racist backlash—at least to inquire, offer support, or partner with their efforts. Yet again, little action was taken by coalition leaders. The talk of a progressive vision backed by a diverse movement for change revealed itself to be nothing but empty rhetoric. The lack of effort on the part of powerful, financially secure, predominantly white national organizations to address the Islamophobia or racism after 9/11 registered with me in a deeply personal way. National leaders I had generally looked up to now seemed distant, cloaked in extreme privilege they seemed unwilling to use in any meaningful way.

It didn't take long for the societal backlash to manifest, either. In the days after 9/11, Middle Eastern and Muslim North Americans faced the burning of mosques, homes, and workplaces, plus both verbal and physical assaults. One moment in particular stands out. I was watching the nightly news and an interview with a Middle Eastern family whose children were facing escalating harassment at school. As the older boy haltingly spoke of what was happening to him, the slight bow of his head, downward-shifted gaze, and hunched shoulders spoke volumes to me. As I continued watching, a heavy sensation expanded across my chest and into my limbs, making it difficult for me to breathe or move. I recognized this boy in my bones. I had been him once.

Out of what felt like nowhere, I began to feel the unexpressed weight of my childhood experiences. On some level I recognized what was happening, but I wasn't yet self-aware enough to understand the full extent. I did what I was used to doing and went into action mode, attempting to save those I saw on TV. It's like this for many activists: working to reset the past as much as the present; childhood wounds giving rise to adult warriors. It's not possible to act from a place of pure motivation, but it is a problem when past and present, wound and warrior, become so deeply enmeshed.

⌒

BEING MIXED RACE ONLY exacerbated the impact of the racist backlash for me. Not having a fixed racial identity meant that I lacked a consistent community of support. What differentiates the mixed-race experience from that of people with a singular ethnic background is the consistent uncertainty about whether you're in or out, as if belonging is an invisible skipping rope one is forever jumping over, from one situation to the next. Self-identity is a Rorschach ink blot, always up for external interpretation. For me, September 11 not only resurrected old ghosts of rejection, it was like stepping on the identity landmine that I'd been carefully tiptoeing around my entire life. Sometimes I could almost pass, cloaking myself in the white part of my identity, until I offered my full name, or was asked where I was from, or watched—again—as someone in power bypassed me to shake hands with my white colleague first. If I disclosed my Iranian roots, I'd often hear well-meaning yet bias-revealing comments from both friends and strangers, such as, "Oh, you don't look that dark," "You could be Mediterranean, Italian, anything, really," or "I didn't really notice your skin colour at all." It was crazy-making. Why would you ask where I'm from if you didn't think I looked different from you? And why comment on my answer in a way that suggests the difference I named wasn't as exotic as you might like, or conversely it was too foreign-sounding and needed to be blurred into "safer" cultural categories? And do you really think it's a compliment when you point out to me that I'm not darker-skinned?! Underlying each of the many responses I've heard over the years is the benign yet always present racism that sees colour but then wants to immediately control or erase its existence.

It was often the small things that drove me nuts. The constant second-guessing—was it all in my head? Or was I really being interrupted more frequently, interrogated more rigorously when returning an item to a store, more often having my pronunciation mistakenly corrected while facilitating a workshop. This was the emotional tax paid for not quite checking the "normal" box in people's heads.

If I travelled even an hour outside of my downtown neighbourhood the signals marking difference became less ambiguous: all heads turning towards me in a restaurant as I entered, no other people of colour in sight. Once, when I returned to Sherwood Park over the Christmas holidays, I was chatting with a Starbucks employee whom I then asked to watch my bag for a few minutes while I went to the bathroom. This person exclaimed upon my return (and not in a positive way), "I'm so relieved. I thought you'd left a bomb in there!"

After 9/11, finding support in other racialized communities wasn't possible either. Four years earlier, during my Ottawa years, I had dated a man whose reclaimed African name was Chitundu. We met one day while he was behind the counter of his father's tiny Jamaican grocery store and immediately hit it off over a shared frustration that the city was still so white, and that most people seemed oblivious to this reality. Yet Chitundu would only see me after dark. We never went out, save for my occasional visits to his father's store or standing at the back of a crowded bar watching his reggae band perform. It wasn't until the end of our three-month liaison that I understood the reason for this furtive courtship. We were hanging around on my futon one night as the news droned on in the background when he mentioned an upcoming wedding that he had to attend.

I asked, "Are you going to take anyone?"

"Nah," he replied.

Thinking it was odd, I pressed on. "I could go with you. I'd love to watch a traditional Jamaican wedding ceremony. Plus, I could meet the rest of your family."

I watched the muscles twitch in his jaw although his face stayed turned towards the TV. "Nah. It wouldn't really work."

"Why not?" I bluntly retorted, caught between hurt and curiosity.

"I can't take you there. No other white person will be in the room."

And there it was. Unconsciously he had spoken the harsh truth that for anyone darker-skinned, I was whitewashed.

Although I understood the need for black-only spaces in a society where the black community was close to the bottom rung on the oppression ladder, I also envied him the shared wordless understanding with his community of what it felt like to be in black skin. Ta-Nehisi Coates describes this connection in his book *Between the World and Me* when, after starting at Howard University and seeing for the first time a spread of only black bodies in front of him, he experienced the comfort of immediate kinship: "Had any people, anywhere, ever been as sprawling and beautiful as us?" I wanted that. I wanted an "us" to belong to. It was hard to feel I had the right to name racism as a reality I had suffered so brutally in childhood, and more benignly as an adult, while having light-skinned privilege and no singular racial identity. The darkness of one's skin colour, though powerful, is only one factor in measuring racial exclusion, an unpopular truth in the world of race politics. Even now, I struggle to write these words, to feel entitled to wounds I have written an entire book about.

I wasn't seen as Persian. I certainly wasn't seen as British. And only some of the time was I seen as Canadian. Feeling the absence of a community that truly reflected my experience only magnified the pain of isolation. I didn't seem ever to check the right identity boxes to be counted "in." Because of the lingering effects of the past, my parents were also a dead end for emotional support. Talking with my mom wasn't very productive; the larger forces of racism remained in her blind spot, or, if she did see them, she wasn't able to recognize their impact. My father, who by 2001 was running a successful accounting business, distanced himself as completely as possible from any of the stigma that came with being a foreigner. For different reasons, both of my parents had shut down awareness of the price we paid for being different, putting me once again in the uncomfortable position of choosing between denial of my experience to keep things easy (for them), and truthfulness, meaning that I left interactions with them feeling even more abandoned. It was infuriating. I found it hard to connect with either of them: the parents who could choose to turn away in their respective directions, while I was left without that luxury.

⌒

MY GO-TO COMMUNITY AT the time was other activists. Shortly after 9/11, I moved into action mode, pulling together a group of organizers to do something in response to the growing Islamophobia and Middle-Eastern racism. Our first meeting was held at Toronto City Hall. We expected roughly a hundred people, and about five hundred showed up: older Sikh men, young hijab-wearing girls, Desi grandmothers, all seated in rows interspersed with the usual leftist crowd. For many, this was their initiation into activism of any kind. I was co-facilitating the session with a friend, Amy, and we had carefully prepared the agenda, even rehearsed parts of it. Before we were more than ten minutes in, some of my peers on the far left of the spectrum (the mostly white, male members of groups like the International Socialists, New Socialists, and Communist League) started heckling us: "What are you doing?!" "We need to talk action!" "This is a waste of time!"

I looked over at them, people with whom I had shared street space and beers, and attempted to reason with them: "We're giving people a couple of minutes to introduce themselves and check in. The rest of the meeting is focused on action."

Yet it wasn't enough. Their voices became louder, and other familiar faces in the room joined in. All of a sudden, this space too had become for me another reflection of childhood. Yet this time the attacks were from people I had thought were friends and allies. "You don't know what you're doing." "Choose another facilitator!" "We're leaving!" It was shocking: such a blatant betrayal by those with white (and mostly male) privilege.

It didn't matter that we, a group of young, women-of-colour activists, had spent hours organizing and calling in favours, while working full-time jobs, to pull that meeting together on short notice. What took over was people's immediate distress. I looked around at the familiar faces at City Hall, no longer believing that if any of us were to gain power we would create a more inclusive society than the one we lived in.

In many ways, activists are like modern-day apostles in the Church of Life. They package thoughts in new ways, reminding all of us of what's most important, inviting society down new paths to barely glimpsed futures. They scatter over people a confetti of ideas that offer fresh beginnings in what often feel like trapped circumstances. Good activists make the world anew. It is a heady promise, an addictive role, and it tips over easily into righteousness. But when it works, when a speech moves through a crowd of people, the promise of a new world can temporarily lift us above the teeming suffering of humanity. It certainly did for me.

That promise of a better world had kept me going through tough moments, and it would have buoyed me through that City Hall meeting as well if it hadn't been for September 11. Coming on the heels of years of accumulated violence on the front lines, layered on top of my own historical experience, my colleagues' responses left me feeling deeply betrayed. In my raw state I wasn't able to put the behaviour of my fellow grassroots activists into any kind of perspective or recognize that they were feeling fearful. I felt angry at being the target of their undealt-with feelings; I was tired of the way we treated each other, especially when times got tough. We created our own hierarchies of worthiness, a mirror image of the unjust hierarchies we were trying to fight in society.

Throwing an analysis of systemic power abuse at every problem—attributing everything, perhaps simplistically, to capitalism, or racism, or homophobia—wasn't enough to excuse people acting out their personal dysfunctions. In a community supposedly built on empathy, empathy often seemed to be what was sorely lacking. I saw more clearly—including in myself—how hard it was to be in relationships of trust across even minor differences in political views. Although our goals were noble, our means of accomplishing them left much to be desired.

Principles minus action, or values without relationship, are no comfort in times of loss. Activist culture needed rehab. That night was the last straw. I knew I needed more, even though I didn't know what the "more" was.

POLITICAL SHIFTS DON'T HAPPEN separate from personal impact. That same week, I got a call from Paul asking me to come over. In his kitchen, while I kept my gaze focused on the rack of Teflon-coated pots and pans behind his head, he sat me on his lap. Thinking it to be a moment of unprompted intimacy, I was unprepared for what came next. Through tears he told me, "I can't do this any more. I love you but I can't give you what you need." I couldn't believe it. Though we'd had our differences—and I knew I had been leaning on him heavily for emotional support—I hadn't seen that coming.

Both of us were political animals who enjoyed debating as a sport. He introduced me to *Sex and the City*. I inspired him with my passion for change. Yet as much as I tried to persuade him otherwise that September afternoon, his mind was made up. Even in the midst of feeling devastated I couldn't help but admire how entitled he felt to name and honour his feelings. How could he do that, I wondered. It seemed such a luxury.

By the end of 2001 it was clear that the ground rules of civil society had radically changed. Political organizing, once seen simply as a democratic right, had become a complete liability. Nevertheless, activists were busy fighting, though surreptitiously, a growing xenophobia and the narrowing of civil liberties. Free trade and corporate accountability were now the furthest things from anyone's mind. The coalition coordinator position I'd held was now rendered obsolete, which meant that by spring I was out of a job. I had rent payments, debt to pay off, and no job security. Increasingly, I was finding it hard to get out of bed each morning.

My family was in the midst of great changes as well. Early in 2002 I travelled to Edmonton to visit my parents, who by that time had been divorced for a couple of years. One morning I met my father for breakfast at a local diner. After watching him struggle with his words (a first!), he nervously told me that his older sister, still living in Iran, had introduced him by phone to a friend of hers whose name was Zary. Not only that, he had flown over to meet her in Istanbul. She was immigrating in a couple of months so they could get married. When he'd finished speaking he looked at me with a rare shadow of vulnerability in his eyes. I realized he was asking for my blessing.

I wasn't sure how to respond. I was glad he was moving on, but at the same time he was marrying someone I'd never heard of, someone from a cultural context I felt completely disconnected from yet not neutral towards. I could see how marrying a Persian wife represented a comforting security for my father as he looked towards his senior years — she would never leave (for reasons both cultural and financial), unlike my Western-born mother. Yet it was as though he was returning to a home we'd once shared, but one that was no longer familiar or welcoming to me.

It was another hard blow to the solar plexus of my identity, altering my place in the world even further. When I go back to visit him now, I encounter a different environment — and father — from the one I grew up with. The man of today speaks mostly Farsi, eats Persian food, and hangs out with Iranian friends. I visit the home I grew up in and feel like a foreigner. He has returned to his roots, even travelling back to the country of our common birth, but with each subsequent step he takes backwards, my siblings and I feel as if we are being left farther behind.

Meanwhile, my mom had moved into a small place by herself in northeast Edmonton. She was getting more involved in her local church and had joined the St. George's Society in the city. It was as if my parents had lived at opposite ends of an elastic band stretched too far by marriage, and once freed, they'd snapped back to where they'd started from.

On top of the losses in work and relationship, the growing racism across North America, and changes to my family structure, by the time I returned from my Edmonton trip I found my small one-room apartment on the second floor of an old three-storey house in Toronto's High Park neighbourhood to be completely overrun by mice. They had got into a bag of flour under the kitchen sink while I was away, and what had started as a small guerilla invasion had become a full mouse-dom; at least it was beneficently granting me honorary citizenship in my own residence. The mice would run laps around the perimeter of the room on a regular basis, and I could always hear them scrabbling if I paused in silence for more than a couple of seconds. It felt as if they were an external manifestation of the fearful and inescapable thoughts running around in my head. I started losing sleep. I was jumping at the slightest sound, and looking for ways to escape my tiny abode as often as possible.

After eating dinner at my tiny, cramped kitchen table, usually forcing myself to purge most of it afterwards, I'd pull up my hoodie to shield my head and face and walk for hours around my neighbourhood. The grand houses near High Park offered a kind of vicarious comfort as I caught glimpses of family life through the picture windows. It was reassuring to see people in routines of normalcy: seated around the dinner table, watching TV, a hand placed momentarily on someone's shoulder, the turning off of a lamp easing the interior into darkness. It was a visual reminder that such stability existed, though it felt like a planet apart from the one I inhabited.

After one such walk I returned home to finish the day with my usual hot shower, the hotter the better. Using my favourite peach-scented shampoo, I dug my fingertips into my scalp, giving myself a luxurious head massage. As I rinsed off, leaning my head against the side of the shower stall, I was suddenly overcome by a rush of bone-deep fatigue. In that moment I couldn't imagine standing any more, never mind finishing and making my way back to bed. Pulling my hand away from my head, I glanced down to see a fistful of hair. I knew one of the side effects of bulimia was hair loss — this had become a normal occurrence — but staring down at that mass of dark-brown strands, I could see the physical evidence of my life unravelling. I remained in the shower, letting the hot water beat down on my skin, yet feeling no warmer inside.

⌒

SHORTLY AFTERWARDS I TRIED something radically different, desperate to find some kind of internal grounding. On the invitation of a friend, I started attending Ashtanga yoga classes once or twice a week at the trendy Downward

Dog studio downtown. Although I wasn't at all sure what I was doing, I'd leave feeling both sore and cleansed. It was not so different from how I felt after bingeing and purging, but it was a much healthier way of getting there. At the end of each class, while lying in my favourite pose, Savasana (or corpse pose, which involves lying on the ground as motionless as possible), one of the assistant teachers would come along and spray some lavender mist before gently and smoothly stroking my forehead. Bliss. I attended those classes as much for that sensory reward as for the preceding ninety minutes of movement.

Alongside yoga, I started meditating—just a paltry five minutes at the start of my day, but it was something. Some days I couldn't quite get myself to sit even that long. Hearing the baby mice running around the edges of the room didn't help matters, but I persevered. Most days I'd plop myself down in a cross-legged position—"Is this the right posture?" "Am I doing it right?" "Is it supposed to hurt?"—not sure what benefits I should be reaping, but desperate for some relief from the constant buzz of anxiety and deeper depression I was feeling.

By January 2002, after a couple months of setting mouse-traps (steel and sticky) baited with peanut butter and other assorted rodent appetizers, plans to purchase a cat, and other assorted strategies I'd entertain at 3 a.m. that never survived the light of day, I knew I had to get out. I had resorted to regular appeals to neighbourhood friends to allow me to stay in their apartments temporarily. Anything to get out of my place. I was sleeping at a friend's house one night and discovered that they had left a stuffed toy mouse propped up against the pillows of my bed. I screamed, loudly, then I tried to strangle out laughter. I had lost all perspective and my sense of humour. I've since read that in some Indigenous traditions mice teach the importance of letting go of the need for control. I guess the joke was on me, though it didn't seem funny at the time.

The question was, once again, where could I go? I knew it had to be a big move. Everything familiar, everything that I had defined myself by, had ended or was coming to an end. I had a couple of job offers for other campaign positions, including one with Public Citizen in Washington, D.C., a corporate watchdog organization founded by Ralph Nader. It was an amazing opportunity, but it felt like a *should* instead of a *want*, a move motivated by ego rather than soul. And I was tired of rescuing; I just wanted someone to rescue me.

Around that time I had a dream. In it, I emerged from underground subway steps with a batch of mail in my hand. I started rifling through the envelopes, trying to remember where I lived and how to get home. I knew my home was somewhere nearby, but I started panicking because I couldn't read the writing on the envelopes, I couldn't figure out where I lived. I don't often remember dreams, but that one felt like a clear message from my subconscious: "You're looking in the wrong places. Home isn't out there, it's something you need to find inside yourself."

A few months earlier I had taken a week-long course at the Massachusetts-based Kripalu Center for Yoga & Health, one of the oldest and most prestigious health and well-being centres in North America. While there, I heard about their three-month, volunteer-based Spiritual Lifestyle program. After my dream, I checked out the program again and applied right away. I didn't know exactly what I was looking for, but I knew it was something deeper, perhaps spiritually rooted. I was accepted as a last-minute addition for their spring 2002 cohort, which coincided with the end of my coalition job. The timing was impeccable. I was all set to exit the world of politics, the country, my city, my apartment, ready to escape and invest hope somewhere new: free, faraway, and focused inwards, truly a holy trinity. Yoga and meditation were the perfect answer, it seemed, to find some internal peace. It was time for the wounded warrior to heal.

PART III

RECONCILIATION

Why not become the one who lives with
    a full moon
in each eye that is always saying,
with that sweet moon language,
what every other eye in this world is
    dying to hear?

— HAFIZ, "WITH THAT MOON
            LANGUAGE"

ELEVEN

Just Breathe

THE SPRING OF 2002 found me travelling by bus down to Kripalu, nestled in the New England countryside. During my journey, I had the honour of being the single candidate pulled off the bus for interrogation at the U.S. border. At 2 a.m., under bad fluorescent lighting, I felt like late-night entertainment for the two droopy-eyed security guards. One of them peered at my passport and kept repeatedly mispronouncing my full name — "Anna-hide?" "Paree-sia?" Dish-gerd?" — as if such a title were a deliberate subversion on my part. "What kind of name is this?" he finally asked. The other one followed up with, "You're from Eye-ran?" (I chose not to point out his mispronunciation.) This continued to the somewhat more predictable conclusion: "How long have you been in Canada? Where did you grow up?" and my favourite, "How many igloos up there?" It felt like a scene from a late-night comedy show, and if I hadn't been so aware of the very real possibility of being denied entry, I'd have been doubled over with laughter.

Eventually, one of the men reluctantly handed over a piece of paper with a tracking number, like a receipt that would expire in three months' time. *Can I get a refund on my time if I don't have a positive experience?* I wondered, but wisely didn't ask. I returned to the bus, officially registered with Homeland Security.

A few groggy hours later, I stumbled off the bus into tiny downtown Lenox, Massachusetts, to see a dirty pickup truck off to the side with the Kripalu logo splashed across its side. My driver was a young Asian guy named Alpha, one of the few people of colour I met during my stay at Kripalu.

"Hey, what's your name?" he asked as I came to stand in front of him. I looked at him before I responded, measuring up whether or not he would "get it," whether he could respect my name by not immediately mispronouncing it or, even worse, taking it upon himself to shorten it back to "Anna."

This was the reason I was there. I felt my back straighten as I heard myself pronounce my full name aloud for the first time in over fifteen years. "Ah-NAH-heed," I answered, a close approximation of how it had been pronounced in Iran. I felt I couldn't go for broke and say "Ah-nah-HEED" as emphasis on the last syllable requires a different rhythm of speech, and it lands like a heavy boot in English. And just like that, I grafted the "hid" — three letters, one syllable — back onto "Anna." Not identifying as a religious Muslim, I couldn't wear a hijab, as many young female Muslims had started doing after 9/11 as a way of reclaiming their marginalized identity with pride in the face of growing Islamophobia and racism—a micro-protest that shouted, "I am here, and I will not let you define me!" But I could still inhabit my full name. I watched with a mix of defiance and anxiety to see if Alpha would pass this first test.

He nodded once, easing the knot in my stomach. I smiled at him as I opened the door to hop on board.

As we neared the end of the short ride, Alpha turned with a screech into Kripalu's driveway, sending a cloud of gravel and dust into the air. I turned to him in surprise when he exclaimed, sounding out of breath as he spoke, "Sorry, I'm experimenting with not wearing my glasses. I can't really see that well."

"Oh," I said, unsure how to respond to this.

He went on, "I read somewhere that if we cease our reliance on external objects we can repair our body's weak spots. I do eye muscle exercises every day."

"Do you notice any difference?" I asked diplomatically, suspecting I already knew the answer.

"Not really!" he cheerfully answered, apparently undaunted.

We pulled up to Kripalu's back entrance, which was between the kitchen and the mailroom. As Alpha groped for his door handle, I took a deep breath and jumped out my side with a burst of energy. It was strangely reassuring to arrive at the unsigned, unpopulated back entrance of a major spiritual retreat, driven by a myopic Asian man in a rundown truck. I felt like Alice tumbling down the rabbit hole into Wonderland.

⌒

ONCE SETTLED AT KRIPALU, I was placed in a cohort with nine other volunteers, all seekers in one way or another. We were embarking on a three-month experience during which we would be taught the practices and principles of a yogic lifestyle. My group included Claudia, a soon-to-be graduate of medical school; Arthur, an older man with white hair and missing teeth who was sunlight on legs; Mark, a guy my age with boy-next-door good looks, who later disclosed that he was battling sex addiction; and Marianne, an older woman estranged from her family who shaved her head while at Kripalu, signalling a commitment to a monastic lifestyle. We were a motley crew, assigned to work in different parts of the centre (kitchen, gardens, housekeeping), and required to attend twice-weekly evening workshops, yoga classes, and a weekly group check-in. I was assigned to the kitchen, where I assisted with food preparation for the more than six hundred guests, staff, and volunteers.

While I loved the New England countryside and the sprawling, sunlit centre that had once been a monastery, our sleeping arrangements were less than ideal. I was assigned a top bunk in a large dorm with about forty other women. This arrangement raised anxiety in me, specifically around the question of accessing the bathroom without waking my bunkmate or others nearby. It was also hard to unplug from the energy of being surrounded by so many bodies each day. I had become accustomed to tuning into others' feelings at all times, yet this was a liability when trying to disengage and calm my own nervous system enough to sleep. The result was that I never fell asleep before midnight, which meant I was exhausted the entire time I was there—and the goal had been to recover from exhaustion.

But it was the weekly group check-ins that became my albatross. For a couple of hours every week, our group of ten would sit in a circle and exercise our muscles of mindfulness—taking special notice of our breathing, sensations, and feelings, and, if we chose, speaking about our observations and experiences in the moment. Each week as we went around the circle, I could feel my heart rate accelerating, palms turning damp, and breath becoming short. It was uncomfortable to feel so conscious of all these sensations, yet at the same time it was impossible to return to blissful denial. I noticed how it was infinitely more challenging for me to tune in to my internal state in front of a small group of people I knew than it was to speak onstage to a crowd of a hundred strangers. More than once, I wondered what the point of it all was; I considered cashing in my tracking number early, returning to the familiarity of the political world.

The oft-repeated catchphrase of Kripalu's founding guru, "Self-observation without judgement is the key to enlightenment," crossed my mind daily while I was there. I could manage the self-awareness part, but I was not so good at letting go of judgement, particularly towards myself. The group check-in felt like shining a thousand-watt spotlight into dark internal corners without access to a dimmer switch. Uncomfortable and anxiety-provoking, these group sessions left me itching to escape my own skin.

In the midst of this discomfort, however, I could also feel that the tools guiding me towards noticing what was happening internally were exactly what I needed to fix my own shaky foundations. Kripalu gave me the keys to begin journeying inward. One of my biggest take-aways was literacy in the language of my body. By offering a breather from the urgent intensity of the political realm, my time at Kripalu allowed me to slow down and notice my own breathing.

During my stay I was lucky to attend a rare talk by visiting guest S. N. Goenka, spiritual superstar and founder of the Vipassana (insight) meditation method. Onstage at the front of the auditorium he looked like a seated brown Buddha. The Vipassana approach to meditation is based on noticing and thus regulating body sensations. In the 1970s it was road-tested in India on prisoners, who were taught to master their anger in constructive ways. Vipassana courses are offered in centres around the world by donation only, in keeping with the principle that all should have equal access to spiritual practices. Goenka put meditation into a context of social activism that had meaning for me.

Shortly afterwards, we had the option of participating in a day-long Vipassana session, alternating between sitting and walking. We were offered basic instructions to slow down movement, to keep bringing our attention back to breath and other physical sensations, and to observe, observe, observe. For an entire day. I was hesitant going in, uncertain whether I'd get anything from it except being bored out of my skull. But I was surprised to find myself wanting more. The silence enabled me to feel as connected to the people I was surrounded by as if we had spent all day in conversation. I felt my mind slowing down to rest in small spaces that anxiety didn't inhabit. Most of all, I started to notice there was a whole other universe of information about who I was beyond just my thoughts. I could let my defences down in the silence and connect to a larger field of being. It was my first time discovering that I found quiet soothing rather than threatening; I began to be able to differentiate between being alone and feeling lonely. Silence, marked by its complete absence of stimulation, was like a lifeline thrown to my drowning nervous system.

Between regular spurts of meditation and the weekly group check-ins, I started to slip away from reactive thinking and behaviour to the feelings and sensations motivating them. A holding of breath, tightening in the shoulders, and a rapid heart rate translated into fear or anxiety. Knotted neck muscles along with slight nausea meant feelings akin to shame. A surge of adrenaline and clenching in my gut usually meant anger. And if I couldn't interpret the sensations, I began to trust that just observing the clenching, tightening, or nausea would allow them to shift. Surprisingly, I also started noticing other parts of my body, where there was spaciousness and strength. Perhaps I was more resilient than I thought.

I also started to perceive that the difficult emotions I carried — anger, fear, anxiety, desperation — weren't monolithic. I began to learn what it was not to abandon myself in the midst of intense feelings, which is the key to undoing damage from prolonged states of stress. It is also the key to being in intimate connection with other people. Kripalu marked the first time in my adult life that I took steps in the opposite direction from what I had learned to do in childhood, which was to distance myself from feeling and find ways to numb out. I started to become aware of a link between physical pleasure and a feeling of inner calm. I had always treated my body as disposable, a way of getting from A to B, of performing tasks for external reward no matter the personal cost. While there, I started regularly visiting the indoor sauna and hot tub, relishing the time with something akin to reverence. It was heavenly to have access to such unabashed sensuality. The heat! The wetness! The ability to sit and take in such sensory gratification with nothing to do, nowhere to rush to.

Such rituals of pleasure started to beat back the old messaging I'd absorbed as a brown girl growing up in a white conservative culture, replacing "Gross! Too much! Not enough!" with "Aaaaaaah, that feels good." For someone who had never been to a spa, rarely had a manicure or pedicure, or indulged much in massage, this access to physical pleasure also planted seeds for a slower, more embodied way of being. Perhaps it was permissible to focus on my own needs at the expense of the collective; maybe it wasn't an either-or proposition in the first place.

As in any place where a lot of single people are gathered with a common interest, there was a lot of hooking up—and breaking up—that happened among the group of volunteers (though this was actively discouraged on the path to cultivating a more ascetic lifestyle). Towards the end of my stay, while working in the kitchen one morning, I was introduced to Nanahme. He was a honey-voiced white guy who had adopted a Sanskrit name, along with the requisite long hair. I fell hard into the usual trap of lust for the distant white guy, the only difference being that this one spouted mysticism instead of Marxism.

For the Celtic festival of Beltane, which celebrates the beginning of summer, the centre held a big outdoor celebration with a bonfire. A group of us told stories in the gathering dark as the flames around us slowly rose higher. As the hours passed, people started to dance around the fire, and this time I was one of them. As my body spun around, arms reaching (often flailing), I felt myself start to loosen up. I stopped feeling self-conscious about who was watching and moved as a form of release, feeling both anger and exhilaration roll through me, dancing until I had no energy left to move. Later that night, I clandestinely led Nanahme into one of the empty rooms on the top floor of the centre and we consummated our flirtation. Although I pined for him for a while afterwards, it was mostly out of habit rather than genuine desire. He had fulfilled his role as consort, and it had been on my terms.

⌒

THERE WAS A SIGNIFICANT limitation to the teaching at Kripalu, an epicentre of New Age spirituality, and it was that the only lens through which we were encouraged to view suffering was that of individual experience. Systemic forces weren't recognized, because individual empowerment trumped all. There is a reason why the vast majority of spiritual teachers, meditators, and yogis in the West are middle- to upper-class white people: they can uphold the illusion that we are fully in control of our own destiny. "You can be anyone you choose to be," they say. But I never felt as though that option was available to me.

All the various therapies offered to me — ranging from the more mainstream, such as massage and homeopathy, to the truly New Age, like soul retrieval, energy healing, dream work, and angel voices — were offered by white folks, most of whom looked as though they had been living for years on a hippie commune. The exemplar was the long-haired, soft-spoken vegetarian with glowing skin dressed in loose clothing made of hemp or some other natural fibre. It was hard for me not to look at them and see walking clichés of unchecked privilege. But I was also desperate to shift out of my inner turbulence, so I tasted what was on offer at the therapy smorgasbord, only occasionally returning for seconds.

I lay in countless dimly lit rooms listening to background tracks of birds chirping, African drumming, or yogic chanting as manicured hands moved over my body and whispery voices informed me that I was "very tense," "holding a lot," or "needing more self-love." During these sessions, I often fell prey to the "wanting to please" spell. I wanted these practitioners to see me as a member of the spiritually evolved club, yet the harder I tried to prove my credentials, the more I could feel them move away, their voices growing silent, their hands less sure. Their healing powers couldn't encompass the range of experience my brown immigrant activist body had lived through. Though I was in that place to process my emotions and feelings, I slowly started to realize that most people weren't going to get it.

The challenge was that useful tools were jumbled in with a lot of psychobabble, and often devoid of any reality checks. One day we were invited for an afternoon session involving some form of regression therapy. There were thirty of us in the room, each lying on a yoga mat. I lay watching as a few wan sunbeams orchestrated tiny dust motes into mini-pirouettes above our heads while we were led through a series of breathing techniques designed to tap into early memories housed in the unconscious mind. After just half an hour I found myself short of breath and curling onto my side. Nicole, one of many wholesome-looking white assistants wearing hundred-dollar yoga pants, came over to whisper, "Please lie on your back like everyone else." I shifted position, only to begin struggling for air once again. After a few minutes I could feel a tightness spreading across my chest.

The instructor at the front of the room murmured, "Now imagine yourself being held by your mother. Feel her arms around you." I couldn't feel any limbs, only the rising of some unidentifiable emotion that threatened to pull me under with its strength. I got up and stumbled out of the room, only to collapse on a chair across the hall, doubled over as ragged, choking coughs escaped me, followed by tears. Nicole followed me out to ask in her whispery spiritual voice if I was all right, though I would have thought the answer was obvious. As I looked up at her, I had the distinct feeling that we were on different planets, that even if I could put into words what was coming out of my body

I knew she couldn't possibly understand. She was looking for a prettily packaged experience of connecting mind to body, in a room full of white bodies. She wanted emotions that were part of a comfortable bandwidth, not the ones spilling out of me as a result of being on the front lines of activism and violence, along with the recently rediscovered memories of childhood bullying and racism. I felt a familiar sensation of anger tightening my shoulder blades. I felt that once again I was somehow "not doing it right." The more I tried to explain my reaction to Nicole, the more I felt myself moving away from the centre to the margins.

The climax of my struggle between political and spiritual world views occurred sometime during the middle of my stay. Nicole organized another workshop session — a pre-Oprah version of *The Secret* — letting us in on the law of attraction, the ability to bring into our lives whatever we desired. The room was filled with forty bodies seated in a circle, all white faces except for Alpha's and mine. Nicole started off by earnestly explaining how we each choose our destiny before birth because of certain soul lessons we need to learn. If my skin were the kind to turn red I would have been on fire. I looked around the room to see a third of the participants nodding, a third slightly confused, and a third pleasantly neutral. Alpha raised his eyebrows at me from across the room.

Always the rebel, I raised my hand to challenge. "But what about people that are born in the Congo and forced to become child soldiers? Are you saying that they chose that destiny?"

"Uh, yes," she answered, with some hesitancy, as if

sensing there was a trap somewhere. "That would be their own karma to work out."

"I find that hard to swallow," I retorted. "That sounds like an excuse for those with privilege to continue doing nothing for the less-fortunate people of the world." Nicole's face was getting red by this point. I continued, "Honestly, I can't imagine any one of us would opt for a life of poverty and violence, given the choice."

This time Nicole flat out ignored me and moved on to someone else. Although I knew how to voice dissent, I was uncomfortable with wearing the scarlet letter that came with the role, marking me as an outsider. That dynamic marked my time at Kripalu as a love-hate affair, an internal tug of war between the spiritual seeker and the activist in me; if I indulged one, I marginalized the other.

⌒

WHILE AT KRIPALU I continued to get offers for jobs similar to the one I'd left behind. I applied to a few but nothing was clicking. At one point, one of the many healers said to me, "Because of your history you might feel that you have to suffer in order to help others in their suffering. Being okay might feel scary, because you might feel you're betraying those who aren't."

Wow! Sucker punch. Was there truth in his words? The activist in me couldn't answer the question. Slowly I started connecting to a whole other aspect of myself that I'd never given myself permission to explore. "Soul of a poet," my friend Arthur whispered to me one day over dinner. I turned, thinking he was pointing out someone else in the room. Instead, he was looking at me. It wasn't until the end of my stay that his words started to sink in.

There was a woman staying at the centre who was there from the Netherlands for a week-long painting course, Tanjeet (another white woman with a Sanskrit moniker). We hit it off right away, and I became a vicarious participant in her course. Apparently, the only instructions offered to her were to stand in front of a floor-to-ceiling blank canvas and just let colour splash out. Every day I'd hear about Tanjeet's progress. On day two, she had to paint over everything and start again. On the fourth night she got up at 4 a.m. to stare in anguish for hours at what was on the canvas, unsure how to move forward. I enjoyed playing the role of coach: praising, inspiring, listening, and reflecting as she talked through the different life issues evoked by her painting.

At the end of the week she took me downstairs to see the finished product. I was awestruck that someone who wasn't an "artist" could create such an image. It wasn't necessarily beautiful, but it was powerful. Taking up most of the wall space, her painting was a seascape—bold swashes of cobalt blue, hovering multicoloured fish, giant bubbles bursting at the surface, and seaweed fronds sweeping upwards, holding all in place. I stood silently transfixed. Her art and the process to get there was the tipping point for the nascent artist in me, giving me implicit faith that I could be creative as well.

Now, a decade and a half later, my home is full of colour, and the colours of my living room carpet are reminiscent of her original painting, with splashes of blue and various shades of red. In each room of the house, at least one thing I've painted adorns a wall. Starting with colour led the way to eventually painting with words, writing this very book. Trusting my interpretation of reality over that of everyone around me.

GETTING THROWN FROM THE heights of intense political activism focused on shifting systemic forces into the belly of an inward-gazing spiritual community meant that I had to struggle to see what was true for me between those diametrically opposed world views. Just as most activist circles saw little merit in psychology, the leaders at Kripalu lacked interest in exploring broad social dynamics. I started to see how each realm had something to offer in terms of how they viewed change; they were indeed folded into each other like the yin-yang symbol. And there were also similarities. In both places, anti-consumerist, vegetarian, and environmental sentiments dominated. Chanting was used in both spaces as a mood manipulator, in one case to motivate people towards external action and in the other to guide people more deeply inwards. In each place, dynamics of competitiveness and self-righteousness ruled the roost, although the respective ideologies of equality and enlightenment preached otherwise. Where humans go, power dynamics always show up.

In activist work the pecking order is often established by how oppressed you are and how loud you can be about it; at Kripalu it was about how much quiet transcendence you projected, and how little you seemed to care about external issues or current events. Activism rewards attachment to injustice; spirituality prioritizes non-attachment to *any* worldly experience. Yet in each community the dominant ideology acted as a barrier to the processing of personal experiences, the actual authenticity that comes from embodying feelings. Really, the doctrine of enlightenment is not so different from a revolutionary manifesto: both require self-sacrifice in order to reach some promised land and a bypassing of the more feminine path to social change, which is wisdom gained through engagement with the messy, emotional life housed in the body.

I ended my time at Kripalu with a realization that any ideology that professes to have *all* the answers to human experience is bound to fall prey to its own hypocrisy or contradictions. What was the point of the tendency in humans, I wondered, to land on a perspective and make it the whole truth, turning a blind eye to its limitations? To create the illusion of safety, perhaps? I felt that I had lost that illusion long ago. It seemed to me that the self is a construct influenced by so many societal and psychological forces that it is impossible ever to place any human being in one single ideological framework and unequivocally claim, "This explains the totality of who this person is." This inability to pin any of us down to a single influence is where hope sits.

After my time at Kripalu, I saw more clearly how we are all islands of diversity, connected not by our thoughts but by our shared emotional nature. There is a reason why the deepest processes of transformation—church rituals,

Indigenous ceremonies, even rock concerts — bypass the rational mind and engage us in communal practice so we can, even if temporarily, share our feelings with one another. Compassion, literally meaning "to feel with," is to temporarily let the other in, to be changed by them, to become our sister's or brother's keeper.

I had entered the worlds of activism and spirituality searching for the keys to create a better, more inclusive world. And although I can say I gained valuable lessons in both places, I left disillusioned by the awareness that each community had its own social hierarchy, with a clearly established group at the centre and others relegated to the margins. I didn't want another pecking order, I wanted to find a community where *everyone* could experience belonging. Remembering my dream, I had the tiny seed of a thought that perhaps it was time to stop searching for home "out there" and instead listen to what was happening inside my own body. For perhaps the first time in my life, I could see how being mixed-race, coming from more than one cultural background, living on three different continents during childhood, and being burdened with experiences of not belonging had actually set me up to see more clearly the holes in the ideological fabrics that others were content to wrap themselves in. My differences allowed me to sense what connected us, the more primal levels of human experience containing clues for individual and collective reparation. I started to think that perhaps my identity wasn't such a liability after all. Maybe, just maybe, I could create what I saw was missing.

PERHAPS THE BIGGEST IMMEDIATE benefit from my time at Kripalu was realized on my twenty-eighth birthday. That afternoon I bought a card from the gift shop and sat at a patio table in the late-afternoon sun as I wrote and rewrote a vow to stop the self-harming behaviour of bingeing and purging. Despite many flirtations with quitting over the years, that day marked my first attempt to externalize the commitment to myself, to put intention behind the decision by creating a ritual around it. There I was, alone in the bathroom stall on the upper level of the centre, just before midnight on the cusp of my thirties. Reading aloud the words I'd written for my ears only, a faint echo in the white-tiled room, I desperately negotiated with myself that the next day would mark a new start. There would be many "take two"s in the following months, but this was my first act to consciously let go of the addiction, the initial step in weakening its grip on me.

It was also the first time that I publicly disclosed my struggles with addiction. The power in any addiction is secrecy, the illusion of full control when the eyes of the world are locked out. I knew I had to take a different kind of risk; I needed to let people in. After this ritual, I shared my intention during our group's weekly check-in circle. Each of my peers in their own way offered support— through poems or notes left in my mail-cubby, or gentle words offered on walks about the grounds, or just simple physical gestures like a hug or a tiny squeeze of my arm as they passed by. I could feel their care seeping in through the cracks in my bravado. My warrior self was beginning to transform.

I had to get away from all that was familiar to be able to take these strides forward. As I learned over time, it wasn't my inner dictator that helped me to stick to the commitment, but rather developing the voice of the nurturer, listening to the whispers of the goddess coaxing me back into the light. Each time I fell off the wagon, beating myself up just meant I was dropping deeper into a black hole of desperation, whereas self-understanding was what always allowed me to pull back. I had to find ways to offer myself the opposite of what I had received growing up: what I was looking for was compassion.

Frequently I recalled the simple advice of Kripalu's founding guru — that the key to enlightenment is "self-observation without judgement" — but the profundity wrapped into those words became evident only after I had come back to them repeatedly over the years.

I left my time in the United States with a lot of seeds planted, unsure which ones would germinate. One thing was clear: although I still felt the familiar urgency pulling me back towards the political community, I couldn't return to its narrow confines. I had become reacquainted enough with the part of myself that functions as a mystic, that needs silence, is guided by intuition and moved by beauty: the artist. It would be a few years before the seeds sprouted enough to have me expressing her through red lipstick, painted nails, and a love of cocktails, but she was there. I could feel her breathing.

TWELVE

First Comes Love

WHEN I ARRIVED BACK in Toronto in the early summer of 2002, I went to stay with renowned Canadian feminist and activist Judy Rebick, who had become a mentor and a friend after we'd met during the anti-MAI campaign (she was one of the panellists on our cross-country inquiry). Judy wasn't someone who only picked up the phone when it was beneficial or convenient for her, as is often the case in politics; she is someone who genuinely cares about personal relationships, who prioritizes supporting young activists, and particularly women of colour (another rarity).

While staying at her place, I slowly scribbled notes for an eight-week Conscious Eating course aimed at women. I wanted to combine awareness of external systemic pressures with a consciousness of internal places of wounding, to offer something unique for women struggling with body image and eating issues. Six months later, after moving

to a light-filled apartment in the city's west end, I had a
handful of women seated in my new living room for the
inaugural session. This course was meaningful for me not
only because it marked the first time I had brought my biggest ideological influences — power and psychology — into
the room together, but also because it was a foray into the
world of adult education, which in time would become my
chosen career. It was the beginning of teaching from a place
of experience in addition to theoretical knowledge: the path
of the feminine, or a more holistic approach, rather than
just another talking head stuck on disconnected body parts.
Because, really, how innovative is that? Words are always
easy; it's vulnerability that takes all the legwork.

I started each night's session with a check-in, a replica-
tion of what I had experienced at Kripalu — an invitation
to notice breath, sensation, emotion, and to share whatever felt relevant in the moment. As I looked around the
circle, I recognized the look of uncertainty in the brown,
blue, and green eyes staring back at me. As each person's
turn neared, the aversion of gaze, slight bowing of the
head, or hunching of shoulders signalled that attention
had spiralled inwards, a terror I recognized — the fear of
being fully present in the moment and trusting that the
right words would come. The desperate need to control
self-presentation reflected something deeper for them, as
it had for me. Living under patriarchy, everybody in the
room was familiar with gender shame. It seemed clear
to me that the various forms of eating addiction were a
dysfunctional language used by the body to reconnect
with dissociated parts of the self.

I also enrolled in a year-long shiatsu bodywork course where I was taught the basics of Traditional Chinese Medicine (TCM), including the different energy meridians, acupuncture points, and the broader Eastern approach to disease. TCM is Western medicine's enlightened sibling, taking into consideration the emotional and spiritual levels of health beyond just the physical. Being introduced to this approach for the first time shed light on physical symptoms I had struggled with for years that had no identifiable cure. For starters, I was able to view the uncontrollable peeing and purging as expressions of past distress manifested on the physical plane but not rooted there. I started to see how limited Western thinking is, not only because of its tendency to divide the physical from the emotional but also because it further underestimates and even denigrates emotional and spiritual intelligence. Descartes's famous proclamation "I think, therefore I am" had done us all a massive disservice. "How much information is lost," I wondered, "when the mind is divided from the body?" While the mindfulness practices I explored while at Kripalu helped me establish connection to my physical body, TCM gave me a road map of where to go and what to look for.

The seeds were sown for teaching mindfulness and the emotional literacy skills that became a mainstay of my later work. I started to wonder if creating a more balanced world wasn't just about shifting external structures of inequality, such as patriarchy (a system that privileges male bodies over female) and white supremacy (a system that prioritizes white bodies over people of colour), but, on a deeper level, whether it was about undoing the internalized hierarchy of cognition over sensation, thought over feeling, mind over body. Any system of oppression is based on dividing the spectrum of human traits—civilized/primitive; rational/ emotional; ascetic/sensual—and assigning the more desirable set to the group with social power and the less desirable to the marginalized. Yet in the imposition of such artificial dualities, everyone loses out. No one truly has the freedom to express their authentic selves in a system of inequality. For example, under patriarchy women are taught early on to limit their assertiveness, men to deny their emotions and vulnerability. Forcing people to outsource their humanity, to separate themselves from their emotional core in order to survive in the established order, also means we are individually and collectively less powerful.

I began to see how personal empowerment fits into efforts to undo systemic oppression. Helping people tap in to their emotions is key. Emotional intelligence isn't just observing and detaching from one's feelings (a potential danger of meditation); neither is it about losing oneself in emotion (a potential by-product of activism). Instead, emotional intelligence is about learning to read emotions as a form of information—signposts towards wholeness.

Scientist Candace Pert, in her book *Molecules of Emotion*, refers to emotions as the "biological substrates of spirit." Pert's understanding of the subject goes beyond the tidy formula for managing emotions made famous by Daniel Goleman (self-awareness, self-regulation, empathy, and relationship skills) to recognize the unpredictable yet transformative nature of growth held sacred by most traditional cultures around the world, requiring one to welcome emotion in order to move through "stuckness," to expand into something...more.

I had experienced enough to know that healing of any sort requires us to confront our wounds. Bravely. We have to chase the wolf of fear into the waters of emotion in order to be rocked and then cradled back to shore. I had dipped my toes in the water, but I still didn't realize that what I thought was a puddle was actually an ocean.

For many women in that initial course, and for thousands of people I've worked with since, the act of noticing breath, sensation, and emotion without judgement is, quite simply, transformative. It's almost as if there is a collective sigh of relief at being able to sink back into skin that over time has grown too tight. Just as a composer needs access to all musical notes when writing a score, so too do we require access to our full emotional spectrum in order to fulfill our potential. These days I think perhaps the most revolutionary act any of us can engage in is to reclaim our birthright knowledge that who we are is enough—who we are has *always* been enough.

IN MARCH 2003, PRESIDENT George W. Bush began bombing Iraq, a foreign policy decision that brought millions of protesters into the streets in cities around the world, including Toronto. My newfound emotional calm was disrupted by his unjust targeting of the Middle East and the resultant rise in xenophobia across North America. I defaulted into rescuer mode once again and stepped into the fray, signing up to coordinate volunteers at the first World Social Forum in Toronto. The event hosted over eight hundred people who came over the course of the weekend to discuss a whole range of economic and social justice issues and alternatives.

I had recently started work as a full-time community health promoter for Planned Parenthood, designing and offering educational programs for a wide range of audiences. So this volunteer activism was my first experience in a political role since I had walked away over a year earlier. It was a strange experience to be in familiar surroundings as a relatively unknown entity. I could feel myself bouncing back and forth between the part of me that relished the focus on politics and another part that had outgrown such a singular perspective — the drive towards urgency was fighting against the more fragile desire for calm. I couldn't yet figure out how to fit old and new, activist and artist, together in one body.

On the Saturday night, a social gathering was held for the conference attendees. I found myself face to face with an overeager white man in his early fifties waving a glass of red wine back and forth while digging into me as if I were his favourite steak dinner. "Where are you from?" he asked eagerly, hitting on one of the most irritating and tired questions of all time. Why did conversations with strangers inevitably start by discussing my difference?

I stared at him, engaged in an internal calibration of how much to offer, not wanting to antagonize but also not wanting to give up ground at a time when it felt as though where I stood was all I had. I offered my polite default response:

"I was born in Iran, and moved here when I was young."

Not receiving my cue to cease and desist, he cheerfully plowed right into my most primal fear: "*Eye*-ran! Do you still have family there? Aren't you worried that Bush might be heading there next?"

I looked at him, incredulous, feeling my eyes widen, slightly in shock that he could remain so completely ignorant of his impact on me. What I wanted to say was something along the lines of, "Dude, back the fuck off. If you had family in a part of the world rapidly being branded as the new face of evil maybe you wouldn't have the luxury of being so insensitive." My reaction was fed by Bush's polarizing language of "shock and awe," his having used unparalleled state powers to "discover" weapons of mass destruction despite the lack of any actual evidence to show they existed, and then using this "proof" to justify attacks on a foreign country much less privileged than America — in this case, Iraq. And yes, on an irrational level, I felt crazy fear that my family, my tribe, my own self could be targeted next. I didn't need to be living in Iran to know how easily certain individuals or groups could rapidly and without rationale become targets for other people's hatred — I was still recovering from the emotional kickback of 9/11.

Seeking support, I went over to the event coordinator, Irindeep, who had earlier mentioned that her husband was going to drop by that evening. I walked up the steps to find her seated beside a brown man with a grey backpack, and I started venting my frustration. After ranting about the conversation I'd just had I launched into the whole hateful political climate. As the words tumbled from my mouth, I felt wetness on my cheeks. (One of the after-effects of Kripalu was that the vulnerable end of the emotional spectrum had become more accessible to me.) It was only after I'd finished and wiped away my tears that I was introduced to the silent stranger: this was Irindeep's friend, Shakil— not her husband, as I'd assumed. The result was that Shakil didn't meet "Supergirl," he met a rather more authentic version of me.

I later discovered that Shakil and I shared an unknown history of near-misses. Shakil's roommate had invited me to his house for dinner three years earlier but I'd had to cancel at the last minute. Another mutual friend had used his basement to store furniture and had asked me to help her move it out, which I'd not had time for. Most significantly, Shakil had intended to go to the anti-racism meeting at City Hall that I'd organized after 9/11, but having missed it, he instead attended the follow-up session, which I was not at. When the same dynamic occurred—an attack on the brown girl facilitators—Shakil stood up as the lone voice defending them and their process. I felt as if he'd had my back even before we actually met.

Two weeks later, as I was walking down Bloor Street around dusk, I heard my name being called by someone on the opposite side of the street, a good half a block behind me. I turned to see a handsome brown face with funky glasses and a familiar grey backpack. My belly flop reminded me it was him: Shakil. That April night was one of the balmy, precious first nights of spring that come after a long, cold winter. We started walking, keeping pace for over an hour, talking nonstop as the full moon rose over our heads. As we parted, I placed my hands together in the universal prayer position and bowed slightly. Without thinking I had lapsed into the goodbye ritual that was the norm at Kripalu, a gesture signifying "I honour the light in you." Suffice it to say, he had definitely caught my interest.

⌒

OUR FIRST YEAR OF dating broke all my previous unhealthy relationship patterns, characterized by the cycle of mesmerization, intensity, codependence, conflict, and then breakup. In contrast, our courtship was marked by a slower pace and lots of playfulness. We talked on the phone only once a week and saw each other only once a week. The space between each contact was crucial, as it allowed me to work through the extreme fear that arose in response to our growing emotional intimacy, and the attendant threat of rejection, without placing it all on him.

We traded responsibility for planning dates, creating a friendly one-upmanship of creative adventuring. For one of our first outings, I brought spades and forget-me-not seeds that we dug into the earth at a small park in the Annex neighbourhood. He asked if he could kiss me. I didn't hesitate, breathing out "Yes" seconds before our lips met over damp soil. In Allen Gardens, he taught me how to estimate the height of a tree using just my hand and a pencil. We went to plays, checked out new eateries, and made up songs together, choosing well-known tunes and alternating verses. Our engagement happened this way two years later

while visiting Cuba, walking on red farming soil with the
sun beating over our heads, as we spontaneously rhymed
words of commitment to one another.

Shakil came from a mixed South Asian (Pakistani and
Indian) background, had immigrated to Canada when he
was five years old, and had roots in community organizing, so he and I tended to see most things the same way.
He was the first person I'd met whom I could shorthand so
many experiences with, from the political to the personal.
As a teacher, he had protested against education cuts
under Premier Mike Harris, Ontario's version of Alberta's
Ralph Klein. Shakil was also fully versed in issues of race,
identity, and oppression, and had been conducting anti-
racism education for years. Perhaps most importantly,
he performed many of the micro-rituals I had grown up
with — washing the rice grains before cooking, always
deferring to elders, insisting on being the one to pay —
and until I met him I wasn't conscious of how much they
signalled home for me.

Shakil was the guy who gave everyone in his close circle
a key to his house, who regularly jumped up on the subway
to offer his seat, and who was once described by a friend
as the "warm fire" people gravitate towards in any room.
While I brought airy, imaginative clarity and joyfulness
to our relationship, Shakil was the grounding force. He
was the first person I met who could hold the entirety of
who I was without making me feel that I had to hide or
compromise myself.

In summer 2003, Shakil wrote an email to me:

how delightful was that!
placing kisses while I sat . . .
facing the screen in my office space
thinking too, of you, your lovely face

your wiles, however, be they crafty or not,
were too late to serve as e-reminders for me
     in this spot,
for your kisses already accompany me
every time I approximate the height of a tree

A few months after I met Shakil, while he was away on vacation in Costa Rica, I was called back to Edmonton as my Grandma Elsie was very sick. At ninety-four, she was still fully lucid, giving clear orders as to what she wanted and how she wanted it. My mother and I were staying with her, taking turns sitting by her bedside. After a few days the instructions gradually stopped, and our time with her passed largely in silence. It was close to the end, and the atmosphere in the apartment was sombre.

I hadn't talked to Shakil since I'd arrived, and then one evening, around 8 p.m., the phone in the apartment rang. It was him.

"How is she doing?" he asked.

As I started to answer, I heard my mother gasp from the other room, *"Ah-nie,* come here! She's stopped breathing!"

I can't help feeling that there was a crossing of spiritual roads that transpired in that moment: the grandmother who had been a refuge for me passing in the exact moment I connected with the man with whom I was building a new refuge. I saw that moment as a kind of blessing, a passing of the baton. My Grandma Elsie was a kind of soul guardian, right to the very end.

⌒

IN 2004, A YEAR after we met, I moved into Shakil's house, making the leap from the increasingly hipster west end of Toronto to the more staid east end. Surrounded by a substantial South Asian and Middle Eastern immigrant community — very near the city's largest mosque — both Shakil and I had our cultural roots well represented. In a three-block radius was everything I needed to live comfortably for weeks on end: grocery store, the restaurants of Toronto's Greektown, gym, hairdresser, coffee shop, hardware store, and library. A fragile sense of home started to seep into my bones.

Arriving into the embrace of Shakil's largely Pakistani Muslim family offered another layer of stability and comfort. I was enfolded in brown culture once again, becoming an adopted Desi even though I couldn't speak Urdu, didn't know that *chana dahl*, *chai* tea, and *naan* bread were redundant terms (you say one or the other, never both), and had not mastered the technique for correctly draping the *dupatta* (scarf). Being a Persian-born immigrant brought me close enough.

Shakil's family was a dose of culture that closely resembled the Iran I had left behind. We celebrated *Eid* and gave money to each of the nieces and nephews in the same way I remembered receiving this gift when I was small.

Though hugs were exchanged as greetings instead of the triple cheek kisses I was familiar with in Persian culture, most other traditions were similar. Deferring to an elder's opinion was always a given. Feminist ideals largely took a backseat to helping in the kitchen to clean, prepare, and serve food alongside the other women. Over-gifting, like ta'aroof-ing, was a fine art, and food, household items, and jewellery were regularly bestowed on me whether they were needed or not.

Though I welcomed the familiarity with his family and background, our relationship cracked open all the underground fissures in my own identity. As much as his Desi family culture became a surrogate for the Persian one I felt estranged from, I still wanted to reconcile with my own background, rather than have my brownness defined by a culture that might look similar from the outside but fundamentally wasn't. Then there was the quiet, nagging question of how much identifying with brown culture meant sacrificing my white, British side (invisible but present). I didn't feel I ever had a choice to identify as Caucasian, but what did it mean to always identify with the opposite? Why couldn't the two parts coexist more easily? Why did I have to keep paying a steep mental health cost because Western society continued to separate and elevate white people above people of colour? My sense of self was still fragmented, so as much as it was wonderful to join forces with someone, it was also confusing to do so when I wasn't confident about where my own identity was rooted.

These schisms were heightened by the various, and sometimes conflicting, family requests that come with any merging. A year after I moved in, Shakil and I got engaged, with plans to get married a year later in spring 2006. Shakil's mother insisted on a Muslim *Nikkah* ceremony, whereas my mom was hoping for a Christian church ceremony. Each decision felt bigger than the two of us, as though we were setting in place foundations for our future without fully knowing the lay of the land. On the one hand, I was terrified of making a mistake and being rejected by Shakil's family, while on the other, I worried about agreeing to something that would imprison me in a set of obligations that overshadowed my own identity. In the time leading up to our wedding I felt increasingly overwhelmed, caught between the twin fears of rejection and suffocation.

As I was still not able to process my feelings consciously, they once again manifested through physical symptoms. The week of our wedding, I got my first full-on migraine. I rushed from work to a final dress fitting, feeling the stirrings of a headache, but since I had no history of migraines I assumed it was harmless and just took an Advil. An hour later the rushing pain was so bad that I was doubled over in the back of a cab counting breaths, praying I could hold off on vomiting until I got home. That whole evening I was unable to rise from the bathroom floor, throwing up every few minutes until I was left dry-heaving and dizzy enough to pass out. Shakil's father, a doctor, drove across the city at midnight to check on me. Finding nothing obvious, he prescribed Gravol pills which finally (and thankfully!) knocked me out so I could rest.

Marriage touched me in the place of deepest wounding. This was a commitment I was choosing but had no control over, and it triggered all my unconscious terror. What if Shakil stopped loving me? What if I couldn't be myself, whoever that was? What if I gave up my lone wolf status only to get kicked in the belly of my fear? The prospect of putting down roots that required me to trust that I was worthy of being loved without working for it, that acceptance was possible without sacrifice, was terrifying. If I didn't earn my right to belong, then I couldn't control it. And if I couldn't control it, then it might all disappear. I couldn't face more of the pain that I still hadn't reconciled from my past. The child in me feared death, the total annihilation of self.

⌐

DESPITE MY (MANY) FEARS, our three spring 2006 weddings were all a success. We officially got married at City Hall, followed by a traditional *Nikkah* ceremony at Shakil's parents' condo. Then, finally, at the very end of May, we hosted family and friends for a weekend shindig of our own design. This event resembled a mini United Nations, gathering people from all aspects of my life, reflecting the entirety of who I had been and who we were together. The planning was a master class in inclusion and trying to balance a multitude of needs! We booked space at the Talisman Resort in the Beaver Valley, north of Toronto, and also rented a retreat centre nearby for friends who couldn't afford to stay at the resort. We wrote our own vows and found creative ways to honour the breadth of our cultural and religious backgrounds: British/Christian, Pakistani/

Sunni Muslim, Persian/atheist (formerly Shia Muslim), and Indian/Hindu. We designed activities to break down the many cultural, racial, religious, age, and other differences—and it worked! By the end of the weekend the most unlikely groupings had formed.

Just before the actual marriage ceremony, I sat with a circle of my closest friends, including my childhood friend, Caroline, family (including the cousin of "Like a Virgin" fame, whom I hadn't seen since childhood), and my two new sisters-in-law. They showered me with blessings and advice, weaving a warm blanket of memories around me. Intermittently, my mom would admonish me not to cry too hard as my mascara was running. My sister, Fariba, sat beside me and held my hand. I felt encircled by so much love, then and throughout the entire ceremony. It was thrilling and terrifying all at once.

It was the first time that Shakil's father had publicly, and vulnerably (considering the extended Muslim family context), shared his faith, through the recitation of a Hindu prayer. My uncle performed a poem in Farsi that he'd written himself, accompanied by Shakil's close friend Chris on guitar. My sister and her partner, Laolu, taught everyone how to line dance, while Shakil's sisters, Bipasha and Monika, organized a group of our friends to perform a Bhangra dance straight out of a Bollywood movie. I designed my own wedding outfit for the daytime and wore a *langha* (traditional Desi outfit) to the evening reception. There weren't enough snacks to go around so neither of us got a single slice of our wedding cake (though I later found out my sister had five!). The song that closed off the evening's festivities was the 1980s anthem "We Built this City" by Starship, at my request—you can take the girl out of Alberta . . . Shakil still cringes at this memory.

THIRTEEN

Anima: Life Force

OUR MARRIAGE WAS ONLY the start of our collaboration. In 2004, a couple of years before our wedding, Shakil had invited me to join a team of educators who were offering a leadership program aimed at high school students through Pearson College in Victoria, B.C., part of the United World Colleges network. I applied and was accepted, and so that summer I flew across the country, thirty-one years old, newly in love, and ready for an adventure.

The leadership program was focused on social justice and included sessions on democracy, feminism, Indigenous history, and anti-racism. It also included teaching skills that could be put into action such as speaking and campaigning, arts and theatre, storytelling, and so on. What had been missing was the third leg of the stool, personal develop-ment—or, as we later referred to it, emotional intelligence.

I redesigned the check-in circles that I had first

encountered during my stay at Kripalu and subsequently used with my women's group. I now called them "power circles." I wrote a set of instructional guidelines for the students, including "Notice your breath," "All emotions are okay," and "It's okay to pass." Participants were divided into groups of ten, and they met with an instructor once a week during the month-long program. I was a little nervous at first. Young people are a tough crowd—open to new ideas, but also quick to jump on anything that smells even faintly of BS.

But I needn't have worried. The power circles were transformational. We always cautioned participants to choose whether to share or not, and to be mindful of personal boundaries. We were clear about what we would need to report to parents and/or external authorities. Yet what we encountered was a deep thirst for authenticity, for a space where people could be themselves and unload. That weekly period of two to three hours made a huge impact on the participants' ability to see themselves—and each other—more clearly and with less judgement.

In one circle I remember a young man named Alan opening up about his parents' divorce, and how he felt pulled between them. "It's like I have to choose. I don't see my dad any more, and my mom is always angry. I feel like I've lost both of them." He couldn't make eye contact with anyone else in the circle, and he was just barely able to drop his clipped words into the pool of collective silence.

The thing is that Alan came from an extremely privileged financial background, he was handsome, and he had already broken the rules about no alcohol on the premises.

He came across as a "bad boy" without a care in the world. His words in the circle changed the way everyone, including myself, viewed him. He was no longer the "bratty rich kid" but a person struggling under the weight of a huge emotional burden. Everyone has their story.

For me, the most transformative part of the exercise was watching how the relationships changed between participants. Not only was there less judgement, there was also more caring. People who otherwise would never have talked to each other now started hanging out—even, and especially, across big divides in identity like race, class, and sexual orientation.

The final proof came during our closing circle. A young white woman stood as she haltingly said to a black participant across the room, "I see you now. I never did before, and I'm so sorry. All I see now are my friends." Difference was no longer a barrier in relationships because people had deeper context—both social and personal—for each other. The power circles almost entirely eradicated the cliquey group behaviours that invariably occur wherever people are gathered.

At the end of that program, Shakil and I were left buzzing. We knew we were on to something with the formula of marrying awareness of social issues with personal development, of the external with the internal. Our end goal was to create cultures of inclusion, communities of belonging, to end systemic barriers holding certain groups back in society, but we wanted to accomplish that in such a way that the means matched the ends, where compassion instead of blame guided people forward. We realized that teaching people statistics and facts about systemic discrimination wasn't enough—they had to be able to clear the resistance to relationships on an emotional level where the ghosts of personal and collective history sit—guilt, grief, anger, blame, shame, and more.

We had already been experimenting with some of these elements, through my Conscious Eating course and Shakil's diversity sessions. All we needed was a catalyst to see the pieces and their impact more clearly—that first program was it. I remember Shakil telling me how he wanted to read a book by Daniel Goleman on emotional intelligence and figure out how to integrate what we had learned through the power circles. With our rough material in hand, unbeknownst to us, that summer sowed the seeds of what later became our company.

⌒

BOTH OF US CONTINUED on our separate professional paths. Shakil was filling in as a supply teacher and taking film classes; I was finishing my master's degree; and we both continued to offer our educational programming on the side. A few months before our 2006 wedding I was accepted into a self-employment training program offered by the federal government. One of our assignments was to brand our business with a vision statement, our raison d'être. I remember writing the words that still represent our company's vision: "Leadership for a world where all people matter and belong." I ran it by the class instructor and he scoffed as he responded, "A little lofty, no?" I didn't think so. Anyone who has ever created change has "lofty" as their middle name.

The fall after our wedding, as I was creating new courses, Shakil was in a similar process of branding his own work. He was planning to call his business "Brown Book Consulting" and went so far as to have logo designs mocked up. It was September, that time of year when life speeds up as the soul slows down, and we were on one of our frequent idea-spawning neighbourhood walks. As we shared plans for our respective companies, I mused aloud, "I wonder what it would be like to join forces?" The idea was electric! Although we had concerns about merging our personal and professional lives, we felt as though our work drew from the same wellspring and was an essential part of what connected us as a couple.

Shortly after we made our decision, we went to see the Blue Man Group perform in Toronto — an experimental musical troupe that was all the rage at the time. During the show, the performers talked about the history of animation: "to animate comes from the Latin verb *anima*, to bring to life." And that was it. I knew the name for our company had arrived. Anima had roots in tradition, had meanings in multiple cultures, and, most importantly, captured the essence of what our work was about: soul, life force, or, quite literally, "to bring to life."

Anima Leadership was our answer to a question: Which is more critically important in creating long-term change, addressing issues on the personal level or on the systemic level? Rather than choosing, we decided to set up an organization that addressed societal inequities while simultaneously exploring their roots in individual consciousness. After all, thought is expressed in behaviour, behaviours affect relationships, relationships build culture, and cultures inform policy: every level of change is interconnected in a continuum. I felt we were creating something truly innovative—a marrying of justice and compassion—in service of a vision of creating environments where everyone, regardless of body, identity, or background, can thrive.

Authenticity was our core value. Every word we wrote for our website or our newsletters or spoke in front of clients—a wide group from executive teams to frontline staff in education, legal, government, non-profit, and even corporate realms—came from our own personal experience. For two brown people, both emerging from the fires of activism, and with heightened awareness of the racial barriers existing across institutions in society, Anima Leadership was our safe space, a professional home where we got to create, have impact, and, most importantly, experience the freedom to be ourselves.

We started with our training programs on different facets of leadership—how to facilitate, manage people, be good at conflict, and create more diverse teams—then branched out with other services designed to create change across organizations. What does it look like to create cultures of belonging, in practice? How do you influence human behaviour? How do you transition—or scale out—one individual doing something differently into a whole system, with hundreds or sometimes thousands of people involved? These were the questions we sought to answer.

We added to our repertoire designing organizational surveys and writing assessment reports, created workplace inclusion tools and user guides, and got certifications in various coaching and mediation approaches. When we didn't know how to do something, we researched, experimented, and figured it out. Slowly we started to grow.

As we both had learned from our own lived experience, and from what studies show, when people feel they can be themselves is when creativity, innovation, and transformation happen. From the very beginning, we knew we were on the right track when we heard from our clients that it was the first time in their workplace they felt they could be vulnerable, or they finally understood where their colleague was coming from, or they noticed people beginning to realize the effect their behaviour was having on others. So much of creating more inclusive cultures is helping people close the gap between good intentions and the impact of their actions! We were somewhat surprised by the feedback—the deep hunger for authenticity and relationship that it revealed. I have come to realize that feeding hearts is as important as feeding heads; the former are sadly often left starving in most communal environments.

Since those early days, our team has had the opportunity to work across Canada and the United States, South America and Europe. We've established a solid reputation as a leader in the field of diversity and inclusion work. And I'd like to think that, through the thousands of lives we've touched, perhaps we've changed a little bit of the world.

ON A PERSONAL LEVEL, the early years of being in the business together were invigorating but also anxiety-laden. As much as we valued the opportunity to create and teach in different contexts, we were also spending more than we were bringing in (typical of any new business) and had no job security. Spending your own money to make things happen is scary. Quickly, you realize the value of every dollar spent. It was like kick-starting a different part of my brain. In the non-profit world, organizations have to spend their dollars every annual fiscal cycle. I never had to analyze programs based on return on investment; the only consideration that mattered was whether they were the right thing to do.

I also struggled a bit with connecting to a deeper sense of purpose. We had our broad mandate, but in those beginning years it was loose. I kept going around in circles: Should I be focusing on women's leadership, facilitation expertise, or organizational change practices? I couldn't get clarity, and it drove me nuts. I missed both the fire of purpose in my belly and the relentless intensity that activism had always provided.

In those years after leaving the bubble of political activism, I was also taken off guard by how much energy I had to spend carving out my territory, fighting for my very voice. Such is the reality of being a self-employed woman of colour. I had been somewhat insulated from systemic barriers in the social change organizations I worked for because there was more awareness, at least on a cognitive level. I remember a meeting Shakil and I had, early in 2008, with a PR specialist, one whom I had contacted. Despite the relational head start, after the first five minutes he shifted his eye contact to Shakil, and that's where it stayed exclusively for the remainder of our hour-long meeting. I would ask him a question and he would look at Shakil while answering. I was fidgeting restlessly in my seat by the end, caught between wanting to get his attention and wanting to skewer him for his thoughtless behaviour. Most of all, I was angry. I wasn't used to being in the back seat, and I did not like it one bit.

Unfortunately, this wasn't a one-off experience. Each time it happened, in all the myriad ways it does—lack of eye contact, being passed over in the shaking of hands, having to repeat a point multiple times—it brought to the surface all the old feelings of powerlessness. Trying harder in the face of these small acts of being discounted—or microaggressions—only served to lower my social status, and yet ignoring them meant my continued invisibility— the classic double bind. My friend Ritu calls it the "toxicity of continuous underestimation" that most women of colour face on a regular basis. I couldn't figure out the secret code to being included in such moments. It was demoralizing— another echo of the past.

⌣

THE UNCERTAINTY ABOUT WORK and purpose, combined with feeling impotent, started to manifest itself through regular migraines. Starting with the first occurrence a handful of days before our wedding and continuing through the next eight years of building our business, migraines became a feature in my life. At best they would arrive with a head-ache and mild nausea; at worst they would force me over the toilet and confine me to hours of bedrest. A full cycle lasted three days, with a twenty-four-hour buildup, a day of being wiped out, and a recovery day.

I tried to identify a whole variety of physical triggers, from gluten to hormones to the weather and lack of sleep. After a couple of years, it was clear that the biggest trigger was my own internal state. Knowing that the root cause was emotional only made the migraines harder to accept. Now that I was no longer forcing myself to purge, my body had found a way of involuntarily releasing the distress and trauma that I still hadn't processed. Usually, the anxiety would follow a similar pathway from stomach, to blad-der, then to my head—from bingeing on fatty or sugary foods, to urge incontinence, then finally into a full-blown migraine if I wasn't able to calm things down internally. And if I was really pushing it, one of my shoulders would dislocate and the hospital visit would force me to rest, at least for a bit.

For me, feeling powerless meant feeling unsafe, so any evidence, subtle or overt, that I was being criticized or somehow didn't measure up would touch on deep-seated feelings of anger, fear, and shame: the rage cocktail. Either the distress would burrow in and express itself through physical symptoms, or it would explode outwards, largely directed at Shakil. He was my fall guy. I would attack him sometimes—often, if I'm being honest—for little or no reason because I couldn't distinguish between a momentary bad mood and a more serious rejection of me as a person.

I was constantly waiting for the other shoe to drop, to be found faulty, to watch another person walk away from me. It was easier to test him than to trust him.

Unconsciously, after all those frogs I'd kissed I wanted Shakil to be my prince. Wasn't he supposed to play his part and awaken the princess from her slumber? To secure that promised happy ending? The sparkle on our relationship began to tarnish as we washed, rinsed, and repeated with varying levels of intensity the same fight: me wanting him to affirm and validate me so I could feel safe; him feeling suffocated and asserting that he needed more space.

Nighttime was the worst. Coupled with a drop in energy levels, my nervous system's vigilance function kicked into a higher gear, a hangover from childhood. I was wired and tired at the same time, and I would often spend way longer sitting on the toilet at night than was required to calm myself down. Inevitably, if Shakil and I had things to discuss, the most contentious topics, such as our finances, would be left until the witching hour of 10 p.m., ensuring a shitty sleep was had by all. It took me years to realize that this dynamic—the time of day when I most needed connection coinciding with a spike in conflict—was all too familiar. The similarity to the years of nightly standoffs with my father was hard to ignore.

Things came to a boil when the political and the personal once again intersected in early summer 2010. The G20 was holding its annual meeting in Toronto and I was asked to facilitate a parallel open forum. Big-name international speakers would be taking the stage, and over a thousand people were expected to attend, including my friend Scott from Edmonton days. I saw it as an opportunity to shine once again in a political role. I seduced myself into wanting my old relationship to activism back; like many first loves, it made me feel invincible. But the reality didn't match my need. Activism remained a culture of political one-upmanship, dominated by invisible white and male privilege (buried under a blanket of politically correct analysis) and characterized by a general lack of gentleness. I had lost my immunity to the dynamics that bothered me. Very quickly it became evident that this was no longer my scene. It was a relationship I still valued but had outgrown. Even with Scott, I felt I was trying to be someone I no longer was, marginalizing in myself newer traits that I was actively trying to nurture. Feeling sandwiched between the familiar and the still unknown was hard. I felt more isolated than usual.

I still secretly placed my bets on the forum. I would dazzle! I would be Oprah! I would once again be publicly recognized for my skills.

The event was packed to the gills. It wasn't a disaster, but it wasn't a success either. It was a casualty of too many political agendas mashed into one short time period, and once again I felt like the fall girl. I turned to Shakil afterwards.

"What did you think? Did it go okay?" (Translation: Did *I* do okay?)

"It was all right," was his measured response.

When you know someone well, you know exactly what they mean by the pitch and tone of their voice. I interpreted his words as "You sucked shit."

The next day I read his private journal looking for

confirmation of his low opinion of me. He was furious. I tried to make him into the villain of the story. On a deep unconscious level, I was replaying the original wounding from childhood, needing reassurance that there was nothing wrong with me but fearing the worst. In his diary I had found his reflections on the evening—fairly neutral thoughts on what could have been improved—but I picked them up as arrows and drove them into my own heart. It wasn't the first time I had projected my sense of failure onto him, but it was the worst. When I confronted him, "DiaryGate" put a real strain on our now fragile relationship. I felt betrayed, while he felt violated.

I had crossed one boundary too many, and although we carried on as before, I had deeply damaged his trust in me. I was back in a familiar place of looking externally for a feeling of security and sense of self—for home—except now it had moved from the level of community to the individual, and in much the same way that 9/11 ended my relationship with activism, DiaryGate threatened the end of my marriage.

⌐

DESPITE ANY STRUGGLES BEHIND the scenes, Anima continued to flourish. We were slowly finding our niche and being called to take on ever-larger projects. In 2010 we landed a contract with the federal government to develop all the materials for the Racism-Free Workplace Strategy through Human Resources and Skills Development Canada. Shakil headed up that team.

For the first time since we'd started Anima I felt as if I was firing on all cylinders: researching, writing, and community building. Shakil and I were able to separate our clients and occupy different office spaces, an important structural adjustment in the process of finding our way back to each other. It hadn't helped our relationship that we were in the same physical environment every day, often working on the same projects.

I was soon offered a long-term contract with a progressive global company wanting someone to advise on organizational development strategies during a time of rapid growth. It was exciting to be thinking in terms of systems change once again, working with an influential organization and managing a team of people. And I was lucky to find a new workmate in the project director, James. James was a visionary, a maverick, a larger-than-life entrepreneur, and I was flattered that he had headhunted me.

During the first months of the project it felt as though we were soaring in every conversation we had together, both of us energized by the rapid exchange of ideas. And yet, gradually, as the high wore off, my relationship with James started to go south. Like many leaders, he remained largely unconscious of his own use of power. He would change his mind every five minutes, and I was expected to intuit his wishes and follow along, discarding hours of conversation, planning, and work. Part of his charisma was speaking whatever was on his mind to whoever was in front of him, meaning that he also gossiped about me to other staff, including people who reported directly to me. It was like working from a base of quicksand. Work was my stronghold, and I had invested a great deal of my time and energy in order to make it a safe haven. I believed passionately in my methods and approach to the company's needs, but the harder I worked to clarify and create priorities and systems, the more James pushed towards flow and impulsiveness. Knowing I was being talked about to others, even though there was no malicious intent, made me feel deeply unsafe. Unused to operating in what felt like conditions of chaos, I faced additional pressures from team members stressed about workload and other organizational changes. While others in my position might have learned to cope, even thrive, I was drafted and recast almost perfectly into the conditions of my childhood: scrambling as hard as I could to fit into my new situation, feeling responsible for my people, and finding that the harder I worked towards finding solid ground, the more it slipped away.

That fall, I caught a flu bug that turned into bronchitis. It was bad. I was feverish and exhausted, but being in survival mode also meant that I felt undeserving of the time I needed to rest. Every sick day I spent at home I forced myself to keep working, operating entirely on adrenaline. Although I gradually got better, my physical resources remained severely overdrawn. I was now struggling to find affirmation at work as well as in my relationship, which meant that my nervous system was on constant high alert. I went from stress to stress, and didn't recuperate over the Christmas holidays either. Even when I had downtime my mind was always spinning.

Three months later, in January 2011, I noticed the first patches of itchy, scaly redness covering my neck. Soon afterwards other scarlet blotches started mushrooming all over my skull, shedding hair and bits of skin, and oozing pus. Half of my wardrobe was taken out of circulation as wearing anything black showed off a dandruff snowfall. The migraines had stopped by then; the energy of distress had burrowed more deeply inward to really capture my attention.

Instead of applying all of my mindfulness skills to stay calm and centred—because how could it be that easy?—I got caught up in an anxious manic whirlwind of healing cures found on the internet. I started off with drugstore chemical shampoos, and natural rinses I ordered online made with herbs planted only under a full moon. The dermatologist I was referred to thought it might be psoriasis and gave me treatments that only made my hair fall out faster. After a couple of such appointments I gave up on the Western medical system. The intuitive part of me knew that my issues weren't rooted in the physical realm, but when I dared to float that idea my doctor looked at me as if I were from Mars.

I went back to my training in Eastern medicine, with its grounding in the intersectionality of mind, body, and spirit, and visited only alternative practitioners, including a renowned acupuncturist who seemed to take pleasure in jabbing unusually long needles into my body and prescribed bottles of Chinese herbs so costly you'd have guessed they were filled with gold. Then there was the naturopath who prescribed at least ten remedies, each to be taken in some different combination with or without food, morning, afternoon, or evening, and the Reiki practitioner who gave me energy-calming exercises. Keeping up with all the prescriptions started to feel like a part-time job. It felt as if I were walking around with a flashing sign over my head saying, "This woman's vibrancy, sexuality, and competency have been compromised. Abort all contact." It was worse than the "helmet hair" days of my youth, and I felt the same shame at not being able to fulfill some external ideal representing access to the "in" group.

Searching for solutions to my skin ailment was a huge expenditure of time and money, but at least the explorations offered me a superficial sense of control, which was helpful. After a few months, I gave up sugar, dairy, and wheat. For someone whose day started with a strong cup of tea with milk and a slice of toast with jam, this was no small feat! The added bonus of this new diet was that I lost a lot of weight very quickly and found myself thinner than I'd ever been in my life. After years of desperately trying to make my body shrink so that I'd look more like Kate Moss, of punishing myself for taking in too much food, losing the extra weight made me feel secretly exultant. Though I was no longer caught up in bingeing and purging, the unconscious belief that thinness equals absolution was hard to erase.

Finally, as I found myself running out of options, I went to visit a psychic around the corner from our office. I followed him inside the house and he gestured for me to sit in a chair in the middle of an empty room directly in front of his desk—it was like a scene from *The Exorcist*. Eerily, he proceeded to whisper that I was in a diseased state equivalent to a stage-four cancer victim. Apparently,

a couple of spirits were attached to me like emotional para-
sites. Luckily for me, he was trained to cleanse my energy
field of them—for a mere few hundred bucks. I wasn't so
desperate I couldn't see the ridiculousness in the situation.
After I paid the psychic for the visit and was walking away
from the house, he called out some last words of advice:
"If you pee into a cup every morning and pour it over your
scalp, that'll help. Of course, you could also drink it."

I did, fortunately, have my limits.

TWO THINGS HAPPENED THAT year that helped me find
some internal balance. The first was visiting Provence,
France with Shakil in the summer of 2011, just after my
contract ended with James's company. Although I took my
Chinese herbs with me, I restricted myself to only five (of
the thirty-plus) bottles of shampoo and ointments I had
amassed, and I decided to also loosen restrictions on eating.

Provence is famous for its consistently warm climate,
golden light, and fields of lavender. People move more
slowly and linger longer, prioritizing the preparation and
sharing of food. The night we arrived at our house exchange
in the small village of Manosque we found that our hosts
had left Tourte aux Courgettes (zucchini quiche) with a
bottle of local red wine. We sat on their front veranda looking over the village below, silently stuffing our faces with
slices of the most delicious pie I have ever tasted. That first
meal set the tone of simple nourishment for the entire trip.

It was relieving, so far away from familiar surroundings,

to feel the lack of a need to perform, to prove something, or to rescue somebody. As in the past, the solution I needed was not to work harder but to give myself permission to just *be*. Shakil and I enjoyed unpressured time together, recapturing the playfulness that had marked the early days of our relationship. There was a Frisbee tucked into our travel sack, so when we weren't chowing down on whatever local flavours were in front of us we'd take in the sights as we tossed the disc back and forth. As we drove through the Luberon mountains, swam in the Gorges du Verdon, and took an unexpected private helicopter flight over the entire region, gradually I could feel some of the layers of stress, shame, and constriction peel away.

We waited until our last week to finally go to Châteauneuf-du-Pape, the small village that's home to the famous wine. Our plan was to visit a variety of vintners and then backtrack to purchase a selection of our favourite wines. After a few tastings left us on the tipsy side, we suddenly realized that the shops were closing before we'd bought anything! One of my last memories of France is careening half drunk downhill on uneven cobblestone streets in my high-heeled sandals, trying desperately to locate the sign for the first winery we'd visited. Crazy Canadian interrupts upscale French wine merchant about to close shop. Not a match made in heaven. But I did get what we wanted.

Our last day saw us wander into the village of Manosque for a goodbye tour. As we were walking through the town square, an impulse pulled me into the centuries-old church I had passed numerous times before. Slowly, I walked inside, awed by the silence, the elaborate stained-glass window scenes, and the worn pews. I made my way over to the alcove where there were rows of glowing votive candles, symbolic of people's prayers. My first thought was to ask for healing for my still red and burning scalp. Instead, what came out of my mouth were the words, "Please, let me birth a healthy child in the year ahead." *Whoa!* I thought to myself, *Where did THAT come from?* It seemed my unconscious mind, or soul perhaps, was putting its cards on the table.

We returned home to Toronto in September, and my old social worker friend, Nancy, took out the utility scissors and chopped off my remaining straggly hair. It went from below my shoulders to about an inch in length. I was Rapunzel in reverse, engineering my own rescue. Though shocked at the sudden change, I felt better than I had in months. Renewed. Two weeks later, I took a pile of tulip bulbs that needed to be planted in the front garden and placed some of my shorn hair in the soil with each one of them. As I did so, I whispered the words of a self-created ritual: "I let go of over-efforting, I let go of the need to be perfect, I let go of shame. And I ask for healing of my body by the time spring arrives with these flowers."

Little did I know that at the time of this ritual I was already pregnant, a mere month after visiting that ancient cathedral in southern France. Talk about an answer to prayer. I was ecstatic. My mind caught up with my spirit so that I felt dizzy with delight, dancing steps at random moments during the day to songs that only I could hear. As my belly grew, colour came back into my face, and slowly the discoloration on my neck and scalp faded, the red, raw patches disappearing of their own accord. Pregnancy is often talked about in terms of the suffering it creates for women; I experienced the healing it can bring about.

⁓

THE SECOND EVENT THAT helped restore my inner balance came when I was six months pregnant, in early 2012. At age thirty-eight, a decade after leaving Kripalu, I finally chose to attend a full ten-day silent meditation course. The Vipassana brand of meditation worked for me because it was based on the central idea that the mind manifests through the body, and I was already more than familiar with that idea.

As Shakil dropped me off at the retreat centre about an hour outside Toronto, I felt time collapse. Suddenly, I was back in my twelve-year-old body being dropped off at camp, wanting to be anywhere else. This time I wasn't confronting a group of my peers but a host of internal demons. I had to summon the courage to go through the motions of registering and dropping off my stuff, pulling myself out of the shadows of the past and into the present.

At the opening orientation session, I scanned the room of, again, mostly white, very serious faces listening intently to the middle-aged man with a British accent going through the instructions with a dose of good ol' Brit wit. "You'll notice that we don't serve coffee here in the morning. Feel free not to panic. There's lots of tea, with milk AND soy milk to meet your every need." I snorted. The gap between people's fears and his exaggeratedly dry manner painted the whole scene in absurdity, and all of a sudden I felt right at home.

Every night they played a pre-recorded video of the founder of the Vipassana meditation method, S. N. Goenka, then in his seventies, giving the nightly dharma lecture. Goenka would start off in his accented singsong voice, "Three days are over. Only seven days left," or "Five days completed. Only five more to go." And even though this practice was designed to facilitate self-liberation, judging by the expressions on the faces of the participants you'd have thought they were hearing their prison sentence every time he announced the days still remaining. One night I had to hold a pillow over my mouth to keep myself from laughing aloud. Meditation is one of those practices that seems so pure somehow, so good to tell people about, except when you're in it. Most of the time it really sucks, especially in the early stages.

On the fourth evening, while meditating in the main hall, I experienced a wave of nausea. I tried to pull my mind back from reacting to it and returned to observing my breath. But I was hit with a second wave a few minutes later, and I rushed out of my chair into the cold winter air, doubling over, coughing and gasping for air. The nausea passed, and then that night I started experiencing cramping in my abdominal region. I felt as if I had swallowed glass. I was scared, given the late stage of my pregnancy, and I told myself that I'd call someone if it continued longer than thirty minutes.

According to Chinese medicine, unexpressed emotions

like anger and shame trap heat inside the body, making what happened next less of a shock. In short order, I had a bowel movement that was a surge of cramping heat, like an army of red ants marching through my lower regions. I wasn't sure what had happened, but it seemed that some deep tangle of feeling had unravelled and been released.

On the last day of the retreat we were invited to come out of silence. People were excitedly chattering in the food hall, a shocking contrast to the previous quiet. I seemed to be in the minority, wishing the silence would last longer. For the first time in a long time, I felt calm. I'd had trouble believing that kind of peace was even possible. It was a moment of inner revolution. I had finally reached a new physical baseline where the waters of emotion weren't threatening to overturn the boat but instead were rather gently keeping the vessel afloat. Such relief.

⌒

MORE THAN ANY OF the things I had reached out towards to "cure" me, my time in France and at the Vipassana retreat brought me back into my body. I didn't need to do or try more, I just needed to give myself a break. By the time spring arrived with the birth of my first child, my hair had grown back to chin-length and was curly, curly, curly, as if life was bursting forth throughout my entire body and my usual light waves weren't enough to contain the energy. Shedding my hair was akin to letting go of the need for external approval, of again being forced to trust that who I was, was enough for the world. It was another encounter with the same life lesson I had confronted before, yet this time it seemed there was no choice whether or not to listen. I was pushed to anchor myself more deeply into the ground of home, to provide a home for others.

FOURTEEN

My Original Face

BY CHANCE, I BECAME pregnant just two months after my close friend Annie. I found out shortly after a girls' weekend away to celebrate her pregnancy news. We were staying at a cottage in Prince Edward County, and on our last afternoon there, as we were sitting on the dock, two white swans swam past—seemingly out of nowhere—just as we were speaking about Annie's impending motherhood. We waxed on about how it was a sign of her mother-baby connection.

Despite bringing along a kit of feminine hygiene products and related pharmaceuticals for the weekend, my period failed to arrive. I was never late. As soon as we returned to Toronto, my first order of business was to purchase a pregnancy test. I was surprised (yet not that surprised) at the little plus sign sitting in the clear plastic window.

Annie was the first person I called, exclaiming, "The swans represented our daughters! They're going to be besties." I was sure they were both girls, and I was right.

It was one of the first signs that my daughter, and later my son as well, would be surrounded by a close tribe. And from the beginning, they absolutely have been, from cousins, aunts, uncles, and grandparents to friends, caregivers, and even strangers. It's been another level of healing to watch the people I love and care for extend their time and energy to my little ones. What is offered to children is usually given freely, no reciprocity required. It is a testament to human selflessness, how deeply our brains are wired towards empathy.

My daughter, Arion, was born six days after my thirty-ninth birthday in May 2012. She was a dream baby. She was sleeping through the night by the time she was six weeks old, and I remember saying to a friend, "I feel like I'm on holiday." Despite feeling tired, I was emotionally buoyed. I took her swimming, to singing classes, on daily park visits, and more. When I watch videos or see photos of myself with her during that time, I'm amazed by how transformed I look by love. Open mouth, singing in delight. Wide googly eyes. A self I wish I could inhabit full-time.

Becoming a mother brought an unexpectedly life-altering shift: the responsibility for another life, the loss of personal time and choice, alongside the physical changes that happen in the body. For me, it was the best thing possible. Motherhood cleared away all the mental clutter, anchoring me to the present in a consistent and lasting way. The love I felt for my daughter kept my heart cracked open.

One of the biggest shifts for me was that work achievement was no longer my core metric for success; it fell below
home and family in the priority list. Rather than seeking
affirmation from others, I was bathed in unconditional love
without needing to work for it. In this way, becoming a
parent started to shift my long-held belief that acceptance
was always tied to performance. Although I wasn't a perfect
mother, I was a good mom.

⌒

A YEAR LATER, IN summer 2013, I was pregnant with our
second child, Koda. I always knew I wanted either none
or two. Yet this time the journey wasn't as smooth, starting with the birth itself. I had to go into hospital early,
as Koda was in a transverse position—in other words, at
nine months his head was still up in my ribs rather than
pointed downwards, ready to exit. I lay in the operating
room while the doctor leaned on my belly to strong-arm
him into position, then drugs were administered to start
the labour pains to get him out—it was an anxious and
alienating process.

Despite all our technology, birthing a child still brings
life and death together in intimate conversation. The process seems to shake loose the hinges on all internally locked
doors, dusty nooks, and dark crannies. As we manifest
another life outside of ourselves, it seems we're invited to
simultaneously renew ourselves in preparation. Ten hours
after Koda was born, enough had been shaken loose that
I was in the basement at home having a panic attack,

hyperventilating as I struggled to return to a feeling of
safety inside my own skin. Old ghosts shaken free. I entered
a state of extreme post-partum anxiety.

I felt the same overwhelming love for my son that I did
for my daughter. Yet the actual experience of parenting
him was harder. Koda was colicky and wouldn't breastfeed.
Or he would feed for five minutes and then start screaming. Every thought passing through my head, from the
moment I woke up to when I finally dropped off to sleep,
was about what and how much he was drinking, whether
I should supplement with formula, what kind of bottle to
use, whether or not I was a good mother, if I should change
my diet, and on and on. I was fully trapped in "monkey
mind," my thoughts going around and around in the ham-
ster wheel that was my brain. My eldest was still under two,
and Shakil was travelling more for work. The result was
that I felt as though I was losing my sanity — except that's
not supposed to happen to brown people (Eastern cultures
often tend to skip over individual experience in favour of
collective unity).

I also didn't realize it, but somewhere along the line I
had slipped Harry Potter's invisibility cloak over my shoulders, and I couldn't take it off. I encountered the reality that
although feminism has created many professional options
for women, it has come at the cost of devaluing domestic
roles. There's a lot of chatter about women having it all,
including the freedom to choose career or children, but in
reality the choices aren't equally valued. Career success is
publicly affirmed; becoming a parent relegates one to the
category of wallflower. What kind of progress is it to value

ambition over nurturing, replacing one set of values with another? Wasn't choice, valuing a diversity of life directions, the whole point of feminism?

Soon after Koda was born I attended a dinner party at a friend's house. I was seated beside a woman about a decade younger than myself who was childless. She spent a full forty-five minutes filling me in on her new overseas job, yet when she asked what I was doing, she tuned out after just three minutes (and that's a generous estimate). I didn't have the energy to dress up my thoughts in fancy clothing to parade out in front of people at social events. I was barely getting through my days as it was. The dual requirement of having to compete with others' work achievements while shuttering the overwhelming experience of new parenthood slowly closed me off from social spaces. Attending events would leave me feeling simultaneously angry and rejected, and that would eat into energy reserves I didn't have. Even having well-meaning friends come to visit often followed the same pattern: trying to pay attention to their words as I was trying to manage two little ones meant that I worked twice as hard for half the benefit. I wanted to be able to talk in a gibberish emotional stream about feeding schedules, food choices, and how to manage sleep deprivation. But I censored myself. Who wants to listen to that?

My inner landscape didn't feel clean or interesting enough to invite anyone in other than Shakil and my family. And since my immediate family lived far away, I leaned even more on Shakil as my primary support. Some days I would count the minutes until he walked in the door, then unleash a verbal stream, because it was the only conversation I would have all day in which I actually felt visible. My sensitivity to feeling criticized also increased in the face of exhaustion and hormones, so we started fighting more frequently. He couldn't do anything right. It felt as though every time my nervous system got a foothold, something else — in this case, motherhood — arrived to push it back towards distress.

ON TOP OF FACING the betrayal of modern feminism as I stepped into the mother role, I found myself isolated in our neighbourhood. The relatively small population of mostly South Asian Muslims was declining as house prices went up, and everyone moving in seemed to be white professional couples buying their first homes. In the early years I tried repeatedly to connect with other moms I met at classes, in the park, or at local coffee shops. Our conversations would always follow the same script: I'd introduce myself, we'd compare notes on children, I'd suggest we get together for coffee, and then nothing. Again and again, I would get lukewarm or ambiguous responses in return.

Part of the reason, I'm sure, was that these other women were also facing the same post-feminist isolation. And yet I would watch them chatter to each other after class or by the swing set with greater interest and ease than they ever seemed to exhibit around me. Given my professional capacity as a leadership consultant and facilitator, I knew my people skills weren't lacking. I was catapulted back to childhood once again, when strong-willed Iranian girls and

anyone non-white ranked lower on the social scale and I
felt as though I didn't measure up. It happened in enough
spaces that I started to realize it wasn't just me; those larger
structures of privilege were operating on the unconscious
level, making it easier for those women to gravitate towards
others they perceived as most like themselves. Humans are
tribal, most comfortable with the familiar.

Realizing this fact, however, didn't stop me from feeling
like scabs were being torn off old wounds. I was excited to
join a women's gym nearby that a few other moms I knew
attended, a seemingly fun way to get back in shape post-
childbirth. Yet it didn't take long for me to feel as though I
was back in high school, as I observed little cliques forming,
often without me. Trying harder to be friendly made me
feel that I was abandoning myself, yet it felt worse to with-
draw and pretend not to care. It was a lose-lose situation.
I'd often return home wanting to cry (and I often would, in
our downstairs bathroom with the lights off and the door
locked) yet simultaneously angry at my own vulnerability.
I eventually gave up my gym membership.

The same exclusionary dynamics also showed up in
other neighbourhood spaces. As a member of a local community Facebook group, one day I posted an article about
Olivia Chow, a Toronto mayoral candidate who had been
the target of an overtly racist cartoon in the local *Sun* newspaper. I didn't post about her politics, but rather how her
race and gender made her a target for attack that her white,
male peers would never be subjected to. I was chided and
told to keep my postings to what I would talk about on
the school playground. When I responded that, actually,

this *was* a topic I'd discuss on the playground, I didn't hear
anything further, and the two white women moderators
went out of their way to avoid me thereafter, walking
across the street when they saw me approach. It was just
another micro-reflection of how identity shapes the scope
of conversation and the borders of community, favouring
the experiences of those who fit the definition of "normal."

Just how raw my internal state had become as a result
of these accumulated interactions was made clear to me
on the day I had to return something to a neighbourhood
store. I'd bought a floral shirt a couple of days earlier, only
to bring it home and find a rip in the sleeve. Finding time
to return it wasn't an easy task with two small babies, but
I managed to get there, only to face the female manager,
who put me through a court-level inquisition: "When did
you notice it?" "How did it get there?" "Was it there when
you bought it?" The clincher: "I don't understand how
this could happen!" (Translation: You obviously did this
yourself.) Conscious that everyone in the space was young,
well-dressed, and white, I had to fight back the shame to
finally lift my voice in challenge: "Why don't you believe
me?" She responded by grudgingly banging out a refund,
refusing to meet my eyes the whole time. Despite my victory, I walked out of the store exhausted and so upset that
I wanted nothing more than to just let myself sob. It could
have happened to anyone, but it felt so personal. I was back
to asking, "Is there something wrong with me?"

In the absence of more tempering positive interactions,
these microaggressions started to eat away not only at my
fragile energy reserves but at the core of the self-esteem I

had been rebuilding over the course of my entire adult life. Microaggressions by their very definition occur beneath the surface of conscious awareness. People move towards, are more lenient with, and less punitive to others they perceive as most like themselves, and on the flip side they are more judgemental and undermining of those who are different. When you are on the receiving end of a microaggression, it's never fully clear whether anything has happened or not, outside of a body echo that says "This feels wrong."

While I was experiencing these moments of undercover marginalization, I was also trying to mitigate the impacts on others who I knew experienced even less privilege. There was a child drop-in centre across the street from us in the basement of an old church. While checking it out one morning, I saw the room was filled with nannies of Pakistani, Indian, Middle Eastern, and Filipino descent. The looks they sent my way were subtle yet confused, as I didn't fit into any clear niche. Racially, as a brown woman with a lighter-skinned child beside me, I fit into their category of care worker, yet my dress and the way I walked confidently into the room probably sent a different message. I spent the next hour slowly introducing myself and doing the non-white introduction dance: "Where are you from? How long have you been here? How many in your family?" (Many first-generation immigrants greet each other with these questions as a way of connecting and replacing the sour aftertaste of foreignness that lingers when the same questions are asked by a white Canadian.)

Over the course of the morning I was able to broker numerous connections, but it came at a cost. Arriving home around lunchtime, I sank into our couch feeling exhausted. It was the first and last time that I was able to muster the energy to visit. Existing in the gap once again between white and racialized communities meant that I was rarely able to just let go in that place of belonging where I unconsciously registered as part of the same group. I wanted more moments of easy connection to fill the yawning gap I felt growing day by day. As the mixed-race girl in the ring I found myself regularly faced with the choice to be Beauty or the Beast, to be accepted or be myself, to be liked or to be powerful. I knew my answer was to stay true to myself, but it seemed to come at such a high cost.

⌁

WHILE THE BABIES WERE at home with me, I focused my attention on house renovations: I poured excess energy into repainting and decorating our living room, having a porch addition built, and getting the front and back yards landscaped. Accomplishing these tasks fulfilled my need to be both productive and creative, as well as mentally stimulated.

Meanwhile, in 2015, Shakil's groundbreaking book *Deep Diversity: Overcoming Us vs. Them*—think Malcolm Gladwell meets racial justice—was published. I was both his biggest cheerleader and his roadblock. No one believed more strongly in the content and the need for this book, and no one resented more the time his increasing travel took away from helping with the constant chaos of childrearing. Writing the book took him further down his career path, while the children took me further into the domestic realm, reigniting issues around power that were our bread and butter but also our albatross to bear as a couple. It wasn't that I necessarily wanted to be front and centre along with him — I didn't have the energy for it at that point — but I envied the affirmation that work afforded him, while I struggled with feeling like a failure at both homemaking and community building.

He was stretched from holding the fort financially, and I was resentful about taking on all the domestic responsibilities, though this was a temporary role division we'd agreed on. In addition, our relationship didn't have much of an emotional buffer because I'd eaten away at that with my constant neediness. Thus our arguments started to take a darker path, from who was on with the kids at what time to whether we should be together at all. It was awful to reach that point, as though we were damaging a sacred trust between us. Our dynamic only served to further tighten my screws of self-hatred, making it harder to see and accept responsibility for what I was unfairly loading onto him. Shakil and I were each the eldest of three children raised in cauldrons of survival as new immigrant families to Canada. How much of our conflict was about us, and how much was a spillover of the distress we had absorbed from our own parents, from having to be cultural translators between our families and the outside world, from having to carry the weight of our family's well-being on our shoulders?

There were many layers to our dance, and, despite trying, I didn't know how to access the more balanced "me" and the relationship I believed was hidden under all that stress. I was flailing, unable to anchor into work as a familiar place of validation, caught in a domestic role I didn't enjoy or feel competent in. My mind was my own worst enemy. Armed with every personal development trick available, I was only more conscious of the ideal self I wasn't able to live up to. All that mindfulness, quite frankly, became oppressive. I felt like a complete failure, and the world once again started losing its colour.

Like the storybook princess, I felt I had been removing mattress after mattress, year by year, searching for the pea—the cause of the behaviours I didn't like in myself but couldn't seem to eliminate. So many times I promised myself if this or that thing happened—if I could move out of the addiction, if I met someone, if my scalp healed, if I got pregnant, if I got that client or lost some weight—I would finally be happy. I felt as though I was chasing ghosts. Every time I arrived at my destination, what I wanted had already disappeared around the next corner. I had put in my best effort—a momentous statement coming from a perfectionist. What was I missing?

⌒

IN THE FALL OF 2015 I went home to visit my family...and dislocated my shoulder. Again. Both shoulders had taken turns dislocating since that first rugby match when I was eighteen years old. Half the time I was able to slide the joint back into the socket, but this was the other half. Once again, I found myself stuck under dingy fluorescent lighting in a tiny emergency room, holding my left shoulder bone hanging halfway down my torso. After more than three hours of waiting, a thousand shallow breaths, and two doses of fentanyl, which barely took the edge off the pain, I passed from shock to trauma. Our bodies keep the score. I was aware, lying in bed after they knocked me unconscious to rest the joint, that my body was calling to me, my shoulder asking me to recognize some injury I was still continuing to ignore. As the Eastern medical model recognizes, our bodies are finely tuned instruments of communication. What we don't process consciously comes out unconsciously through body symptoms, pain, and even accidents. As with other hospital visits, I felt the aftertaste of vulnerability, as if someone had forced a wedge into the patched-up seams of my soul, whispering that the sutures were infected and the pieces needed relocation in order to become whole.

My forty-year-old self mentally threw her hands up. How much more could I possibly unearth in those subterranean depths? By that point I had been in and out of therapies since I was twenty-two. I had been to talk therapists, somatic therapists, alternative therapists, psychics, nutritionists, naturopaths, and energy healers. I was a competent businesswoman who could capture the attention of any audience I was placed in front of, and yet here I was waiting for my mother to pick me up, feeling no more than seven years old with the same question looming over my head: *Why is this happening to me?*

It was the last straw. My marriage was stretched. My body had snapped. And I felt as if I couldn't stay upright in my own life.

After I returned to Toronto, Shakil and I went for our first couples' counselling session. Gord, our therapist, was a gay man with a sensitive soul buried underneath a theatrical exterior. He could swing from compassion to humour, from depth to lightness, in a heartbeat. He was a balm, and one of the biggest gifts he offered was a correct diagnosis. In our first session, Gord turned to me and asked about my childhood history. After ten minutes of giving a cursory description, I looked over at him. His eyes were filled with tears. I felt exposed and surprised. He gently and matter-of-factly leaned forward, looked me in the eye, and said, "What you're telling me about is called trauma. What I hear you describing is post-traumatic stress disorder."

Whoa.

"I don't think so," I replied. "I'm not sure that applies."

No one had ever said those words to me before. I associated trauma with people who were, quite frankly, down and out. Broken, dysfunctional. Surely that wasn't me. It was the first time anyone had put my experience into such a context. I heard his words, but I still felt resistant to what they meant. By contrast, Shakil seemed relieved. The burden of fixing things was off his shoulders and onto mine; it was up to me to mend my own past. Yet I had trouble identifying with a label that seemed so extreme. Additionally, I felt vulnerable at being diagnosed the "damaged" one in our relationship. I couldn't see it.

Soon after that first visit to Gord I started reading Peter Levine's seminal book *Waking the Tiger: Healing Trauma*. One night, after yet another argument with Shakil, I went down to our tiny downstairs bathroom, watching as a potato bug

made its way across the floor. I squished it. I was in a state
of familiar post-conflict emotional hangover where I felt
simultaneously angry and ashamed, unable to differentiate
past from present. As I sat trying to sort through the conflicting emotions, I started feeling rage towards the entire
psychological world. How was it that I had reached midlife
and no one had ever diagnosed this before? I'd done my
due diligence. I had gone to my first therapist more than
two decades earlier. Sure, I'd been hit with labels such as
depression, anxiety, and "daddy issues," but no one had
ever put the pieces together to spell "trauma." The beginning of every change starts with naming. You can't heal
a broken leg with a Band-Aid—you have to know what
you're dealing with. I felt cheated out of the opportunity
to have potentially lived a better life, to have been a better
version of myself, to at least have lived with greater ease.

After a few minutes of feeding the unquenchable beast
named "regret" I began to feel an impulse move through
me. I said to myself, "This is your work! You have to name
this for people. You have to wake people up." I didn't know
exactly what "this" was, but I knew I was being called to
something bigger than my own experience. I stood up,
looked in the mirror, and whispered aloud to myself, "I'm
a high-functioning trauma survivor." Then I repeated it
over and over again until I started to believe it.

⌒

SINCE WESTERN THERAPY FOCUSES largely on individual experience and is offered for the most part by white,

middle-class practitioners, for me, the larger social forces of exile, immigration, racism, and sexism had never been added to the mix! Each of the therapists I had visited over the years had looked at micro causes of my problems: family life, childhood bullying, cognitive beliefs. No one had ever before looked at the larger, systemic picture of the ongoing impact of having an outsider identity. What made Gord different was that not only had he been trained in trauma, but he was also the only one who held an anti-oppression lens over his work. It was a synergistic turning point in self-understanding where systemic forces met individual psychology. The political once again became personal, because I could see more clearly how our social identity — the body we're born into and how that body fits into the tribe — shapes our emotional baseline, giving us differential access to nervous system regulation.

Identity (or systemic) trauma is different from other forms, such as those arising in the private sphere (sexual, physical, or emotional abuse) or the political (war, geno-cide), in that it happens in day-to-day interactions. Negative signals can run the gamut from the more subtle, usually unconscious forms, such as others averting their gaze, to the extreme, including verbal or physical harassment. And it isn't confined to a single incident. Identity trauma is the sheer inundation of being told — directly and indirectly, over and over again — that you are different. And it is expecting that you will receive more punitive treatment if you step out of line, that you have to work twice as hard to have any hope of the same degree of acceptance enjoyed by others. I realized that when wounds are caused by people rejecting who you are, the triggers are hard to escape, for we are open-loop systems. We are designed to regulate each other. When we face social exclusion on a regular basis, our deepest loss is the capacity to rest inside our own skin. And what we inherit is a constant self-doubt that can permeate every moment. Dealing with identity trauma requires both a focus on personal inner healing *and* a recognition of the ongoing forms of systemic discrimination that keep people in a "less than" position.

Viewing my experiences in the context of trauma, particularly identity trauma, was life-changing for me because it finally put my suffering into perspective. I realized I was buried under shame because, despite knowing all about the therapeutic effects of meditating, journalling, chakras and energy meridians, managing triggers and gratitude practices, and so on, it wasn't enough. I couldn't dig myself out of emotional desperation. I felt as though I was a bad person because I still felt anxious so much of the time, and that came out especially in my closest relationships. The diagnosis of trauma allowed me to breathe more easily, because it wasn't about me not doing enough, or *being* enough; it was about an invisible wound that I wasn't aware of, that kept getting kicked repeatedly by others around me. I could finally see what I was dealing with. And it was so relieving to know it wasn't about some deficit on my part.

I finally understood why finding a state of calm was so difficult for me, why I couldn't clearly remember big parts of my childhood, why my emotions often churned from neutral to volatile in just a few seconds, and why it was so hard to let in the good stuff or have it hang around for long. These were all physical symptoms of a nervous system set to hypervigilance mode. Rather than feel ashamed of my history with unexplainable physical symptoms that ran the gamut from obsessive-compulsive toilet-going and other controlling behaviours to struggles with addiction, migraines, hair loss, and shoulder dislocations, I now had a frame that could put those symptoms into focus. I was able to begin unravelling the last clinging threads of shame, the biggest barrier to growth.

I felt profoundly hopeful knowing that my body, in particular my nervous system, could actually return to a state of equilibrium under the right conditions. Trauma is marked by prolonged stressful experiences that flood the nervous system's ability to handle emotion. If fight-or-flight doesn't work, the system goes into freeze mode, where the capacity for calmness and connection is disrupted. I learned that self-regulation is challenging because even small things can be interpreted as a threat. Controlling behaviours grow in compensation. Conflict (whether internal or external) is always present. In fact, conflict becomes its own addiction. Trauma survivors often feel bored or anxious if intensity is lacking, because the nervous system has become accustomed to running on adrenaline. I found out that the answer to all of this is integration. You have to process small doses of the difficult emotions to eventually resolve the impact of overwhelming experiences. If this doesn't happen, trapped stress just continues to come out in unhealthy, addictive, or self-sabotaging ways.

I learned to identify more quickly when my anxiety was ratcheting up, and rather than berating myself or pushing harder, I learned to be more gentle, to talk to that part of myself the way I would to a small child: "It's okay. You can be anxious, fearful, angry. We can take a break. I got you. You're just fine." The way we speak to ourselves, especially in the face of distress, plays a huge role in either calming or escalating the body's response. When our wounds have their origin in social rejection, the tone of our internal voice is especially important; because we have absorbed the belief that we are unworthy of love, we never learn to offer ourselves compassion. This was a big step, changing how I met my own shame, learning to embrace it. Over time I would get better at sharing this vulnerability with others as well. On the horizon, I could see how walking the path through my own trauma would deepen my work in addressing wounds of racism and other forms of oppression that I knew affected countless other lives in even harsher ways.

⌒

I HAD TO GO deeper to do the trauma-related work. I decided that I didn't need to talk more about what had happened, but rather to find a more consistent way of changing the physical settings on a nervous system still geared towards fight, flight, or freeze. I could recognize when I was triggered by something in my environment and, on a cognitive level, put the incident into perspective. Yet I couldn't prevent the physical after-effect of switching into hypervigilance mode, as my body was flooded with the familiar emotions of anger, shame, and fear, even when the external event was relatively insignificant—such as being questioned by the store clerk when I returned the blouse.

I was referred by a friend to a somatic therapist, Kristi, who offered a form of therapeutic bodywork. A couple of months after the shoulder dislocation that happened in Edmonton, I found myself lying on her massage table, experiencing her healing hands working around my shoulder blades. As Kristi gently prodded my skin, I started to experience waves of icy-cold tremors sweeping from head to toe, alternating with bouts of shivering. According to Eastern medicine, fear manifests as cold in the body, so I knew that strong emotions were starting to move through me. The words "It's easier to dislocate than to feel the pain" floated into my consciousness. Images started flashing through my mind like an old TV set on the fritz.

I saw the little girl whom I had been, walking in our walled garden in Iran. I could smell the orange blossoms. I could feel the intensity of my anger towards Ayatollah Khomeini, forcing us to leave behind family and home, my known universe. I saw myself a month later in a tiny English village with a grey sky, alone on the playground. And then I saw another image of me running through the forest in Sherwood Park, panting, escaping, still alone, and so very cold. As I reached the last image, my chest started to heave and the raw sounds of a trapped animal filled the room. It took me a few moments to recognize that the sound was coming from me. I turned onto my side, allowing myself to grieve what I later realized was the loss of my "original face," a Buddhist term referring to our most authentic self. Who might I have been if I had grown up in a community that reflected and accepted me? Leaving the

Persian girl behind to become the "foreigner" had broken my heart and cleaved my spirit in two. Before I could move forward, I had to let myself break open, to heal.

Stepping back into the past to connect with unresolved feelings was some of the hardest work I've ever done. It was not an overnight process, and it continues to this day. Although the adult in me was ready to move on, I had to slow down and learn to listen to the seven-year-old who wasn't. I had to honour the fifteen-year-old who seemed to fill my world with her needs, to support the young woman who was angry at feeling so powerless. I thought the cumulative grief of my many selves would never end.

But slowly, as I was able to recognize the full extent of the wounding and therefore take responsibility for its impact, things began to shift around me, starting with my relationship to Shakil. He was my litmus test. As difficult as it sometimes could be, neither of us avoided the vulnerability of speaking what we felt was our deepest truth. This ability is our superglue. I had to do a lot of stepping back, giving him more room to also be messy. Trauma can suck up a lot of oxygen in any relationship, and in ours, Shakil hadn't had a lot of breathing space. The most difficult thing to do was to start trusting him, not in the day-to-day aspects of our lives but in the hurt places. I was so used to being alone and having to fight for everything that when I got angry I threw him out of our nest. It took me a long time to wipe away the fog of shame so that I could see my own behaviour clearly and with compassion.

Shakil would say, "I'm on your side. I can see when you're spinning even if you can't. Why do you have to fight me?" To let someone else into that place of wounded vulnerability and trust that they could have my back was excruciating. Shakil went into the trenches with me. Slowly, we began to climb out together.

That spring our son Koda turned one, and was suddenly (and miraculously) less fussy and more independent. We spent more time as a family actually enjoying ourselves instead of just trying to get through the day: walks in the Don Valley, bedtime stories snuggled in with each child, laneway running races. As a mother, I was able to keep my head more above water.

Gradually, I noticed something new infiltrating my thoughts during unexpected moments. As I was walking to get groceries or lying in bed at night, I started replaying different scenes from the past, and before I realized it, I was forming the script for them in my head. It took a couple of months to realize that I was starting to excavate my own history in the form of a story. Stories had always led the way: What would it be like to place myself at the centre of my own?

FIFTEEN

Belonging

IN EARLY 2016 I started writing, and then writing some more, in spurts of time stolen between naps and client calls, travel and bedtime routines. As I embarked on the journey of organizing all these memories in one place, I found myself tested by the still-present fear of being found faulty. It left me winded and re-examining my default coping mechanisms.

Three incidents stand out for me from this time; they each magnified the core beliefs I had developed as self-protection during my childhood years: "You will never be accepted." "You will never be safe." "You are unlovable." Like the pigs listening to the wolf blowing at the walls of identity, by the third incident I had found my brick fortress, a sense of comfort inside my own skin.

In spring, I had an altercation with my sister. Like many sisters, we tend to squabble often and frequently, and move past the conflict just as quickly. This time was different. Fariba had moved with her husband and two toddlers to Nigeria a year earlier and was there during the Ebola health scare. Days after the World Health Organization had declared the country to be in a state of emergency, her husband was due to travel by himself out of the country for a week, leaving my sister behind with the children. I went into full big-sister mode, going over her head to admonish her husband in an email. It was not my finest moment. It was just over a year since my son's birth, and I was still deeply exhausted, hormonal, and anxious. I was doing what I'd always done: trying to protect her. The conflict came to a head when she threatened to end our relationship. I was devastated. Even though I knew I'd gone too far, I couldn't understand how she could abandon me for playing the role I'd always played. Why was I being punished for trying to be the rescuer?

A couple of weeks later I attended a neighbourhood moms' dinner. I was sitting at the table enjoying a second glass of wine, listening to the conversation ebb and flow around me. At some point I turned to Leanne, an acquaintance sitting next to me, and asked what I thought was an innocuous question. Leanne abruptly and loudly exclaimed in front of everyone gathered, "You ask really weird questions! Why would you ask that?" Seemingly, I had inadvertently touched a raw nerve, and her reaction left me feeling shamed in front of the group. Instead of being able to move past it, I left immediately. At home, I spent the next few hours locked in the bathroom feeling anxious, jittery, and in tears. I couldn't understand what I had done wrong. Why did I feel like the transgressor, when surely it was the other way around?

The third incident occurred when Shakil and I were called (again) into our daughter's daycare as she was refusing to listen and causing a ruckus during naptime. Irrational fear took over that my daughter, who is fiery, verbal, and pushes boundaries just like her mama, might be marginalized as a result. I got lost in a whirlwind of visits to other daycares, exploring our options. I was scared that she might somehow be found faulty and face even a fraction of the rejection that I had. Why was I adding more to my plate when I knew rationally how deeply my daughter was supported by all the staff?

I was in a tailspin where past and present were enmeshed but I couldn't immediately pull myself out. By the third incident I was fully in the trauma vortex—a state of internal panic, a veritable spin cycle of fear, anger, and self-loathing. I was a bad sister, a bad friend, a bad mom . . . a bad person. I was bingeing on food, repetitively visiting the toilet late into the night, and snapping at Shakil. I felt out of control, as though my nine-year-old self was once again running the show. This time I was faster at reaching for supports: one-on-one sessions with Gord, writing a lot, daily attempts to breathe in a quiet room by myself. Gradually I was able to put the brakes on. It took some time to fully see the constellation of childhood coping mechanisms mapped out in mandala-like form in front of me. The early survival code: rescue; absorb blame; work harder. It was exhausting. I kept cycling through the same old steps. I had never seen the pattern so clearly before.

After a couple of months, I approached Leanne to talk with her about what had happened at the dinner. I apologized for any unintended impact and then was taken aback as she went on to accuse me in general of being too curious, asking too many questions, being, in essence, "too big." I found myself falling down the old rabbit hole of shame, but this time I was able to stay present. Here, in front of me, was my original wound—that I was somehow not right, this sense that I had to erase my feelings, my truth, my *self*, to survive. What did I need to convince her of? The irony is that to find belonging we have to make peace with rejection. Pausing, I looked her in the eyes, and in that moment—a reverberation of so many other moments—I simply pulled out of the vortex. I was done. Finished with downplaying my Persian fieriness, through with apologizing for aspects of myself that were what defined me, tired of wearing the cloak of identity shame.

"Leanne," I said in level tones, "I recognize that I'm not everyone's cup of tea. Clearly I'm not yours, and that's okay. Let's leave it at that."

And just like that, I felt more free.

No prince. No magic. Just me, on my own terms. I had to cut through the thorny brambles of all the projected rejection I'd received over the years to rescue the unblemished part of myself that was ready to take tentative steps out of the shadows.

I HAD SPENT SO long chasing after the desired state of acceptance, I couldn't see that, truthfully, I didn't want to just "fit in." Membership often comes with its own restrictions, and blending in with the crowd requires smoothing out the sharp edges that make us unique. That oft-required, barely visible sacrifice can be suffocating. Without realizing it, I had come to rely on my outsider status. Like the moth who knows not to get too close to the flame, my soul knew what it was to get burned. I much preferred the freedom to fly.

That girl, whose ancestors defied social norms, who herself crossed ocean, country, and culture to get here, was finally able to see how belonging is worlds apart from acceptance. With the former you can settle more deeply into your own bones, whereas the latter requires countless invisible nips and tucks to the very shape of self. Belonging does not require marginalization; conformity does. With inner impunity, I could finally choose authenticity over acceptance, choose to be myself over being liked. For many, it's not an either-or. For women of colour—and most people facing systemic discrimination—it often is.

Soon after that period of emotional heavy lifting, Shakil and I had another session with Gord. I spent some time describing the recent spate of events. As I finished, I looked over to see that Shakil's face was cracked open, a smile crinkling the corners of his eyes, lightening his irises to a golden brown, a sign he was at his most vulnerable. He held my gaze as he croaked softly into the stillness, "You've always been my cup of tea." There they hung. Simple words that shone so bright I imagined I could feel them scorching new pathways into my brain. A moment that, because it couldn't be earned, I knew would never be forgotten. It was more than enough redemption for any real or imagined sins of inadequate identity.

LATER THAT SPRING I flew down to visit some friends in Portland, Oregon. It was my longest vacation without the kids, and it became known as the "cocktail caper." My friend Julie took me to a trendy downtown restaurant the night I arrived, and I broke my usual wine-drinking habit by ordering a speciality cocktail to kick off my holiday. Tangy, bitter, and citrusy, the cloudy orange drink came with a radish garnish. I was assaulted by five levels of taste, transported to gustatory heaven, and spent the next few days in a pretty constant state of inebriation as I travelled from place to place educating myself on different liqueurs and possible mixtures.

Over the weekend we went to a popular downtown brunch spot, and finding a lineup of people outside we decided to go to the sister bar next door while we waited for a table to open up. The bartender was the quintessential Portlander: a friendly foodie who was well travelled. As we got into conversation he started pulling bottles off the shelves, giving us a down-and-dirty lesson in esoteric liquors. I lifted my shot glass, containing a murky green liquid, up to the light and listened raptly as he told us the story of a formerly medicinal elixir brewed by monks in the Carpathian Mountains, where the recipe has been passed down from generation to generation since the early 1600s. Already hooked, I took a sip. "Whoa!" I gasped. "That packs a punch! I love it." And so began my obsession with Green Chartreuse, as liqueur and as metaphor. Bottled fire. A liquid soulmate.

Back in Toronto, I happened on a silver ring in my favourite jewellers' collective. It was a slim, rough-hewn band representing a branch with a small silver leaf perched on the top. I bought it and special-ordered three tiny emeralds to be placed inside the leaf. I've never been one for jewels—they've always seemed too ostentatious—but the tiny leaf felt like a fitting reminder that growth is always possible, and is, in fact, a constant. The ring became a talisman.

It made me think about my father. That year I purchased a card for Father's Day and inscribed a list of memories: the many times he had us giving one-minute off-the-cuff speeches across the dinner table until we sounded like mini politicians; how he taught me to mix kebab meat to just the right consistency; his commitment to push me through extra math problems. Most of all, I remembered his ability to pull up his shirt sleeves and just get the job done, no matter the obstacles facing him. I am his daughter in many ways.

That June my father called as I was out for a neighbourhood walk. He thanked me for the card, choking up as he spoke of our past for the first time. "Those times were so hard for all of us. I wish I could go back and do things differently." I swallowed, knowing this was as close as my father could get to apologizing, to acknowledging his own vulnerability and the role he played in my suffering during those early years.

"It's okay, Dad," I finally responded. "We're okay now. I love you."

I thought, also, about my mother—how she came for a month after the birth of each of my children, holding my son for long stretches when his colic pushed me beyond the end of my own rope. I visualized the countless times she tirelessly washed, cooked, shopped, and folded. The fact that her phone line and kitchen table are spaces where I am always unquestionably accepted, no matter how I show up. My mother asks so little of me and is always there. She may not share my understanding of what it is to live in a brown body, but she supports my work without question. I sometimes wonder how the journey to reconcile my Persian identity has overshadowed my British roots, and by extension my mother's influence. I am my mother's daughter, too.

I became a perfectionist to survive, and that meant that I expected everyone around me to be perfect as well. When I held both my parents and myself to impossible standards I felt as if I was keeping all of us safe in a cocoon, when we could have been testing our wings for collective flight instead. The past is, unfortunately, unalterable. The trauma happened due to fate and others' cruel and neglectful behaviour, but the reality was that no one could clean up the internal shards but me. I didn't want to be held hostage any longer to the part of me that had internalized the belief that I was somehow inherently wrong; I didn't want to keep absorbing this projection from others, keeping me locked in a smaller version of who I felt I could be. The bars of the cage still existed, but there was also room for freedom within. I had to imagine a future in which all parts of myself were represented, the visionary as well as the victim, where joy could take over from grief. I wanted a different kind of future for all of us.

This future includes my siblings, who live many miles away from me. My brother is a geology professor on the west coast of Canada, married to an Edmonton-bred Alberta girl; he's now a father of two. My sister is a freelance journalist married to a Nigerian Brit; they live in London, England, with their three girls. I married a South Asian Canadian. We chose partners who represent the full spectrum of skin colour from light to dark, perhaps reflecting a future norm where race and identity are no longer fixed, where we will be forced to make room for more possibilities than the narrow categories we grew up with.

This fluidity of identity offers hope for new approaches to old problems, innovative ways of seeing the world outside of narrowly prescribed world views, a forceful push to go beyond the usual and comfortable stereotypes. Perhaps a maturing beyond the infinite possibilities of us versus them. Individuals who don't fit the mould are often more comfortable taking necessary risks, a valuable trait in a world whose future is uncertain, where the only way forward seems to be a radical departure from what has come before. As an adult, in the city and country I inhabit, I've found communities reflective of this multiplicity, signalling that peaceful coexistence is possible. Twice a year I take our children to celebrate *Eid* at the Noor Cultural Centre. We attend the *khotbah* (sermon), my daughter and I in our jewel-toned *chalwar kameez*, camouflaged in the rainbow spread across the carpeted floor of worship, women seated alongside the men. Sometimes I also attend the Metropolitan Community Church of Toronto, one of the first and largest Christian LGBTQ congregations in the world. Both of these communities are outliers in their respective contexts, reflected in part through their acceptance of those people—trans folks, refugees, same-sex families—not yet as welcome in other mainstream religious environments. These are little pockets where inclusion is not just a word but a way of a being.

⌒

THAT SUMMER OF 2016, Shakil and I went with the kids on our annual week-long getaway to the cottage with a group of close friends. This time, I was outfitted with a cocktail kit, key liqueurs, and a variety of recipes. Cocktail hour started about 11 a.m. every day. On our last night, the adults sat gathered in our cottage's rustic living room for a last night of revelry. Bon Jovi's "Livin' On a Prayer" wafted through the speakers and I swayed to the music, belting out the words with our friend, Sandy, while offering a spontaneous interpretive dance (somewhat) synced up with the music. Graceful I was not. After a couple of minutes, I found myself succumbing to the eruptions of laughter emanating from my belly, gushing from my mouth. It is powerful medicine, to laugh like that.

The next morning, our last day there, I went for a run along the tree-lined gravel side road. The sun was shining through the trees, the lake winking at me as I ran past. As I rounded a curve, up ahead I saw a deer, framed by leaves, right in the middle of the road. The deer, sunlight, and green of the leaves all converged in a single, perfect moment. I smiled as I felt a shadow lift from my heart. *Hope, thy colour is green*, I thought. *More precisely, chartreuse. And thy nature, growth.*

⌒

THAT FALL I WAS called back to Ottawa for the first time in over a decade. I found myself facing an audience of a couple of hundred people all representing federal employers looking for best inclusive hiring practices. I wore my favourite Mac fire-engine-red lipstick (a.k.a. "Ruby Woo"), a 1950s-inspired form-fitting red dress with black polka dots, and four-inch black patent Kate Spade heels. It felt powerful to deliberately showcase my body, letting the colour shine. No more second-guessing being in the spotlight. As I stepped up to the podium, I heard my inner voice cheering, "Go get 'em, goddess!"

I thought of my strong female friends who, in different ways, had reached a similar point: Indy, with her diamond nose jewel; Asmaa, with her funky purple glasses; Au'drey, with her hair arranged like a dark halo around her face. All of us had landed on these small yet visible ways to signal our presence, to occupy space none of us takes for granted. Although more women have started to appear in leadership roles, they are still, by and large, white women. For visible minority women the glass ceiling is more like concrete.

Although I still didn't see myself reflected at leadership levels in most organizations I walked into, I was not going to go gently into that good night. My relationship with activism was no longer in the lustful, tempestuous, often conflictual early stages, but had matured to a point where all parts of me could walk together on the path towards social change. That internal reconciliation allowed me to use my own experiences as a bridge for others.

In the keynote session, I shared my own story as a way of illustrating the power of stereotypes, inviting others to reflect on their own experiences with exclusion. At the front of the room, a Jamaican Canadian woman described sending her children to an all-white Catholic school. Because her children spoke with an accent, they were regularly slapped with a ruler in front of the class for not speaking "proper English." Her voice broke as she stumbled through the rest of her words. Another woman described growing up Métis, yet not disclosing her Indigenous status to others until she was an adult. Her eyes narrowed as she described how much discrimination she faced afterwards, simply for holding a different identity umbrella over her head. Finally, a tall, middle-aged South Asian man described growing up in poverty as one of the only non-French-speaking families in his neighbourhood in Quebec. "Each day on the way to school, the boys would be waiting for me, sometimes with tools in their hands."

In each of their stories, I could feel echoes of my own past, see the resonance with others in the room: wide eyes, forward-leaning bodies, pin-drop silence. I felt a rush of gratitude for being able to open such spaces, to host them, and in the process to be honoured with a glimpse of people's authentic selves, their quiet yet universal struggles. I knew, even if they didn't, that my professional ability in such moments was the result of peeling off successive layers of the old trauma in order to be present, to welcome the spectrum of experience in the room as I'd had to do inside myself.

We are, all of us, able to guide others only as far as we have journeyed ourselves, to regulate others as much as we are regulated. Inviting and navigating vulnerability is my hard-won superpower, and one I use intentionally because I know this is where true transformation occurs. There is a quality to this level of conversation, a shared feeling, a kind of communion. Story is the original teacher, the oldest recipe for inclusion in the books.

When the session ended, one of the corporate sponsors came up and whispered in my ear, "Thank you for what you said. I moved here as well from England when I was a little girl. I was bullied too, and I also coped through an eating disorder." I looked at her face, around the same age as my own, her blond hair cut and straightened into a bob, her blue eyes and pink cheeks. It was a face I imagined would carry only privilege, yet her words reminded me how none of us has the territorial rights to exclusion. My heart stirred with compassion hearing her all-too-familiar story of not fitting in. And yet at the same time the activist in me reared her head, reminding me of the macro perspective that for brown and black immigrants these experiences are ubiquitous.

While it's true that marginalization is a universal experience, for some whose identities fall outside the norm marginalization *is* their universe. White skin versus dark. Christian versus Muslim. Straight versus gay. Any individual can experience the exclusion that we call discrimination. And then there are systems of oppression that operate across the board, in every societal institution, and privilege certain identities over others. The truth is that belonging is a complicated beast that straddles the individual and systemic levels of existence, toggling between the psychological truth that we are all the same and the political truth that we are divided by access to power. Having a foot in the world of whiteness, where racial privilege is taken for granted, and the other in the racialized world, where you always feel your difference, has made me acutely aware of these polarizations. I spent the first half of my life wanting to be more white and the second half wishing I were more brown. Perhaps the biggest gift in growing up mixed race was being forced to navigate these polarities internally. Every day I have to work to hold brown and white, Persian and British, dominant and marginalized identities together in some coherent narrative.

At this point, I'm no longer stuck in this Catch-22 because the goal is no longer harmony but connection. The idea of an integrated self where all parts of who we are remain in perfect lockstep is an illusion, an idea born of Western psychology that takes for granted a uniform cultural context. Instead, I try to honour each of the contradictory aspects of my identity, give them voice, let them have their time onstage. For to truly shift external structures of oppression, we have to reclaim all the lost parts of ourselves, to recover the inner fluidity that enables us to occupy our whole selves. As Audre Lorde famously observed, "the master's tools will never dismantle the master's house."

I've discovered over time that the more I'm able to bring the injured parts of my identity into conversation, to make visible what was shamed, the more I notice my physical symptoms dissipate. It is rare now that I catch myself over-eating because of underlying anxiety. Once in a while I'll get mild migraine symptoms when something happens to touch the child inside who felt so powerless and furious at the same time. I can still sometimes find myself sitting on the toilet for longer than necessary late at night because it is a familiar space to unwind in. But the difference is that I'm better at decoding what these symptoms are communicating, more practised at catching the signals from a hyper-vigilant nervous system to slow down and recalibrate. If I catch the wave, it will carry me forward. When I resist, I go under.

⌒

I LOOK BACK NOW and want to praise the young girl I used to be for her temerity and resilience. I want to share with her what I've learned since, to help her understand that those symptoms were an appropriate outlet for expressing the frozen terror she felt each and every day. I'd congratulate her for finding rituals that allowed her to drop the armour of bravado and connect with the vulnerability underneath. The compulsive behaviours, which carried through into adult life, were a way of regaining control, compensation for circumstances in which she felt none. I would let her know that belonging is never a destination but a journey, something we commit to anew every day, to embrace that which most scares us, both inside and out. To love what has been rejected, otherwise it will keep interrupting, eventually tearing us apart.

This is true for all of us. We cannot break the ocean. We are not meant to live separated from parts of ourselves that we learn to hide, punish, or rebel against. To do so is to live in a smaller home than the one available to us: we end up with less energy and more suffering. A wise healer once said to me, "Every living thing—plant, animal, and human—desires nothing more than to truly be listened to." This is our most human job: to step out of the seductive fray to listen to the inner tugs (sensations, feelings, thoughts) bringing us back, over and over again, to our deepest soul self—the site of greatest possibility for reaching out across difference, tucking the other into our heart, and offering love. True justice is born out of love. And any belief system that marginalizes parts of the self, parts of the world, is an enemy of life itself.

Epilogue

I AM STANDING BY the schoolyard fence with Shakil on my daughter's first day at elementary school. As I watch her twist and spin away, my tears drop into a moment where past and present collapse, forming a peculiar cocktail of familiar grief, apprehension about the future, and fragile contentment. It's the best I can hope for.

I've realized that the larger forces of trauma will never completely disappear, but they are no longer the dominant notes in the music score of my life. I think back to the story about the Buddhist monk who finally gave up fighting his demons, instead inviting them out of the closet to sit down with him for tea. Squinting in the sun, I try to freeze the moment in my mind like a memory bowl I can dip back into when fear returns. I look over and catch Shakil's eye, offering up a watery smile. He looks relaxed and at ease, and for that I am grateful.

The people dropping kids off this morning are not only

parents, there are some grandparents as well. I imagine mine growing up thousands of miles away and continents apart: Talat and Abdullah, Elsie and Allan. From generations of established British Christians and Iranian Muslims down to me, a secular first-generation Canadian immigrant. It seems a miracle in moments such as this to have landed here. I imagine them above us somewhere with all the other ancestors watching our messy human lives unfold, beyond such concerns because they now inhabit a place where everyone lives with a full moon in each eye, where all know their place in the tribe, where they sit blowing patience into our thick human skulls. For just a moment I feel my grandmother's lips pressed to the top of my head.

At some point, I hope to return to Iran, having cleared away enough of the tarnish on the Persian part of myself, and I hope that little Annahid will once again shine brightly as she dances on the soil of her birthplace. For now, it's enough to feel her finding her feet again inside me. I take a deep breath and let it go, glancing one last time at my daughter twirling in the sun at the edge of the schoolyard fence, surrounded by children with all shades of skin tone, reflecting the possibility that is Toronto, the promise of Canada—the home I have come to inhabit. I remind myself silently that, after all, she is my daughter, part of my ancestry. Inheritor of all I have walked through. This moment is a new beginning. And my ability to recognize it, to hold it, and to love it is my happily-ever-after.

IMPOSSIBLE MISSION
(written at age eight, a year after leaving Iran)

One day I saw a notice and it said that the circus was coming to town. Then I went to the circus field.

One of the clowns showed me to the owner of the circus. When I got to him I asked can I do an act in the show tonight?

He said yes as long as you're very good at it. When I told my friends they just laughed at me.

When show time came and my act was announced I went on the tight rope. I went on one leg and swung round which is impossible but I did it.

And I did a lot of other impossible things.

After that they never teased me again.

The end.

Acknowledgements

I AM LUCKY TO have found kindred spirits all the way along my journey. Breaking the usual order of these things, I have to mention first and foremost my life, business, and adventure partner, Shakil Choudhury. He is the best community-builder and relationship-holder I know and has loved me through not only my best times (where, I must say, I can be pretty awesome) but, more importantly, my worst (where I can be the opposite). As you will have read in these pages, unfortunately my worst got a lot — too much — space in our relationship. He deserves the Annahid Dashtgard Lifetime Achievement Award. This book would not exist without him.

My immediate family, all mentioned here, were hesitatingly supportive of the writing of this book, which is more than I expected. If someone told me they were writing a memoir, the first thing I'd ask (or demand) would be to read it. They answered my questions, gave me space, and (mostly) understood my purpose in writing it. Whatever details I have shared have been in service of telling a complete story, rather than placing any blame or exposing any of them to scrutiny. I'm sure if you met any member of my family on the street, you'd want to invite them over. They each have their unique brand of charm. I am indebted to them for their support, respect, and love throughout the years, impossible to capture in a two-dimensional telling such as this. To the moon and back, Mom, Dad, Shah, and Yars. And to my extended family as well, scattered across Canada, the United States, England, and Iran, I so appreciate all of you. And thank you, Uncle Shadfar, for our conversations.

I am also lucky to have a small and deeply cherished group of close friends. Special mentions go to: Nancy Rubuliak, the first one to put me on the path to understanding the connection between mind and body; Kim Brodey, who normalized trauma for me; Annie Simpson, a loyal friend throughout; James Beaton, my friend and our office manager, who is unfailingly cheerful, patient, and up for anything, including getting the podcast connected to this book (*Breaking the Ocean: Soundwaves of Belonging*) up and running. A big thanks as well to other members of the Anima team who were cheerleaders throughout, including Brook Thorndycraft, Dasha Kotova, and Dan Bashaw.

Other friends who have played a role in bringing this story to life include: Barb Thomas and D'Arcy Martin (you rock), Julie Diamond (love you), Ritu Bhasin (sis-in-arms), Sandy Yep (surrogate family), Parker Johnson (your solidarity), Farah Malik (always on my side), Vanessa Reid (for the deep dives), Irene Vandertop (up for anything!), Kristen Roderick (spirit support), Chris Kay Fraser (writer guru), Indy Batth (parallel journeys), Florence Pastoor (one of my oldest friends), Rachel Johnston (soul sister), Caroline Davies (my oldest friend), and of course my loving surrogate sisters (a.k.a. sisters-in-law) Bipasha and Monika Choudhury and brother-in-law Sundeep Chauhan. My online writing community also stepped in at crucial moments, especially Minelle Mahtani, Carrianne Leung, and Julia Horel.

As well, a shout-out to Julie Diamond and Gary Reiss, who have revolutionized my approach to conflict and polarization. Judy Rebick, I can always count on you to have my back, and that was especially true around this book. Thank you, Devyani Saltzman, for believing in me right off the bat. Danielle Martin, Jay Pitter, Ayelet Tsabari, Kamal Al Solaylee, and Angela Pelster-Wiebe, thank you for your writing and publishing advice. Thank you, Jael Richardson and team for creating the amazing FOLD festival for literary diversity — and not too far from Toronto! Tonya Surman, Adil Dhalla, and others at the Toronto-based Centre for Social Innovation, I appreciate your unfailing support of our work. The Only Café, thank you for letting me brood for hours in your cozy corners. Thank you, Gord Bricker, Kristi Magraw, Julie Simmons, Janine Sindrey, and Nouha Ali Ahmed for your supportive healing powers over the years. And to all the Anima clients I have the privilege to work with: I love the work I do, and I thank you for the great pleasure of ongoing learning.

Boy, did I learn about the (very white) publishing world in this process, but hey, that's the subject of another book.

As in any journey, it's the people who support that truly stand out. Honestly, I wouldn't have arrived here without a great deal of editing support, starting with Mary Newberry, who was the best first reader I could have imagined. Amanda Lewis of Page Two plowed through early drafts even though she was in the midst of moving across the country. Caroline Starr, my neighbourhood editing rock star, stepped in for a third and final revision before I sent it off to publishers. Julie Devaney, thank you for the final push. Amanda Tucker at Between the Lines, Lisa Lyons at Kids Can Press, and Noelle Allen at Wolsak and Wynn, I really appreciated your advice.

And last, but certainly not least, my awesome editor at Anansi, Douglas Richmond, who saw something in a much earlier draft of this book and welcomed it back later on. Along with Shakil, you're the other knight in shining armour for this piece of work — deep gratitude. Thank you also to my lovely publicist, Holley Corfield, the talented managing editor, Maria Golikova, and amazing designer, Alysia Shewchuk. And to the rest of the Anansi team led by Sarah MacLachlan whose commitment to publish the often missing and invisible stories in a time period of rising xenophobia is...everything. I am honoured to be part of your stable.

Finally, I have to say that finding courage to put my story into the world comes in no small part from other truth-speakers, writers who have risked exposing their own underbellies, trusted their own voices despite...a lack of any evidence that it would matter. I want you to know: it has always mattered to me. The influences are too countless to name here—I've done so many drafts of this paragraph and realize I can't contain it—how far back do I go? Fiction, non-fiction? In the end, you'll all stay named in my mind and heart (and littered around my house), but just to say that words on paper have been my bread crumb trail home. Seeing myself in others' stories has always helped me encounter, name, and then reclaim some part of myself, so thank you, writer tribe.

Lastly, Shakil's mum and dad (known to me as Amma and Pa), Saeeda and Anil, deserve special mention. They are not only grandparents but like second parents to our children, and always step up no matter how tired or busy they may be. I hope to be like you some day. The staff at Dandylion Daycare, who by looking after my children allowed me to do this; I am grateful for all of you. Also Jamie Saunders and Fazila Kasam. And very last of all (but certainly not least) a written smooch (x and x) to my children, Arion and Koda, who share my heart between them. This is also for you. For your generation. And for that new beginning.

ANNAHID DASHTGARD (M.ED.) is the co-founder of Anima Leadership, a highly respected international consulting company specializing in issues of diversity and inclusion. Previously she was a leader in the anti–corporate globalization movement, responsible for several national political campaigns and frequently referred to as one of the top activists to watch in the 1990s. She is the host of the podcast series *Breaking the Ocean: Soundwaves of Belonging* and the director of two award-winning documentaries, *Buy-Bye World: The Battle of Seattle* and *Bread*. Her writing has appeared in the *Globe and Mail*, the *Toronto Star*, and *Briarpatch* magazine. Dashtgard lives in Toronto with her husband and children. *Breaking the Ocean* is her first book.

www.breakingtheocean.com
Twitter: @annahid
Instagram: @annahiddashtgard